Mexican American Girls and Gang Violence

D1602998

Mexican American Girls and Gang Violence

Beyond Risk

Avelardo Valdez

palgrave
macmillan

First published in hardcover in 2007 by PALGRAVE MACMILLAN® in the United
States — a division of St. Martin's Press LLC, 175 Fifth Avenue, New York, NY 10010.

Where this book is distributed in the UK, Europe and the rest of the world, this is by
Palgrave Macmillan, a division of Macmillan Publishers Limited, registered in England,
company number 785998, of Houndmills, Basingstoke, Hampshire RG21 6XS.

Palgrave Macmillan is the global academic imprint of the above companies and has
companies and representatives throughout the world.

Palgrave® and Macmillan® are registered trademarks in the United States, the United
Kingdom, Europe and other countries.

ISBN-13: 978-0-230-61555-7

Library of Congress Cataloging-in-Publication Data

Valdez, Avelardo.
 Mexican American girls and gang violence : beyond risk / by Avelardo Valdez.
      p. cm.
 Includes bibliographical references and index.
 ISBN 1-4039-6722-9 (alk. paper)
 ISBN 0-230-61555-4 (paperback)
 1. Gangs—Texas—San Antonio. 2. Female gangs—Texas—San Antonio. 3. Mexican
American women—Texas—San Antonio. 4. Female juvenile delinquents—Texas—
San Antonio. 5. Family violence—Texas—San Antonio. I. Title.
 HV6439.U7S258 2006
 364.106'608209764351—dc22   2006044807

A catalogue record of the book is available from the British Library.

Design by Scribe, Inc.

Jacket photo © Mike Kane / San Antonio Express-News. Used by permission.

First PALGRAVE MACMILLAN paperback edition: April 2009

10 9 8 7 6 5 4 3 2 1

Printed in the United States of America.

Transferred to Digital Printing in 2009

For my mother Adeline, my wife Cecilia, my daughter Rebecca,
and my granddaughter Azucena

Contents

Foreword

Joan W. Moore

I am very pleased to be able to contribute something to this book. I think that it is among the rare works that might have real impact on researchers in a well-established field—the study of street gangs. Let me briefly explain why I think so.

The study of gangs has its roots in an odd mixture of journalistic storytelling and social science research. Criminal gangs were a hot public issue during the Prohibition era of the 1920s, and were seen, in a sense, as the precursors to current youth street gangs. The journalist Herbert Asbury's 1927 book *The Gangs of New York* ultimately became the basis for a Hollywood movie (or at least its title did). In the same year, the University of Chicago Press published Frederick Thrasher's classic study of virtually all of Chicago's youth gangs. Thrasher took a social work perspective, examining the wide variation in gangs and their locations in the social space of the city.

Later writings focused more intensely on gangs as venues for juvenile delinquency, but the two strands—journalistic and social science—persisted. To this day, popular writers continue to find a rich source of often sensationalized material in street gangs, especially as gangs have become increasingly associated with inner-city Hispanic and black youth—the "others" of our society. Among social scientists, gang research has become more and more the province of criminologists, with sophisticated sampling and systematic measurement added to a continuing thread of qualitative studies.

A funny thing happened in both realms. Gangs came gradually to be viewed almost as self-contained minisocieties. This view was particularly prevalent in the journalistic works: in many of them it is as if once a teenager joins a gang all other social ties become irrelevant. To be sure, social science researchers sought to explain the gang in terms of larger systems—as artifacts of working-class or ethnic cultures or as inevitable outcomes of the deteriorating fortunes of inner-city communities, for example. But by and large gangs—male gangs, at least—were portrayed as deviant versions of "adolescent societies," sometimes even tending toward the "corporate." Like studies of formal organizations, research has focused on recruiting, internal social structure, and the activities, norms, and motivations of members.

I am exaggerating, of course. Ethnographers have continued to look at the family, community roles of gang members, and the community context of gangs. I did too, particularly in an unpublished study of the impact of gang members' incarceration on their parents and siblings (1981). A rare few studies have discussed the ways in which gangs affect the community as a whole. Several researchers draw a distinction between "core" and "peripheral" or "fringe" members—although they almost never study the fringe. Field studies and surveys of high school students find that for many youth, actual membership in the gang is a short-term fling. However study after study leaves the impression that members' ties to the adult world are only marginally relevant. Joining a gang means joining a total institution, but people in the surrounding community are somehow indifferent toward the gang.

Girl gangs have been of much less interest to researchers. This is partly because they are less common than male gangs are, and partly because their boundaries are often far less tight. In fact, researchers— Avelardo Valdez included—often fail to find "real" female gangs at all. Female gangs are almost always portrayed as adjuncts or "auxiliaries" of their male counterparts. The extent to which they are following their own agency or are pawns of the boys is often an issue, as is the question of whether or not the girls who are studied are "really" gang people or are "just" hangers-on.

In this book, Valdez has done something different. He doesn't dismiss the importance of the hangers-on. He has creatively and painstakingly sampled not the "auxiliaries," but the whole plethora of female hangers-on—those many rings of girls that orbit the male gangs of Chicano San Antonio, Texas. These are girls spread rather widely throughout the community. They have very different relationships to the boys, but all are under their influence. Valdez has looked in detail at their day to day interactions, with each other, with their families, and with the boys. This is truly innovative. We know from several field studies that male gangs are often shadowed by crowds of hangers-on, male as well as female, but Valdez looks at those satellites as of real interest in their own right.

Valdez's approach puts a different spin on gang life and on the place of gangs in the community. Two major points struck me forcibly. First, this book challenges the assumption that youth gangs are crisply bounded. In this study, the male gangs are looked at sideways, so to speak. They are a major part of the social context of the girls' lives. Not surprisingly, the gangs turn out to be more like everyday adolescent cliques than like formal organizations. Their members are seriously involved in violence, drug use, and criminality, which certainly helps to set them apart from the conventional world. They are thus "beyond risk," as are the girls that hang around with them. So are most of their families. In fact, one begins to wonder why gang researchers haven't been paying more attention to the immediate social context of gang members—to *cholo* families and extended kin. Gangs and other deviant adolescent cliques may emerge from an increasingly well-established subculture in which the formal institutions of social mobility and social control often operate punitively. By contrast, street socialization and street controls offer short-term status rewards to frustrated kids. Gang members get caught up in their own mythology, which gives them a spurious sense of being of consequence. One of the functions of the cloud of female hangers-on is to reinforce this sense. The quasi-institutionalized gang is the core of what Valdez calls a "risk network." Risk networks are among many social factors that preserve an intergenerational cycle of dysfunction.

Second, throughout this book Valdez portrays the grittiness of the lives of the *cholo* families and adolescent cliques. In these communities, street norms compete with traditional values to provide the boys with a kind of precarious legitimation for treating some of these girls as trash while others are ostensibly paid more respect.

It's the good old virgin/whore dichotomy. But Valdez makes the uncomfortable point that all of these girls, not just the stigmatized "hoodrats," are engaged or closely involved in violence, criminality, and drug use. Some of this material is hard to read. There is a constant reminder that these are little more than children, who cry when they're hurt. But many of them also learn an odd combination of submissiveness and aggression. They're the target of fights and the victims of violence and sexual abuse, but they also fight back and even instigate fights. This is a highly nuanced view of what it means for a girl to live in this kind of environment. And it reminds us that the girls are embedded in families and cliques of female friends that are also fully engaged in this sorrowful but dramatic way of being young.

Valdez chose to broaden research on girls and gangs by studying girls who hang around with gang boys, rather than those who form themselves into independent gangs. He focuses on one-on-one relationships and gender roles, and the details of what he finds shatters many stereotypes. But to me one of the most innovative aspects of the study is that he moves the spotlight from the gang to the surrounding social world. This includes the families. He has done so with extraordinary attention to sampling and to data collection, as well as sensitivity to and involvement with the community he studies. It is virtually impossible to dismiss—or to forget—his findings. I think this is an important book.

References

Asbury, Herbert. 1927. *The Gangs of New York*. New York: Alfred Knopf.

Moore, Joan. 1981. *Barrio Impact of High Incarceration Rates*. Los Angeles: Chicano Pinto Research Project Final Report.

Taylor, Carl. 1989. *Dangerous Society*. East Lansing, MI: Michigan State University Press.

Thrasher, Frederick. 1927. *The Gang*. Chicago: University of Chicago Press.

Acknowledgments

This study would not have been possible without all the persons involved in the research team. Special recognition goes to the field-workers who were responsible for contacting and recruiting the study's sample of three hundred Mexican American females. Field-workers for the study included Richard Arcos, Maria Alvarado, Rosie Olivarez, Ramon Vasquez, and Katrina Kubicek. Also, I am indebted to John Alvarado, who was the field director of not only this project but also others in our San Antonio field office, and James Codd, our project adminstrator. Special recognition goes to Richard Arcos whose community contacts with this population made the study possible. Richard was also the primary field-worker on the male gang study that preceded this study. These staff have been especially generous in providing thoughts, insights, and experience on the topics of this book.

Faculty associated with this research project include co-investigators Dr. Alberto G. Mata at the University of Oklahoma and Dr. Rebecca Petersen at the Kennesaw University. Consultants associated with this project are Dr. Hortensia Amaro at Northeastern University, Dr. Richard Cervantes at Behavioral Associates, Inc., and Dr. Joan Moore at the University of Wisconsin-Milwaukee. Research assistants on the project included George Lara, Maria Munoz, Raquel Flores, Laura Bermudez, and other staff including Melissa Heinz-Bennett and more recently Yolanda Villarreal here at the University of Houston. Dr. Alice Cepeda's contribution to this study was invaluable in the initiation of the proposal, research implementation, analysis of data, and assistance in completion of the manuscript. Special thanks to Melissa Navarro who transcribed all of the open-ended interviews. I would also like to recognize Dr. Charles D. Kaplan, research scientist at the University of Houston and Masstricht University for his scholarly insights, inspiration, and contribution to this project. On a more personal note I would like to recognize my family and friends for their support, encouragement, and ideas during this research process.

I am especially grateful to the one hundred and fifty young women who agreed (with their guardians' consent) to be interviewed for this study and to be the subjects of this book. These young women willingly discussed aspects of their life that they seldom shared with others. I would like to personally thank them for that privilege.

This report presents findings from a study funded by the Center for Disease Control, National Center for Injury Prevention and Control (R49/CCR621048), aimed at developing a scientifically based understanding of sexual- and intimate-partner violence among high-risk Mexican American females from fourteen to eighteen years of age. This was initially funded through the University of Texas at San Antonio and later the University of Houston. The study builds upon an earlier study on drugs and violence related to Mexican American gang-affiliated males in San Antonio and Laredo, Texas, funded by a National Institute on Drug Abuse (NIDA) grant (RO 1 DA08604).

The findings from this project are seen as critical to the development of effective prevention programs that are culturally responsive to the needs of this rapidly growing minority population. The book is intended to shed light on the etiology of sexual- and intimate-partner violence by comparing behavior and personal characteristics of a sample of high-risk, gang-affiliated females.

The Office for Drug and Social Policy Research at the Graduate College of Social Work, University of Houston, anticipates that the knowledge gained from this research will lead to a richer, more thorough understanding of the relationships between multiple risk factors and sexual- and intimate-partner violence among high-risk adolescent females.

List of Tables and Figures

Chapter 1

Introduction

During the last decade, there has been a great deal of national attention placed on adolescent delinquency, in particular as it relates to the use of violence. Much of this attention has focused on the subgroup of delinquents associated with street gangs, given their association with violence. Evidence indicates that youth street gangs have proliferated in the United States in large and small cities, suburban and rural areas. Hispanics make up a disproportionately large number of existing street gangs due to the increasing numbers of Mexican, Central American, and other Hispanic young males living in geographically dispersed communities recently occupied by this population. These Hispanics often reside in neighborhoods characterized by unemployment, poverty, welfare dependency, single-headed households, and other socioeconomic characteristics that are traditionally associated with street-gang formation. While gang youth violence has generally been addressed as a male phenomenon, in this book I am concerned with understanding the experiences adolescent females in these same disadvantaged communities face on a day-to-day basis.

During the 1990s and early 2000s, an increased participation of women and girls in high-risk behaviors such as drug abuse, violence, crime, and gang-related activities was observed (Curry, Ball, and Decker 1996; Klein 1995; Sanders 1994). This was a significant shift from earlier periods when only a minority of adolescent girls was involved in antisocial behavior. Researchers such as Jody Miller (1998) discuss how female participation in gangs has increased the likelihood that they will become violent offenders and also victims of crime. Through Miller's research emphasis has been placed on how gender inequality and sexual exploitation shape the risks found within street-gang culture that play themselves out in these impoverished communities. Females in this context are particularly vulnerable to risks as they transition from late childhood to adolescence. They find it difficult to reconcile the status that their peers assign them via their connection with, and attraction to, young men, with the denigration and stigmatization for engaging in deviant risk behaviors such as early sexual activity. As we shall see, the risks are exacerbated when adolescent girls in such low-income communities participate in gang activities and other delinquent lifestyles.

Most research on females connected with male gangs has focused exclusively on female gang members and has overlooked the large number of females who are not members but participate in the street-based activities of male gangs (Campbell 1995; Chesney-Lind 1993; Miller 1998). There may actually be more of these hangers-on than female members, especially in Hispanic inner-city neighborhoods. Since few studies on gang-affiliated females exist, this book seeks to explore the relationships and processes of how these young women are influenced and integrated into the social groups of male gangs. How these relationships play out for adolescent females is presented here within the larger backdrop of the structural conditions of low-income, urban, barrios. Structural changes in these urban areas (and in other communities as well) have increased the social isolation of residents, especially adolescent females. This social isolation has compounded the negative social and health consequences the adolescent girls are exposed to in these communities.

Beyond Risk

I identify within this Mexican American community the emergence of a *beyond-risk* adolescent female. The meaning of beyond risk for the adolescent females is rooted in the fact that changes in gender roles and sexuality are transforming male-female relationships in this society. For instance, in the United States, and in society in general, sexuality has seen some important transformations. This is evident from the increased media representation of sexuality in its repeated advertisement of contraceptive methods and pharmaceutical sexual enhancers, as well as the frequent representation of scantily dressed young women performing provocative sexual dances and moves in music videos on television. These factors have, in a sense, created a social space in which the portrayal of sexuality is acceptable and oftentimes encouraged for young women. Similarly, we are seeing more and more adolescent females engaging in delinquent and criminal behavior—activities that are viewed by the larger society as antisocial even though they are highly glamorized in the mass media.

In general, these social transformations are important to understand within the context of conventional society's understanding of a person's life trajectory for adolescence and early adulthood. That is, the emphasis is placed on the development of a person through socially constructed age-graded stages and normative orderliness and expectations. Transitions are normative because they are expected to occur in a given order and at a particular age in the course of life. They are typically associated with social relationships and the person's role in society. For females, the normative life trajectory is expected to include such stages of life as completing school, dating, finding employment, getting married, and becoming a mother, all at appropriate ages.

As you will see, this normative course of life is not an option for the young women presented in this book. Their involvement in risky behavior—such as the perpetration of physical fights, early onset of sexual behavior, substance use, and/or other delinquent behavior—is characteristic of growing up in these environments. In a sense, for some of these adolescent females engaging in these individual risk behaviors is perceived as contributing to an increased autonomy in regard to male counterparts. This is further evidenced in that the Mexican American adolescent females I present here are not the typical self-identified gang members or affiliates but rather have created new roles for themselves within the gang context. These new roles revolve around associating or "hanging out" with male gang members via their personal relationships with members (that is, as girlfriends, sisters, relatives, and so on). Hanging out and associating with male gang members becomes a daily routine in the lives of many of these adolescent females. Intimate relationships and peer social-support networks are established within this social context.

During this process, however, some adolescent females are exposed to further risks associated with negative social and health consequences, which place them beyond risk. First, the traditional patriarchal characteristics of male dominance and female submissiveness inherent in Mexican culture is magnified in the male gang, which further isolates the adolescent female. Second, the females I examine here lack the social support and constraints imposed on typical adolescents by prosocial adults and community institutions of social control. For the adolescent females whom I looked at, their sexuality and participation in deleterious behavior is established and reinforced by the street-oriented environment they have been exposed to throughout their lives. This street culture, however, is detrimental to the young women's safety. For instance, drinking and getting high at a party may be normative behavior within this context; but doing it in the presence of violent, intoxicated adolescent males increases the risk of victimization. Finally, the patriarchal ideology of the larger society has imposed the cultural norm of "connectedness" to males. That is, even among this young female population, their lack of ability to hold significant control over unwanted sexual encounters is associated with the need for connection with males, which has traditionally been emphasized by gender role expectations. For instance, as you will see, the risk of jeopardizing existing sexual relationships with male partners contributes to the sexual victimization of these young adolescents. In summary, in this book I depict how these adolescent females' association with male gang members compounds the volatile situational context and places them beyond risk for sexual and physical violent victimization.

My primary aim in this work is to render first-hand experiences of the social, cultural, and contextual dynamics that are affecting poor urban Mexican American adolescent females living within the social milieu of gangs. In doing so I explore how each adolescent female's level of delinquency is mediated by the quality of their connectedness to parents, siblings, boyfriends, common-law husbands, and friends. This book therefore offers insight into a population that has rarely been looked at—*beyond-risk* Mexican American female adolescents.

Mexican American Female Gang Members and Other High-Risk Girls

Although the focus of this book is on girls who are not formally integrated into a gang, it is important to present existing knowledge of Mexican American female gang studies. Mexican American female gang members are likely to have strong connections to family networks, highly gendered relations, and strong identification with their ethnic culture. For instance, not only are husbands and boyfriends important influences in generating and confirming women's deviance, but also family lifestyles and adolescent peer groups. Traditional Hispanic values may deter the majority of Mexican American women from using drugs or participating in other antisocial behaviors. Nonetheless, among families with histories of drug use, crime, and incarceration, traditional values may actually drive these women into a deeper lifelong involvement with a street lifestyle because these values form the basis of labeling and social isolation (Moore 1994). Chicano youth gangs or adolescent crowds similar to gangs become important groups to affirm the street lifestyle for female adolescents from these types of families. Once involved in the gang, girls are stigmatized by traditional Mexican American gender norms that label them as a "bad girl." This reputation narrows their social options, especially as they transition to early adulthood (Cepeda and Valdez 2003; Rosenbaum 1985).

Mary Harris (1994) found that Mexican American gang members rejected traditional images of a Hispanic woman as a "wife or mother" and substituted the gang for family and school ties. These girls identified themselves with a more "macho homegirl" image. She found them willing to fight and face the enemy. Joan Moore (1991) found a similar pattern among Chicana gang members in East Los Angeles where gangs provide an avenue for respect, status, and recognition. However, even within a gang, girls were described as "bad" and "good" girls, and "bad girls" like to fight and to drink—the very thing that confers prestige on male members. Bad girls were the ones who were more likely to move to harder drugs, such as heroin, as adults. These observations suggest that gang girls are experiencing major shifts in traditional gender roles. Their roles may be converging with those of Hispanic males in what some have identified as an oppositional femininity (Portillos 1999). Such shifts in gender roles create conflicts, especially among intimate partners and family members. The conflicts are often resolved through violence.

National data consistently reveal that the prevalence of drug use among Hispanic females is lower than it is among white and black females. It has been argued "that traditional Hispanic values seem to be protective factors against alcoholism (and by extension, substance abuse) in women" (Canino 1992; Caetano 1994). However, for Chicanas, gang membership is associated with more frequent involvement with substance use (Long 1990). Harris's study of female *chola* gang members found they engaged in heavy drug use parallel to the men (Harris 1994).

David Brotherton (1996) found Mexican American female gang members had a broader range of drug use in comparison to black and El Salvadorian gangs. Moore's study (1994) that focused on adult Chicana female heroin addicts, found that youth gangs became a significant locus for heroin consumption. Mexican American girls who use drugs tend to be labeled as the "wilder girls" whose "social life tends to be confined to other drug-using girlfriends and the wilder, more *cholo* boys" (Moore 1994, 1117). *Cholos* are Mexican American youth who have adopted a distinctive street style of dress, gestures, tattoos, and graffiti (Vigil 1988). As a whole, these studies suggest that not only is drug use higher among these girls who violate gender norms, but also that drug use has serious repercussions for Mexican American females, leading them into a more long-term, street-oriented lifestyle.

Much of the Hispanic gang literature points to the fact that tradi- tional Mexican American gender norms are very important in channel- ing sexual behaviors as well. For instance, Ruth Horowitz describes how young Mexican American females "account for their loss of virginity and their public behavior with and toward motherhood" through "bounding" and "unbounding" sexuality (Horowitz 1983, 125). Bounding refers to the projection of an image that sexuality is restricted to a man whom they love. Girls whose sexuality is bounded retain the respect of peers and family. Unbounded sexuality means giving in to her passion and failing to meet community norms and criteria. Hortensia Amaro and Carol Hardy-Fanta (1995) explain how this need for con- nectedness to men among low-income minority women increases initi- ation to drugs, disappointment in men, failure to provide for children, and violent victimization. Mexican American females associated with gangs in these types of social milieus are highly susceptible to physical violence and sexual victimization.

My interest in this book is on those who are not gang members but who are nonetheless connected in some form or another with male gangs. In low-income neighborhoods, young females may be attracted to male gang members because of the status associated with their member- ship (Palmer and Tilley 1995). However, the majority of these other girls are loosely associated with male gang members through brothers or other relatives, neighbors, life-long friends, classmates, or acquaintances from their neighborhood. These nongang girls may be structurally incorporated into the activities of a male gang differently than girl gang members, but they are just as prone to illicit drug use, violence, and high-risk sexual behavior as the gang members (Quicker 1983; Murphy 1978; Moore 1990). Research on female gangs focuses on self-identified female gang members, ignoring the high-risk, nongang girls associated with this social milieu. As a result, previous studies of gang girls have ignored a large segment of the female delinquent minority population who are connected to male gang life in other ways.

Female Gang Members and the Role of Gender

Generally, most social scientists agree that Mexican American culture reinforced by social context magnifies the differences between gen- ders to a greater degree than many other cultures. Gender roles reflect a family–ethnic community complex tied to structural features of the family and to more general conditions of social solidarity that stem from Mexican Americans' subordinate status. Patriarchy (male

domination/female subordination) and machismo have a complex interaction with class and ethnicity. Patriarchy refers to the development and
institutionalization of male dominance over women in society, a characteristic observed to some extent among all groups. Machismo is how
patriarchal ideology is operated by males of Mexican descent and other
Hispanics. Young women associated with these gangs—regardless of
how they are associated with the gang—must mediate privileges and
opportunities through an imposed patriarchal structure.

However, traditional gender roles are dynamic and are changing
among Mexican Americans (Davenport and Yurich 1991). As in the larger
society, gender roles have become more egalitarian (Williams 1990). The
majority of Mexican Americans continue to be situated on the lower end
of the class hierarchy. But even at this end of the class continuum, independence and autonomy vary among these young women. Ethnographic
studies show that Mexican American working-class girls are "a generation
of young women who don't expect to be supported by a man—a generation who see men in their working-class community often unemployed or
underemployed, men who too often dealt with this hardship by abandon-
ing their obligation and responsibilities to women. This generation is not
waiting for a man to save their lives" (Bettie 2000, 2). Therefore, some
girls may experience a contradiction. On the one hand, they want to be
more independent and autonomous but, on the other hand, they face
internal and external pressures based on culturally prescribed, traditional
gender norms. As a result, they are likely to experience considerable internal conflict, as well as conflict in their relationships.

More recent research takes the position that the lives of Mexican
American, street-oriented women (such as drug users) cannot be reduced
to a traditional, gendered stereotype of dependency on men and subordination to them. These females vary widely in the extent to which they
control their criminality, drug use, sexuality, and access to resources.
Specifically, these contemporary "deviant" females involved in antisocial
behaviors seem to be exhibiting a greater variation of autonomy than
their counterparts in the past. This autonomy is noncelebratory. That is,
this relative autonomy from those personal relationships, which are based
on traditional Mexican American gender roles, does not relieve them
from the overwhelming burdens of supporting a drug habit or subsisting
economically (Valdez et al. 2001). Collectively, these women continue to
live in an ethnic community that continues to impose clearly defined gender and class barriers on women. Thus, their relative autonomy from men
has not necessarily resulted in a freer development of self, as a celebratory
autonomy would assume. I define it as *paradoxical autonomy*.

Multilevel Theoretical Approach

There is no single theoretical approach that can fully explain why Mexican American females affiliate with gangs and engage in high-risk behaviors. In recent years, several theoretical paradigms have contributed to our understanding of females' participation in behaviors previously more closely associated with males. This includes the feminist perspective that posits the convergence in women's and men's patterns of crime brought about by the greater gender equality in the larger contemporary society (Miller 2001). The orientation of my book is less theoretical and more empirical in that it takes the perspective that multiple levels of factors are continually interacting with each other to exert influence on an individual's susceptibility to these deleterious behaviors. Levels that comprise these factors include; community-level, individual-level, and situational-level factors (Sampson and Lauritsen 1994). Approaching the book's subject from this multilevel theoretical perspective substantially increases our opportunity to understand these girls within the greater context of the complex social system in which they are embedded.

Macrosocial and Community Level of Explanations

The macrosocial or community-level helps define what it is about community structures and cultures that produce behaviors such as interpersonal violence, drug use, high-risk sex, etc. It examines whether it is the characteristics of the community that produce high rates of drug use or whether it is the characteristics of the persons living in the community. The macrosocial perspective goes back to Shaw and McKay's social disorganization model of delinquency in ethnic communities in Chicago in the 1930s and 1940s. In this model, the goal of the research was to identify social-structural characteristics that lead to social disorganization and then to high rates of crime. Such characteristics included low levels of income, ethnic heterogeneity, and lack of residential mobility. Social disorganization was defined as communities experiencing the deterioration of traditional institutions. Shaw and McKay argued that this disorganization contributes to the isolation of communities so that legitimate economic opportunities and social services are not readily available. Such a process "leads to the rejection of individualistic explanations of delinquency and focuses instead on the processes by which delinquent and criminal patterns of behavior were transmitted across generations in areas of social disorganization and weak social controls" (Sampson and Lauritsen 1994, 45). This ecological perspective was confirmed to various degrees by researchers in many studies that followed in the 1950s and 1960s.

What was distinct about this macrolevel approach was that it focused on neighborhoods as the unit of analysis (Jencks 1990; Mayer and Jencks 1989; Morenoff and Tienda 1997; Quane and Rankin 1998). More recently, research along similar lines has focused on social capital factors (Sandefur and Laumann 1998). Economic downturns can increase inequality and therefore increase poverty, joblessness, and welfare dependency in urban minority neighborhoods. William Wilson (1987) and others (Rickets and Sawhill 1988) argue that the constellation of these characteristics have produced what they identify as an "underclass."[1]

Female-headed families, declining marriage, illegitimate births, and welfare also increased compared to previous decades (Jencks 1990; LaFree and Drass 1996). Concomitantly, more economically stable minorities moved out of these inner-city neighborhoods to more middle-class areas open to them now as a result of the civil rights legislation. Residents of the older racial enclaves were now more socially isolated and susceptible to behaviors such as substance abuse, crime, and violence. Wilson and his colleagues argue that deviant behavior can be traced, in part, to the social disorganization associated with collective social characteristics such as neighborhood cohesion and trust, informal social control, structural lack of educational opportunities, and unstable family relations (Latkin and Curry 2003; Quane and Rankin 1998; Sampson, Raudenbush, and Earls 1997).

The characteristics of social disorganization are also related to what is described as institutional completeness. Institutional completeness refers to the extent that there exists a full range of social institutions such as churches, community businesses, neighborhood associations, schools, and intact family and kinship that organize and support the daily lives of the community's residents (Tsukashima 1985; Valdez 1993). High levels of institutional completeness, even in the face of poverty, may create a protective factor against crime and violence by providing a buffering safety net against an urban atmosphere of desperation and powerlessness (de Swaan 1988; Ross, Mirowsky, and Pribesh 2001; Ross, Reynolds, and Geis 2000; Thompson and Seber 1996).

Individual Levels of Explanations

The individual level of explanation refers to characteristics that explain antisocial behavior. In discussions of individual risk factors, researchers typically focus on ascribed and achieved characteristics of individuals statistically associated with violence and crime. For example, researchers may be interested in how risks for homicide are distributed across characteristics such as age, gender, marital status, lifestyle, and socioeconomic status. Individual-level risk factors associated with gang membership include early onset of such delinquency as theft, burglary, fighting, and destruction of property. Excessive use of alcohol and drugs is often associated with crime, fighting, and other deviant behaviors. Childhood trauma makes youth susceptible to commit such offenses. If a young male has a history of aggression, violence, rebelliousness, and other risk behaviors, his chances of perpetrating violence and violent victimization within the gang context are increased.

For adolescents living in poor urban communities, street gangs often provide the social context that encourages violence, crime, drug use, and other deviant behaviors. However, increases in delinquency and violence among these adolescents may also originate in the quality of family relations (Robbins and Szapocznik 2000). The family is believed to play a pivotal role in the evolution of behavioral problems. Some researchers even argue that differences in family relations may be more important than even psychopathological factors in understanding such adolescent behavioral problems as acting out, unwillingness to follow rules, early sexual involvement, and chronic drug and alcohol use (Brook et al. 2000).

Certain characteristics of family structures and processes are associated with juvenile crimes. Family structure is related to the makeup of the family and household (e.g., two-parent household vs. single-parent household). Family processes are connected to the relations between members, including parental involvement, conflict resolution styles, and other communication characteristics. Recent research suggests that family-process variables such as communication skills are more important than family-structure characteristics in preventing delinquent behaviors.

Within Hispanic families, the extended family has been identified as the most influential institution in the culture. However, many Hispanic families are experiencing structural changes and acculturation stress moving them away from traditional characteristics. This is especially the case among families with multigenerational members. Thus, family-level risk factors, family structure, and instability or disorganization (e.g., divorce and lack of adult prosocial role models) will be considered in this research. Issues such as the history of multigenerational familial involvement in gangs, substance use, illegal activities, arrests, and incarceration such as found in Mexican American barrios in the Southwest also will be considered.

Situational Levels of Explanation

Situational-level factors refer to those factors that have an immediate influence on the initiation or outcome of violence or other deviant behavior. Understanding the situational level processes that instigate violent acts among high-risk adolescents is a major focus of this study. Situational-level analyses treat the incident as the unit of analysis. In their discussion of violent events, Robert J. Sampson and Janet Lauritsen focus on such factors as the presence and types of weapon, the presence of drugs or alcohol, the role of bystanders, and the victim's degree of resistance and retaliation (1994). This would also include a discussion of victims' and offenders' past histories, present behaviors, and relationship to one another. Such considerations add to the individual-level data to provide a more complete framework for understanding the context of violent events.

Such microlevel considerations suggest mechanisms and properties that can contribute to a deeper understanding of violence. The microlevel explanations are expected to be more important in subcultures (and societies) that are less well developed and less binding and constraining. As James Short states:

> Microlevel processes probably are more important to the explanation of the behavior of gang members, individually and collectively, than they are for young people who are involved in more formally and effectively structured, adult-sponsored institutions. (Short 1985, 65)

The situational approach is highly appropriate for violence and other behaviors among females who are involved in street gangs and marginalized and segmented from the majority of society.

The Present Study

This research on females began in 1998 looking at one hundred and fifty females associated with male gang members in San Antonio, Texas. At that time, there were few studies that focused on Mexican American female gang members; such studies include Joan Moore's *Going Down to the Barrio* and several others, which I will discuss in the following chapters. Moore's subjects, however, were older gang members and the study was largely retrospective. Up to the late 1990s, the majority of research on gangs had focused on Mexican American male gangs in the

Southwest (Spergel 1995). Mexican Americans have a long gang tradition, especially in Southern California. Many of the street gangs in Southern California have existed within particular localities as extended families or clans for three or more generations with connections to family networks and community-based institutions (Murphy 1978; Vigil 1988). Some of these gangs have evolved into highly organized criminal networks engaged in heroin distribution (Moore 1991). Other gangs have evolved into adult prison gangs whose illegal activities now extend beyond correctional institutions. The majority, however, are territorially based youth gangs concerned with protecting their turfs from rivals.

The research that does exist on Mexican American females or other Hispanics generally tends to be among populations in Los Angeles or cities with long gang histories (such as Chicago and New York). In the first half of the last century, urban areas were characterized by waves of European immigrants and southern blacks. Today, Hispanic immigration has given rise to diverse and multiethnic populations that affect every aspect of public life: schools, politics, public health, housing, and the workplace. These demographic changes have generated competition for limited resources between these new immigrants and more established minority groups like African Americans. The consequences of these social dynamics—especially how they influence youth street gang formation—are not clearly understood. This research is unique in that it has given me the opportunity to explore gangs in a new urban setting with a majority Mexican-origin population.

San Antonio might be described as an example of a budding gang "city where the young people's creation of and involvement in gangs has occurred since the mid-1980s" (Miller 2001, 16). In addition, most of San Antonio's Mexican-origin population is largely nonimmigrant, which is different from other major cities with large Hispanic populations and gang traditions. Nonetheless, like other cities it has experienced macrolevel shifts during the last three decades. This "economic restructuring" is often described as a loss of manufacturing jobs as they became internationalized, giving rise to the service economy (Moore and Pinderhughes 1993). I will explore and compare how these macroeconomic changes are related to microlevel processes in regard to their influences on the nature of gangs and girl's involvement in gangs. Also, I will consider how the ethnic community imposes clearly defined gender and class barriers that may differentiate them from girls in other communities. Many studies on female gangs have focused on older populations, although much current information points to girls becoming involved in gangs at a much earlier age. What is distinct about this book's population is that they are mostly girls in their early teens.

The chapters presented in this book are organized to describe the design and procedures used throughout the research and findings, which address the aims initially proposed in the research. Chapter 2 describes the ecological—or macrolevel—context from which Mexican American youth gangs emerged in this community. The context considers a framework that is both historical and contemporary. Portions of this chapter originally appeared in a book chapter entitled "Toward a Typology of Contemporary Mexican American Youth Gangs" in *Gangs and Society: Alternative Perspectives* published in 2003 by Columbia University Press. Chapter 3 details methods by which entry was gained to this population and the recruitment and sampling procedures used in the research. In addition, it includes an overview of the demographic characteristics of the adolescent females. A portion of this chapter first appeared in a peer reviewed article entitled "Using Snowball-Based Methods in Hidden Populations to Generate a Randomized Community Sample of Gang Affiliated Adolescents" in *Youth Violence and Juvenile Justice*, Vol 3:2 with Rebecca Peterson. Chapter 4 shifts to more individual-level factors by focusing on the effect of the family. Individual family experiences may differentiate the risk behaviors among these girls. Chapter 5 presents a qualitative typology of the high-risk Mexican American females that shows how girls with different degrees of association with male gangs behave in risk-prone social activities. A version of this chapter originally appeared in the *Journal of Adolescent Research* (Vol 18:1) as an article entitled "Risk Behaviors among Young Mexican American Gang-Associated Females: Sexual Relations, Partying, Substance Use, and Crime" with Alice Cepeda. Chapter 6 continues this individual-level analysis by examining sexual victimization and how gender structures girls' victimization in relationship with boyfriends, gangs, and family members. Chapter 7 focuses on situational processes associated with intimate-partner violence. An original version of this chapter was published as an article in *Sociological Focus*, Vol 38:2 and was entitled, "A Situational Analysis of Dating Violence among Mexican American Females Associated with Street Gangs" with Raquel Flores. Chapter 8 provides an analysis of distinct psychosocial predictors of violent victimization and perpetration of intimate-partner violence using the Conflict Tactics Scale (CTS) as a dependent variable. This chapter is distinct from the others in that it is much more psychological and quantitative. The book concludes (Chapter 9) by discussing the implications of the study with an emphasis on prevention and intervention strategies for girls in these types of marginalized communities. Finally, it provides some concluding comments and suggests a theoretical framework for understanding sexual and intimate violence among this special population of females.

Notes

1. The concept of the underclass has seen numerous nuances in its development and has been hotly debated in its meaning and application to Hispanic communities (Moore and Pinderhughes 1993).

Chapter 2

Life and Gangs on the West Side

San Antonio's West Side Mexican American Community[1]

San Antonio, Texas is located one hundred and forty miles from the U.S.-Mexico border. The population in 2000 was estimated to be 1.2 million, with approximately 60 percent of Mexican descent (U.S. Bureau of the Census 2000). The West Side community in San Antonio is comprised predominantly of Mexican-origin persons and is one of the poorest urban areas in the United States. According to the census data, the per capita income was $5,098 and the median household income was $14,352 for twenty-two census tracts that comprise this community. Of West-Side families, 55 percent had children living in poverty and only 23 percent of the families received public assistance (U.S. Bureau of the Census 2000, 2001, 2002).

The adolescents in this study live in impoverished neighborhoods concentrated in approximately ten census tracts located on the West Side of the city with a population of around fifty thousand persons (Brischetto 2000). Neighborhoods in this area are characterized as having the highest concentration of low-income, Mexican-origin persons in the city. It is also an area that has a high concentration of crime, violence, substance use, and some of the highest rates of teenage pregnancy in Texas (and the second highest in the nation) (Alan Guttmacher Institute 1995; Yin et al. 1996). More importantly, in these neighborhoods is the highest concentration of delinquent behavior and gang activity.

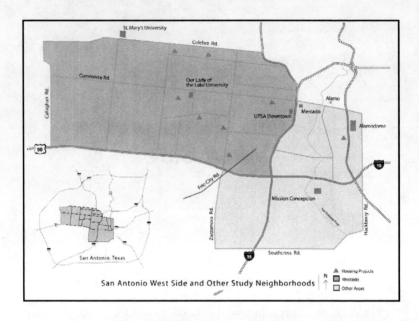

San Antonio West Side and Other Study Neighborhoods

The Social Etiology of San Antonio's Barrios

The economically marginal condition of this population has its etiology in the early twentith century. The West Side was the traditional settlement for Mexican immigrants beginning in the 1920s when they arrived in large numbers, escaping the political turmoil and poverty of Mexico. This migration steadily increased through the 1940s as San Antonio experienced an urbanization process. However, unlike other newcomers to the city, Mexicans were segregated into limited geographic areas that were primarily in neighborhoods on the near West Side, adjacent to the city's central business district. These neighborhoods were characterized by inadequate housing, inferior infrastructure (water, sewers, electricity, etc.), and limited public services (schools, police, clinics, hospitals). In the 1930s, San Antonio's barrios had some of the highest rates of tuberculosis, venereal diseases, and infant mortality in the United States (Garcia 1989).

The Mexican barrios of San Antonio were adjacent to the city's' vice district where most Mexican businesses were located. This area was west of the downtown area and the San Fernando Plaza, which holds San Antonio's main Catholic cathedral. In this sense, San Antonio was similar to other cities such as New York and Chicago, where vice districts were typically segregated in minority ghettos or barrios. According to one historian, in the first half of the twenty-first century, this area of San Antonio had over ninety bordellos, saloons, gambling dens, and small shacks where prostitutes plied their trade (Bowser 2003). These establishments were sustained by Anglo clients from throughout the city. The district was also the entertainment center for the Mexican population where Spanish language theaters (vaudeville and film), cantinas, restaurants, outdoor markets, and dance halls were situated. It was the primary source of liquor during prohibition and marijuana beginning in the late 1930s. The red-light district operated under the approval of the city until the early 1940s when under the pressure of the military it was closed (Bowser 2003).

Opportunities to engage in illicit activities during this time for Mexicans in this city was facilitated by the proximity of the vice district and their limited access to other conventional opportunities imposed by a de-facto Jim Crow social structure (Montejano 1987). One criminal activity in which Mexican Americans were able to flourish was drug trafficking. Within this market, Mexican Americans had an advantage over others in that they shared a common language and ethnic background with drug wholesalers in Mexico's border regions and interior. Beginning in the 1940s, Mexicans began to be associated with the drug market enterprises that extended throughout the United States (Redlinger and Michel 1970). Drug selling and buying continues to be a major illegal activity among segments of the population, especially the young gangs and the adult prison gangs with whom the females in this study are associated.

Despite discriminatory barriers and sectors of this population's involvement in illegal activities, the majority of residents in the barrios managed to find employment in the fringe sectors of the city economy, especially after World War II. Nonetheless, employment did not necessarily mean that families escaped living in persistent poverty. Mexican Americans engaged in various adaptation patterns finding innovative means to subsist economically. For instance, many of these families migrated to the Midwest to work as seasonal agricultural workers for two- to three-month periods. Strong extended families were the major sustaining social structure in San Antonio's West-Side barrios. Mexican American neighborhoods were residentially stable and had a high proportion of home ownership. There were also greater interclass relations found in Mexican American neighborhoods (Garcia 1989). These social factors, along with a strong ethnic identify, created a strong sense of community structure. As a result, these families were "institutionally complete" (Valdez 1993, 193). The structure tended to break down in the following decades as the result of macrofactors influencing San Antonio's economy leading to more socially dysfunctional behaviors.

The West Side's Economic Transformation

As many other urban metropolitan areas of the United States, San Antonio was impacted by the process of deindustrialization during the last decades of the twentieth century (Valdez and Halley 1996; Wilson 1980, 1987). During this period, the city lost most of its industrial base and therefore many of its blue-collar jobs when major manufacturers and livestock- and farming-related industries closed. At the end of this transformation, the city's economic base shifted to services mostly centered on the burgeoning tourist industry, a phenomenon which continues to this day (U.S. Bureau of the Census 2000; Valdez, McCray, and Thomas 1994). This economic base is sustained by one of the lowest wage structures in the United States. Compared to other cities, San Antonio has one of the largest populations of "working poor," which means people that work but earn incomes below the poverty line.

The reason for the large population of working poor is that Mexican Americans, although working, are disproportionately concentrated in lower status occupations. For instance, during the 1980s over 40 percent of Mexican Americans were either employed in craft or labor occupations. On the other hand, 67 percent of Anglos were employed in occupations as managers or technicians. In service occupations, the proportion of Mexican Americans is nearly double that of Anglos. In jobs with the highest status, those of management and professionals, 73 percent are Anglos compared to 22 percent Mexican Americans. In the occupational category of laborers, 64 percent of employed persons are Mexican Americans and 30 percent are Anglos. Clearly, Mexican Americans are working, but at poverty levels.

The low occupational status of Mexican Americans in San Antonio begins to explain the exceptional high poverty rates among this group. In 1980, 24 percent of all Mexican American families fell below the poverty level compared to 12 percent of Anglos. Ten years earlier, 25 percent of all Mexican American families fell below the poverty level compared to 7 percent of Anglos. Hence, while poverty levels did increase for Anglos during the 1970s they still remained half that of Mexican Americans. Correspondingly, Mexican Americans tended to have higher unemployment rates during the late 1970s—it is suspected that this was also true during the 1980s—than those of Anglos. Based on these data we can only project that socioeconomic differences between Mexican

Americans and Anglos have not significantly changed from the late 1970s to today.

The quality of a job indicates whether its holder is fully integrated into the labor force or has marginal participation in it. More importantly, as stated by Roberto M. de Anda,

> Having a job does not guarantee full participation in the labor force. For example, persons having part-time or irregular jobs also show inadequate participation. Similarly, those with full-time jobs who do not earn enough to cover their basic needs are also marginal participants in the labor. (de Anda 1996, 42)

That is, having a job does not guarantee that workers will be able to sustain their families economically, resulting in a population of what is described as the working poor. But even this precarious connection to the labor force by Mexican American workers in San Antonio was broken with macroeconomic changes that occurred in the 1990s.

Such changes were embodied by the closing of the city's major employer, Kelly Air Force Base, which employed up to twenty-five thousand military and civilian employees with a payroll that exceeded $721 million in 1990. At its peak, Kelly Air Force Base, a maintenance business, made $8 billion per year, employing multiple members of the same family, many of whom were second- and third-generation workers. Kelly Air Force Base was the largest employer in the city for forty years (Smith 2001). It was the economic lifeblood of the city. Most of the workers at this base were semiskilled Mexican American males that serviced the aircraft fleet. Many of them were second-generation World War II, Korean War, and Vietnam War, veterans. Access to these jobs was facilitated by deferral civil rights legislation that ended de facto discrimination policies at the federal bases. Jobs at the base were considered the most stable and lucrative positions in the city and were highly coveted by blue-collar workers. Many of the children of these workers provided the basis for the emerging Mexican American middle-class of the 1980s and 1990s. It was the children of the Mexican American middle class who metamorphosed into the Hispanic generation at the end of the twentieth century (Rosales 2000).

On the West Side, this industrial transformation destabilized the precarious economic stability of the community and its institutions. Many of these residents were not necessarily employed at primary industries such as Kelly but did find work as unskilled and semiskilled workers at the hundreds of smaller shops and manufacturers that existed. As a result, these workers were able to economically sustain their families, purchase inexpensive homes, and support neighborhood businesses. These low-income neighborhoods displayed high levels of "institutional completeness" such as residential stability, high numbers of home ownership, and participation in local institutions (Valdez and Kaplan 1999). Although sectors of this population during this period were involved in crime, gangs, drug use, and other deviant behaviors, the amount of such activity was minimal. This relative social stability changed in the 1980s with the transformation of San Antonio's economy.

The comparatively low levels of infusion of governmental investments that would alleviate these conditions further exacerbate San Antonio's poverty. For instance, San Antonio has one of the lowest educational achievement levels and largest illiteracy rates among large U.S. cities. San Antonio Independent School District, one of the largest school districts in the city, has an average of 93 percent of low-income students compared to 49 percent for the state. Among the population twenty-five years old and over (696,022), 49 percent have a high school education or less. Yet, school districts in this city have some of the lowest per-student expenditures in the United States. The city also lags behind in other public services such as libraries, recreation programs, job training, and adult educational programs. Until very recently, municipal and county governments failed to adequately invest in the city's infrastructure, resulting in dilapidated streets, run-down public recreational facilities, lack of affordable housing, and environmental hazards. The city also has some of the lowest health indicators in the nation including high teenage pregnancy and birth rates, diabetes, and cancer. Health problems are exacerbated by the comparatively high proportion of the population without health insurance.

The economical marginalization of the Mexican Americans can not be blamed on the influx of Mexican or other Hispanic immigrants. Among cities with large Mexican origin populations, San Antonio is one of two cities (the other is Albuquerque) with a relatively low percentage (16 percent) of foreign-born Hispanics, or immigrants. San Antonio has failed to attract a large number of documented and undocumented immigrants over the last three decades compared to other cities with large Hispanic populations such as Houston (50 percent) and Los Angeles (56 percent). This may be because of the low-wage structure and unavailability of access to entry-level jobs in manufacturing, construction, and services. As a result, many documented and undocumented Mexican immigrants in Texas bypass San Antonio and instead go to Houston, the Dallas–Arlington–Fort Worth area, or cities farther into the U.S. heartland where there is a much greater concentration of immigrants and where there are more economic opportunities.

Frio City Road Community

A typical community in which the girls in this book reside was the Frio City Road area of the West Side. This street runs alongside one of the major railroad lines, which served industries formerly concentrated on the West Side, to the now-closed air force base. The street is flanked by the railroad tracks on one side, and on the other, abandoned buildings that once housed businesses, which catered to the workers and residents in the area. Immediately to the west of the street is a neighborhood of one-story clapboard houses. Adjacent to these modest homes is San Juan Courts, a public housing project with approximately 204 units. In the larger study target area there are over 2,954 housing units in eight public housing projects (San Antonio Housing Authority 2003). Some of San Antonio's poorest families and elderly residents live in these homes. Today, the only businesses in this area are bars, icehouses, storefront churches, auto repair shops, and convenience stores. One of the striking aspects of the convenience stores are the barrels and bins filled with ice and quarts of beer, large confectionary selections at the counter (gum, candy bars, etc.), and huge displays of cigarettes behind the counter. In these stores it is cheaper to buy a quart of beer than a bottle of water.

From the late 1940s to the 1970s, supply warehouses, produce distributors, shoe manufactures, garment factories, and meatpackers were located along this corridor. South Texas's major stockyards and slaughterhouses (Swift, Armor, etc.) were located just blocks to the east. During this time period, these industries were a major source of employment for residents. However, approximately ten to twenty years ago most of these industries began to close, resulting in thousands of workers losing their jobs. For instance, the Levi's plant that displaced approximately three hundred Mexican American women was one of the last major industries to leave this area. The plant workers were largely uneducated and unskilled women from the adjacent neighborhoods. Levi relocated the production and jobs to the Dominican Republic where wages were much lower. The workers and unions, and Mexican American civil rights groups representing them, met the closing of the plant with protests and demonstrations. However, except for some token job-training programs provided by the federal government and administered by the city, there was no compensation or other reparation to these women or other workers who lost their jobs. Although less dramatic, thousands of other workers in the area found themselves in the same situation. Harold Baulder states that, "Wage levels in San Antonio are so low that many young people and potential entry-level workers drop out of the formal workforce altogether or do not even bother looking for work in the first place" (2002, 26).

There was strong evidence that low-income residents living in the Frio City Road community and others on the West Side were developing characteristics associated with the underclass. Based on John Kasarda's (1993) lead, five social indicators of the underclass were calculated using the 1990 Census for the areas comprising the West Side. The indicators include the percentage of individuals below poverty level; unemployed males; teenage high school dropouts; households receiving public assistance; and female-headed households. Compared to other cities, these data clearly indicate that there was a trend toward developing underclass characteristics on the West Side that emphasize a shift to public-assistance dependency and joblessness. In the underclass discourse, persons identified as belonging to this group generated a distinctive set of values, attitudes, beliefs, norms, and behaviors (Moore and Pinderhughes 1993). Another characteristic of this persistently poor sector of the population was its inability to escape from poverty, making it different from other classes of the poor. The image of this population was that it was prone to crime and welfare dependency.

San Antonio's Mexican-origin population and other urban areas of the United States during this period were experiencing declines in economic status similar to African Americans in large urban areas such as Los Angeles, Houston, the San Francisco-Oakland area, and Chicago. The concentration effects of increased male joblessness, welfare dependency, single-headed households, and decreases in governmental services had a devastating impact on poor and working-class segments of the Mexican American population. Among the effects was the loss of the Mexican American middle class, which fled to higher-status neighborhoods and suburbs leaving traditional barrios to poor Mexican Americans with limited opportunities or resources to escape the communities. In regards to socioeconomic status, San Antonio is one of the most segregated cities in the United States (Abramson and Fix 1993). It is within this socioeconomic context that this study was initiated.

West-Side Mexican American Youth Gangs and Other Criminal Activity

Mexican American youth became increasingly marginalized as a result of this economic transformation. Reduced economic opportunities forced many youth and young adults to turn to the underground economy as a means of material subsistence. During the 1980s and 1990s, a greater proportion of such youth was drawn to criminal activity associated with street gangs. The attractiveness and resources associated with gangs, crime, and drug use attracted both young men and girls including the subjects in this study.

At the time this study was conducted there were twenty-six active Mexican American youth gangs and two adult prison gangs in San Antonio, Texas. The study sample consisted of one hundred and sixty male gang member participants ranging in age from fourteen to twenty-five years with a mean age of eighteen-and-a-half years. Approximately, 43 percent of the respondents reported living in single-headed households with a large proportion living with mothers (39 percent). Only 21 percent were living in households where both parents were present. The remaining 37 percent were currently living by themselves, friends, or other relatives including grandparents, spouses, uncles, and aunts. Thirty-one percent of the subjects reported having children. Only 26 percent reported being currently enrolled in middle or high school. Of the male sample, 56 percent reported getting a girl pregnant at some time in their lives.

As discussed earlier, the girls in this study were selected based on their association with gangs. In a forthcoming chapter, we discuss extensively the relationship of these young women to the gangs. However, most of the gang members involved in the study seem to be involved in long-term relationships with females they were living with in a common-law relationship. Others had serious relationships with someone they considered a girlfriend. A third of these relationships produced at least one child. The other set of girls were those who were loosely associated with male gangs as "hangers-on." These were girls who partied with the guys, which meant drinking, using drugs, having sex, committing crimes, and selling and buying drugs. As we will discuss in the following chapters, many of these girls were involved in gang-related criminal activities such as stashing weapons, holding drugs, assisting in burglaries, and car thefts.

In the tradition of the Chicago School of community field studies, this typology is based on qualitative data derived from actual interaction with gang members. The identification of these gang members is associated with the previously described study that focused exclusively on male gang members. This community field-study method, discussed more extensively in the methodology section, allows for the discovery of the research dimensions used in the construction of the typology. This methodology allows us to acquire an understanding that goes beyond that of most studies on gangs that are often more narrow in their methodological approaches.

Construction of the Gang Typology

The process of typology construction employed methodological techniques for the conceptualization of typologies suggested by Kenneth Bailey (1994). This typology is defined as a constructed type in that it represents a heightened representation based on common characteristics among the gangs. Building upon existing research, four classifications of Mexican American gangs were constructed from the analysis. The classifications included criminal –adult-dependent gangs, criminal non-adult-dependent gangs, barrio-territorial gangs, and transitional gangs.

This gang typology is multidimensional and conceptual in that its construction was based on five distinct dimensions or variables. The variables are illegal activities, gang organization, drug use patterns, adult influences, and violent behavior. These dimensions were used to distinguish the variation of gangs found in San Antonio's Mexican American community. This analysis produced four polythetic classes of gangs that share an overall similarity around these dimensions. What follows is a description of these dimensions as they were applied to the construction of the typology.

Illegal Activities

Each gang in San Antonio's Mexican American community reported participation in various criminal activities, including drug dealing, auto theft, burglary, car jacking, robbery, fencing, and weapon sales. Gangs differed on the basis of whether the illegal activities were controlled by the gang or were controlled on an individual basis. Organized gangs were identified as having a distinct division of labor that assigned members specific tasks associated with criminal operations. Profits were dispersed according to each member's status, role, and the needs of the gang. Unlike these organized gangs, other gangs engaged in criminal activity that was more individually based. In some cases, there were groups of individuals, or crews, that functioned as a subset of the gang. In these types of gangs, the gang provided a cover for the activities of the individual or crew. For instance, it provided protection within a physical territory or market in which they were operating. The subset typically kept the profits; however, those members were obligated to contribute to the gang for organizational needs such as the purchase of guns.

Organizational Structure

The organizational structure was based on type of leadership, hierarchy, and the rules among gangs. The type of leadership may vary from those gangs that have leadership ranging from very diffused to highly structured (Jankowski 1991). The twenty-six gangs varied regarding the existence and enforcement of rules and regulations, violations and sanctions, cliques and sets, frequency of meetings, collection of money (dues), and division of labor and territory.

Drug Use Patterns

A third dimension was the extent and nature of each gang's drug use patterns. On an individual level they had exceptionally high rates of lifetime use of most controlled substances. For example, the majority had tried marijuana (98 percent), cocaine (90 percent), heroin (57 percent), hallucinogens, and various prescription pills such as Rohypnol, Valium, and Xanax. However, gang members differed on current use patterns by frequency and type of drug. Marijuana and alcohol were consumed daily by a majority of gang members as part of their everyday routine. There was little variation among gangs on this type of substance use. Cocaine and heroin use and abuse were perceived differently by individual gangs. Some gangs had strict regulations prohibiting the use of heroin, seriously sanctioning members who violated this rule. Sanctions included severe beatings by other members. Other gangs tolerated the use of heroin as long as it did not interfere with the individual's responsibility to the gang. Other gangs generally were known for partying and polydrug use, including cocaine and heroin.

Adult Influence

Another characteristic used to construct this typology was the extent to which the gang's illegal activities were adult dependent. The level of dependency on adults influenced the nature of the gangs' illegal activities and organization. Typically, those types of gangs that closely associated with adults displayed higher levels of organization and sophistication with regards to criminality. These gangs were organized more as criminal enterprises than delinquent groups.

Violence

Finally, the construction of this typology included the type of violence committed by members of these gangs. Violent incidents were differentiated as purposeful (expressive) versus random (personal) acts of violence. Purposeful violence refers to that which was planned or premeditated. Such acts were often associated with illegal activities and the customers who refused to pay drug debts. Other acts of violence tended to be more spontaneous and gratuitous, often centered on perceived acts of disrespect. Consideration was also given to the severity of the violence with emphasis on the use of weapons. Attention was paid to the frequency of the violence committed.

Criminal Adult-Dependent Gangs

Of the twenty-six gangs, four are identified as criminal and adult dependent. In these gangs, adults provide access to illegal drugs, weapons, drug-dealing networks, and U.S. and Mexican markets for stolen merchandise. Adults provide other important services such as protection against rival gang members and adult criminals. Drug dealing—especially the dealing of heroin—is this type of gang's major source of income. Relative to other gangs in the community, these gangs are highly organized in that there is a distinct membership hierarchy, leadership, and organized criminal activities. However, the organization is based more on a criminal enterprise with a distinct hierarchy and a distinct leadership structure. Heroin use is generally discouraged, although, as the gangs began to deal heroin, many members became addicted. Violence among these types of gangs is more purposeful and revolves around business transactions.

There are two types of adult criminal networks associated with gangs in this community. One type of criminal network consists of relatives of gang members such as fathers, uncles, in-laws, common-law relations, and other extended family members. In some cases, the adult may have been a long-term neighborhood associate. Another type of criminal adult network consists of organized prison gang members who operate in the Mexican American community. The prison gang controls a significant segment of the heroin market in specific neighborhoods through direct sales. They impose a surcharge on drugs sold by others in areas that they control.

The Nine-Ball Crew: Prison-Gang Dependent Gangs

The Nine-Ball Crew is located in one of the major housing projects in San Antonio. This gang was distinct from other adult gangs in its direct ties to a Chicano prison gang that controlled the heroin trade in the community. The gang leader's stepfather was one of the heads in the prison gang called the Chicano Brotherhood. The Brotherhood began in the Texas prison system in the early 1990s among Chicano prisoners. Throughout the following decade they established a criminal network outside the prison that controls the heroin trade in San Antonio and other southern Texas cities. On the West Side of San Antonio, it is common knowledge among heroin dealers that they must contribute ten percent of all sales to the Chicano Brotherhood. Over the last few years, they have recruited several youth gangs to sell heroin for them. The control they have over the Nine-Ball Crew is their most successful.

The Nine-Ball Crew is highly organized with a leader and two second-heads or lieutenants, a hard core membership of twenty members and approximately thirty others. Fieldwork revealed that there were about twenty girls affiliated with this gang. The leader of this gang is Juan, who tightly rules the gang. He is twenty-three years old and has been described as "cold blooded and vicious." He lived with his long-term girlfriend who occasionally sold drugs out of their home to mostly other girls. His control of the gang is solidified by the support of his five brothers who are active in the gang.

The selling of drugs is coordinated by one of Juan's brothers and another member identified as a hardcore member, or an original gangster (OG). The hardcore members, under the direct supervision of the two heads, are responsible for the distribution and sale of the drugs. Most of these transactions occur in the Carranza Courts and the nearby vicinity. When one of the Nine-Ball Crew members was asked if any one person was in charge of the drug selling, he responded:

> There is one guy in charge of selling. Yeah, he's the main guy that controls the drugs. He says who is going to sell and who ain't going to sell. If you're selling without permission and don't bring money to him your going to get in trouble, get a v [violation].

The Nine-Ball Crew is also used by the Chicano Brotherhood against gangs who refuse to cooperate with them. For example, the leader of the Chicano Boyz, one of the largest gangs in the area, was shot by a rival gang for refusing to pay the Brotherhood a percentage of his profit. The hit was an attempt by them to solidify their control of the drug trade in this area. The Chicano Boyz at this time was one of the largest gangs on the West Side and selling large quantities of heroin. If the Chicano Brotherhood could control this gang, they would assume control of most of the heroin and cocaine trade in this area of the city.

The Gangsters: Criminal Adult-Dependent Gang

The Gangsters had previously been known as one of the most violent gangs in the city. The Gangsters identified themselves in interviews as having ties to a Chicago-based gang, although, this was never substantiated. The gang has evolved into a highly organized drug-dealing criminal enterprise with several independent cliques. Each of these cliques has a head that was responsible for the operation of that group. Every clique operated relatively independent from each other, but they did answer to the Gangsters' leader. Fieldwork identified about thirty girls that were involved with this gang as wives, girlfriends, party girls, and criminal associates. At the time of the data collection, the gang was experiencing a crisis in that many of the gang's hardcore members and leadership had been incarcerated. Allegedly, the leader was running the gang from prison. However, according to members that were interviewed, several of the cliques were breaking away from the Gangsters and were forming their own gangs. One Gangster, commenting on several of the cliques forming their own gangs, stated:

> To hell with the S. Perez Boys, Dallas St. Killers. Screw all of them. That's why there is so much problems in the organization ... because of shit like that. They got to have their own gang.

The Gangsters' constituency is among the emerging Mexican American and Mexican immigrant neighborhoods forming on the fringes of the diminishing black community on the East Side of the city. The gang's membership is distinct in that it has a mixture of Mexican Americans, blacks, and Anglos. The gang operates in areas adjacent to territories controlled by two black gangs: the Crips and the Bloods. Nonetheless, there did not seem to be any conflict between the Gangsters and these two gangs.

Unlike the Nine-Ball Crew, which associated with adult prison gang members, the Gangsters were highly dependent on adult family criminal connections in the southern Texas region. The fathers of the two founders of this gang were both well-known underground figures with extensive criminal records including sentences in the state and federal penitentiaries. These relatives provided the gang with access to a network of adult criminals not as accessible to other gangs. These contacts facilitated the acquisition of criminal resources such as illegal drugs and markets for stolen goods. One of the Gangster's uncles was a high-level drug dealer in South Texas and Mexico. This provided the gang a safe and consistent source of marijuana, cocaine, and heroin directly from Mexican dealers. Moreover, the Gangsters were purchasing these drugs at wholesale prices, often on consignment. This level of accessibility to illegal drugs gave them an advantage over other drug-dealing gangs. These adult relatives were a key factor in the evolution of the gang from one whose primary illegal activity was the fencing of stolen property (e.g., weapons, audio, and video equipment) to a powerful drug-dealing gang.

The Gangsters were distinct from other gangs in that they were not concerned with territorial issues such as turf violations or random personal violence. For instance, little importance was placed on identifying their territory with gang tags, or preventing other gangs from tagging their neighborhoods. One Gangster likened tagging to a "dog pissing on a fire hydrant. Another dog is going to walk by and piss on it too. At least we know whose pissing on the wall." In other words, the Gangsters utilized tagging as a vehicle to determine "who's in our hood and who to look out for." Tagging itself was often a source of violent conflict among other San Antonio gangs. The Gangsters generally viewed tagging as a distraction from their illegal activities.

The Gangsters perceived themselves as a criminal organization that was primarily concerned with making money. One Gangster expressed these views:

> You're not going to be a Gangster unless you got some sense. You ain't gonna just be a thug. I mean there is no such thing as a thug (in the Gangsters). If you ain't making money, bringing something to the boys that's profitable for everyone, then we don't need you. If you don't want to be productive for yourself, then you won't be a Gangster.

This attitude gave the Gangsters an advantage over other drug dealing gangs.

The Gangsters were distinct from most other gangs in several other ways. The gang leadership discouraged the use of heroin. One member of the Gangsters described his gang's feelings toward heroin. "We don't do it, but we can sell it.... We don't want to be known as *tecatos*. We don't want to be like the Chicano Boyz." (*Tecato* is a derogatory term used by Mexican Americans to identify injecting heroin users). As opposed to other gangs, there was not a high value placed on heavy drug use or alcohol consumption.

The Gangsters were also distinct from other gangs in the nature of their activities. Although they had a reputation as a violent gang, their violence was highly instrumental and often related to drug dealing. Members were discouraged from engaging in more expressive acts of violence such as drive-by shootings, random assaults, and personal fights. According to several members, these types of violent acts tended to draw unnecessary attention from the police, which could disrupt their sophisticated drug-dealing operations. One member stated:

> We're not evil. I mean hell, we're just like any other man out there. We got to fight for what we can get. You know nothing is free. I know it's not right to go out and steal, but we're not going to go out and shoot somebody, just to shoot them. People think that we drive around, just to shoot someone. Like we ain't got nothing else better to do. There is always two sides to the story. Don't think that somebody is sitting on their porch and just got shot. That's bullshit, they're not an innocent bystander.

Criminal Non-Adult-Dependent Gangs

These gangs are similar in organizational structure to the criminal adult-dependent gangs. However, they are more loosely knit with a flexible leadership structure. There are a total of five gangs in this category. They differ from the previous group in that they are not as influenced by adults. They are involved in more independent and personal illegal activities such as drug dealing, stolen cars, robberies, and carjacking. The gangs offer an organizational structure to protect the interests of individual gang members, not as a centralized criminal enterprise. Members display higher rates of alcohol and drug abuse, especially heroin. The members are involved in more minor personal fights within the gang and with rival gang members. Often their level of drug dealing will determine the purposefulness of the violence. This gang may be more territorially based than the gangs described previously.

There are two categories of criminal non-adult-dependent gangs. One of these is loosely organized with a weak leadership structure. The other is highly structured with a clear hierarchy and strong membership.

Chicano Boyz: "Loosely" Organized

The Chicano Boyz were one of the largest and most violent gangs on the West Side of San Antonio. There were approximately fifty-nine members at the time of the study. This gang controls a large portion of the heroin and cocaine market in a large West Side public housing unit. The Chicano Boyz are organized into five main sets/cliques that comprise the main core of the gang. Each of these sets has a head, hardcore members, and other members including beginners and marginal members. The set is under the control of the head that in turn answers to the leader of the gang. This was a very popular and organized gang that attracted a large number of female associates. At its peak, the study estimated that there were over sixty girls integrated in the various cliques of the gang.

The leader of the Chicano Boyz is Mark Sanchez who took control of the gang after the previous leader (Ernest) was sent to prison for attempted murder. Sanchez has a reputation among the community as being extremely violent. In the initial months of his leadership he had a physical confrontation with two adult members of a notorious adult prison gang whom he viciously beat with a two-by-four. Subsequently, he "kicked a lot of the younger members' asses," which solidified his control of the gang by gaining loyalty among the sets' heads. His wife's family was deeply involved in drug selling and trafficking in these neighborhoods and facilitated important drug connections to her husband. She was known to sell drugs herself, mostly to other women in the barrio. There was also a large contingent of "bad girls" that hung out with the Chicano Boyz who were into heavy partying and drug using including snorting and injecting heroin. It was common practice for these girls to exchange sexual favors for drugs with gang members. Gang members were careful to separate these two sets, the "bad girls" and the "good girls," from each other.

The Chicano Boyz is organized as a federation whose primary activities are drug distribution and dealing. These illegal activities are conducted on an individual or subgroup basis, not as an organized gang. Therefore, gang members are not expected to share their profits with the gang as a whole. The gang provides a drug market within a geographic territory that it protects through intimidation and violence. Members are expected to support and defend the gang's collective interests often through violence. Violating this expectation could be serious as one field-worker's notes recount:

> Last night an ex–Chicano Boyz who turned Brotherhood got an order to jump on a Chicano Boyz who broke a car window of a sister of a sergeant in the Brotherhood. He went to do his work, and he took his best friend, who is still a Chicano Boyz, with him. He did his job, and roughed up Tony, the one who broke the window. The Chicano Boyz who went along, Robert, didn't do anything but observe the situation. This all happened

around 9:00 p.m. at 11:00 p.m. Mark the head of Chicano, sent a group of seven boys to find Jesse, the ex Chicano now Brotherhood, and beat him. The group did find him, and did beat him. They also found Robert, and beat him for watching.

Members may be required to participate in a drive-by shooting, an assault, or gang fight. One member of the Chicano Boyz described an incident about catching a rival gang member selling drugs in their area:

> This dude was a Nine-Ball. We had already kicked his ass I don't know how many times. We were saying fuck Nine-Ball and all this shit. We started laughing. We let him get up. He took off and started running.... My homeboy took out an AK from the truck, my other homeboy took out a 9mm. My homeboy got on his knee, aiming at him. He shot him in the head. My other homeboy just ran up and shot him in the back too.

In some circumstances, the gang members are required to contribute monies, or pitch in, to purchase weapons or other gang needs. This usually takes the form of an informal "pitch-in" by all the members present. In most instances, the gang gets to keep all their illegal income. One member states, "Everybody is making their own money. So you don't have to be giving money to the gang. You just have to pay for your drugs and that's it."

The heads of the sets and the gang leader meet occasionally to discuss important issues affecting the gang and violations of gang rules. The Chicano Boyz had specific rules to which it expects its gang members to adhere. One of the rules that was often mentioned was the "no fighting with fellow gang members" rule. One member commented: "Everybody knows about it, its been established. If there is any fighting, it's one on one. Not everyone has to be there, just the heads and the guys that are going to fight. Nobody wins, its just settled." At a typical meeting of one of the sets the members address various issues affecting their gang:

> Jake and Carlos begin the meeting by talking about the drug profit or loss for the past week. The money is counted and given to someone to hold. The plan is to buy a "cuete" (gun) next week. A few other matters are discussed, who's messing up at Rosedale (high school), the prison gang's 10 percent, violations for Xanax abuse etc. After about an hour of chatting the meeting is closed.

Gang members were restricted from instrumental acts of violence against rival gang members without permission from the leader. Members needed approval of the leader to commit a drive-by against another gang. Such acts were likely to precipitate a war with the other gang that would disrupt the drug trade. In other situations, the gang makes a conscious decision to commit an act of violence against another gang, understanding the consequences.

The gang initially had rules against the use of heroin and inhalants. Both drugs were highly stigmatized but for different reasons. The use of inhalants was thought to cause people to lose control and do "stupid things." No one seemed to have much respect for "spray heads." Additionally, most gang members believed that using inhalants caused brain damage. When asked about the heroin rule, one member stated:

> Because if they do heroin, they get too fucked up. They start stealing shit from one another. They start stealing from their own people. Doing all kinds of shit. We don't want them doing none of the shit. We start losing.

One veteran member expressed the ambiguity of the gang's drug rule:

> You can do cocaine and weed. Heroin is something that is up and down with us. Sometimes we say nah, you can't use it. But, they use it anyway. What can you do? *Les gusta* [they like it]. They can't stop, so that's something we live with. You just try not to let the "juniors" get involved.

In reality, many of the original gangsters (OGs) were regular users of heroin and had become addicted. One rival gang member, commenting on the demise of the Chicano Boyz, stated, "They're nothing anymore because of the heroin."

One of the distinctions of the Chicano Boyz was its independence from the adult prison gang that operated in the same area as they did. The prison gang attempted to control the Chicano Boyz over the years, particularly its drug trade. The leader of the gang, Mark Sanchez, was one of the few gang leaders in that community to stand up to them. He did this through his own violent behavior and was backed up by several loyal hardcore Chicano Boyz who were not intimidated by the adults. Only recently did this independence begin to waiver when Sanchez was seriously injured in an attempt on his life by a rival gang associated with the Chicano Brotherhood. Nonetheless, the ability and willingness of the Chicano Boyz to stand up to the adult prison gang financially benefited those members who were involved in dealing drugs, especially heroin.

Varrio La Paloma: Strong Leadership

A second type of non-adult-dependent, criminal-enterprise gang is that with a dominating, hierarchical leadership. An example of this type of gang is the Varrio La Paloma (VLP) located in the San Miguel housing project and the Indigo River subdivision. This is an older gang that has multigenerational ties. It is one of the few gangs whose members had parents and relatives who had been involved in the same gang in the past. The San Miguel projects have been traditionally identified as the territory of the VLP. The Indigo River faction is a more recent development that occurred after families were displaced from the San Miguel housing project to the working-class suburb by public housing authorities.

There are approximately one hundred hardcore and eighty marginal members in the VLP gang. These gang members are generally characterized as polydrug users—they use marijuana and alcohol daily and occasionally use cocaine and heroin. Most of the activity described by the members includes the use of drugs. Given its location and long-term stability, this gang had over forty girls who were associated with it in a various ways.

Organizationally, the gang has several sets. One principal set is located in the Carranza Courts and another in the Indigo River subdivision. Each of the sets has a head that is under the command of the leader of the gang. This is a highly organized gang with a distinct division of labor among its members. There are several cliques of members who are responsible for various tasks associated with the gang's business. For instance, there is a drug-dealing clique that is responsible for the distribution and dealing of drugs. There is also a shooting clique that coordinates all the organized violence that is initiated by the gang, including retaliation against rival gang members.

During the three years of the study, the gang was involved in a war with a rival gang located in the residential neighborhood adjacent to the San Miguel projects. One respondent describes an incident with the rival gang:

> In the beginning of January one of the homeboys got jumped there outside the neighborhood by a couple of Nine-Balls. We caught one of the guys and beat him up pretty bad with a lead pipe and car jack. If we would have had a gun, we would have killed him. But there were too many bystanders around.

Several individuals from both sides were murdered as a result of this conflict. They were also involved in a serious conflict with the adult prison gang, which was attempting to take control of the heroin market in the Carranza Courts. Two adult gang members were murdered by a VLP member when they refused to cooperate with him. One of our field-workers described the time he met the VLP member soon after the shootout incident:

> Georgie walked with the help of two crutches as he approached the car. The Brotherhood put out a contract on him because he refused to pay the 10 percent commission on his drug sales. Georgie had started out selling dime bags of heroin. Shortly thereafter, he was selling three to four ounces of heroin and coke a week. That's when Brotherhood started asking for their 10 percent. He said, "They sent two hit men. The men shot first hitting me in the thigh and the knee. I was shooting on the way down and killed them both. I gave the gun to Ray-Ray, who stashed it before the police got there." Georgie was upset because none of the VLP got down for him.

Eventually, the VLP reached a compromise with the adult gang. The VLP would be allowed to sell cocaine and marijuana, but the heroin trade would be the exclusive right of the prison gang.

The distribution and dealing of drugs were largely controlled by the leader of the gang and his close gang associates. The associates were older hardcore members including two of his brothers. These individuals had connections to wholesale drug distributors that were associated with independent adult criminals with ties to Mexico. The actual drug dealing was conducted by other gang members who were fronted the drugs by the gang's leadership. Except for a small percentage of the total, profits were turned over to the heads who passed them on to the leader of the VLP.

Control of the VLP membership was maintained through the strong leadership of Charlie, the leader of the gang. The leader held periodic meetings with the San Miguel set to discuss any problems either internally or with rival gang members. As in other highly organized gangs, the group had strict rules that they had to abide by to retain their privileges. Violation of the rules would warrant a physical beating from other gang members. During the study, Charlie was able to defuse a potentially violent situation when two Chicano Boyz beat up some VLP members in the Indigo River area.

Charlie explained in a meeting to a researcher in his apartment, "[I] don't want to take care of this with guns." However, Charlie emphasized that he would encourage his own people to strap it on with members of the Chicano Boyz if they confronted them again. He added that the prison gang has told him that "if there is any crossfire in the courts they will take care of the VLP and the Chicano Boyz."

Barrio-Territorial Gangs

These gangs are traditional territory-based gangs located in various types of neighborhoods ranging from public housing to residential single-family home neighborhoods. Twelve gangs are categorized as bario-territorial gangs. These are not as hierarchical as the previously mentioned groups although they still adhere to gang rituals. Most of their criminal activities include small scale drug selling, burglary, vandalism, criminal mischief, and other petty crimes. These crimes tend to be more individual initated, less organized, and less gang directed. The gangs' violent behavior tends to be more random and personal. Except for gang turf disputes, most violence is centered on interpersonal fights and random situational acts of violence often associated with male bravado. Even gang drive-by shootings tend to be more spontaneous and predicated on issues such as defending the gang's honor. These gang members use drugs similarly to the other groups with the exception of the low prevalence of heroin use. These gangs tend to operate independently of any adult-gang influence. Territorial gangs comprise the majority of the gangs in the study.

The Invaders

The Invaders are located in a low-income residential area characterized by modest single-family homes in ecologically segregated neighborhoods with long-term residents. The neighborhood is accessible by car through a couple of major streets, making it difficult for rival gang members to enter the area unobtrusively. The gang consists of approximately twenty members ranging in age from fourteen to eighteen years old. This gang is relatively young compared to the gangs described previously. Various sources generated by project researchers indicated that the gang is in its second generation with many of the previous generations either maturing out or incarcerated. Maturing out refers to the process by which the persons involved in drug use, crime, or other delinquent behavior become less salient as they age (Winick 1962). This is a gang that has only about ten girls who attached to it, many of whom are wives or girlfriends.

The gang seems to have a loosely organized structure. Members claim that it does not have a leader although two individuals appear to make major decisions regarding the gang. The gang will hold an occasional meeting if necessary, but they do so reluctantly since the police tend to hassle them if they are seen in large numbers in public. The gang has some informal rules that include the prohibition of heroin use, spray use, and "ganking." "Ganking" loosely refers to robbing fellow gang members. "Violations" are formal sanctions used against gang members who break these and other rules. The violations usually result in a beating by fellow gang members for a designated amount of time. At the meetings, the gang may require that members "pitch in" if the gang needs to purchase guns or other things.

The Invaders' major criminal activities center on car theft, robbery, and burglary. For instance, one member recalls how they stole a low-rider bicycle from a rival gang, the Crowns:

> We were drinking that night and took a drive downtown. I was drunk. We saw three Crowns who had shot my friend. I went to the first one that was closest to me. He threw down his bike. I just popped him and told him, "fuck the Crowns." We started fighting and three of my homeboys jumped in and started beating him. My friend started hitting one with a hammer on the head. He just fell down. We threw two of the bikes in the truck and hit the highway.

This type of random violence is not seen among the more criminal gangs described previously because they do not see it as economically smart and becuase it often results in arrests and convictions.

A few of the members are involved in small-time drug dealing, primarily marijuana sales. Drug dealing is done on an individual basis, as opposed to collectively. The gang activity that seems to occupy most of the member's illegal creativity is "gang banging." This includes protecting the gang's turf from rival gangs, drive-by shootings, fights, and assaults. When asked why they committed a particular drive-by a member responded, "At the time they were our main rival. After we shot them, they stayed low. Then the Vatos Locos came up. They became our main enemy." Their rival gang is the Vatos Locos with whom they had numerous violent incidents during the course of the study. Their other main rival gang is the Crowns, the largest and most violent active Mexican American gang in the city. However, that rivalry has diminished after several violent altercations left members of both sides seriously wounded.

The Invaders also have a reputation as a party gang. The members are known to be heavy users of marijuana, cocaine, and alcohol. What distinguishes them from more criminal gangs is that partying is often their central activity. In fact, members often discuss how a night of partying usually results in committing an act of violence. The following description is about a night of partying by the Invaders that resulted in a shooting:

Interviewer: Okay so lets back up a little bit. So you guys were, You and a *camarada* were in a stolen car?

Respondent: Yeah we had it was like three o'clock in the morning.

Interviewer: Okay.

Respondent: We were already all wasted and shit.

Interviewer: Where were you in what in your hood, or somebody else's hood?

Respondent: In somebody else's hood…. I just started shooting.

Interviewer: Okay, so your reaction was, you know, you just started shooting?

Respondent: Yeah.

Interviewer: So you shot a few times and then you guys took off and went down the street?

Respondent: Yeah.

Transitional Gangs

This category encompasses several gangs in transition relative to a trajectory, that is, either growing in membership and reputation or fading organizationally. In some cases the gang is a temporary phenomenon, such as only when school is in session. The six gangs that fit into this category are usually smaller and semiorganized with a loose hierarchy and loose leadership structure. Often, the gang centers on a charismatic leader. The formation of these groups may be based on residential factors such as living in the same building or subarea of the projects or neighborhood. There is a lot of partying in which alcohol and drugs are consumed. Criminal activities such as drug dealing, stealing cars, and burglaries are individually based as opposed to more organized gang activity. In some cases, certain gangs may have relationships with adult criminals that supply them with guns or drugs. These adults are often parents or other relatives of gang members.

School-based gangs are a subset of the smaller, less structured gangs. These gangs are formed and maintained in the junior high and high schools. Membership is geographically more dispersed. Violence revolves primarily around personal fights and girl-boy differences. Many of their activities occur in school-related settings such as after-school hangouts and parties with school friends.

Up And Above: From Delinquent Group to Gang

Up And Above (UAA) is a gang that in the initial months of the research project had been classified as a "tagging crew." They are a group of individuals whose major activity focuses on spray painting walls, alleyways, street signs, and buildings in a highly individualistic style described as "graffiti art." Tagging-crew art is often confused for gang graffiti by the general public and school and police authorities. In fact, tagging-crew art is much more elaborate than gang graffiti, which is primarily used to mark territory. The primary objective of tagging crews is to display their artistic ability. These tagging crews are often in competition with each other for the most elaborate tags and for the best location. Prestige is bestowed on those that display their art in the highest places, that is, the tops of buildings.

Members of tagging crews vary according to the roles played in the organization. At the top of the tagging hierarchy is the "bomber" who does large-scale colorful paintings with spray paint, markers, or chalk on public and private buildings. Crew members assist the bombers in their work. There are also members who are considered "partyers." These are attracted to the gang because of the group's social activities, which include the frequent use of marijuana and alcohol and the occasional use of cocaine. Because of the partying nature of the gangs, females are an intricate part of the scene either as girlfriends or just those that hang out to party and get high.

On one occasion, a rival gang accused a UAA member of painting over their gang signs and operating in their neighborhood without permission. As the tension mounted, UAA members began to organize themselves more as a gang. They identified a leader and began to recruit persons to their crew for factors other than their artistic talent. As the crew began to diversify, the group's activities expanded into more illegal activities such as drug dealing. The crew's identity as a gang was solidified when they successfully defended themselves in a gang fight with one of the most notorious gangs in the area.

UAA began to evolve into a gang as it was forced to physically protect itself from other gangs. One member talks about an incident with a local black gang:

> We were cruising in our van with the rims. We cruised in it all the time before it got stolen. Some black Crips pulled up next to us. They thought

we were Crowns because we were dressed in black. They were talking shit and threw their fucking beer bottles at the van. We were like "fuck," you meet us over there ... we both parked and all started getting out. And one of them looked like he was going to reach for a gun. We were like, "ah damn man!" So, I was in the back. I hooked one of the UAAs with a Tech 9 that my uncle got for me. So we fired on the whole car and they took off. We only shot a couple of rounds, just enough to scare them.

Incidents such as this have transformed this tagging crew into a full-fledged gang.

The Killing Crew: Decline of a Gang

The Killing Crew is a gang that experienced a significant decline during the course of the research. The Killing Crew started out as a territorial gang located in a public housing project (Martin Homes) and the adjacent residential area. At the height of their organizational career the gang had at least twenty members, including a large number of "little rascals" who were considered too young to be full-fledged gang members. Gang members were involved in a wide range of illegal activities focusing primarily on drug dealing and arms sales. The gang has been known to protect its territory from encroachment by rival gang members with violent means. Only eleven girls were known to be associated with this gang at the time of the study.

The gang's organizational structure was not highly evolved. Most of the members functioned independently of the gang structure. One of the leaders said of their meetings, "Yeah, we have meetings every month. But the guys don't want to get together. They're too busy or don't have time. It's kinda too impossible. I mean, not everyone shows up." The gang had two exceptionally strong leaders whose functions seemed to be drawn toward coordinating instrumental acts of violence against other gangs. They would also mediate problems as they arose among Killing Crew members. There were no distinct sets or cliques with heads that answered to the gang leaders. Meetings were held when an assault or a more coordinated act of violence was needed to protect their drug markets and territory against violations by rival gang members.

The Killing Crew was known primarily by Martin Homes' residents as the sole source of marijuana and weapons. Guns were not only sold but also used by gang members. One member involved in the gang's gun trade said:

We do a lot of gun smuggling. We get many different arms, like grenades and armor piercing bullets and guns like "cop killers" and AK-47's. A lot of these guns we use ourselves. Once we get busted, they start taking away the guns. Guys start fucking up. By the time I know it, I look into the case and there is nothing there no more.

The gun trade described is controlled by the previously mentioned individual and the gang's sergeant-at-arms. The sergeant-at-arms makes sure there is enough money and acts as a bodyguard to the gun dealer who knows where to purchase the weapons.

Members sold marijuana individually or in small groups to area residents in the Carranza Courts and adjacent neighborhoods. Profits were not distributed to other gang members or the two gang leaders who themselves were known to sell large volumes of marijuana. As long as the gang only dealt marijuana and not cocaine or heroin, it did not draw the attention of the adult gangs in the area. This is how they were able to maintain their independence from other adults. Marijuana dealing was organized in the same manner as the weapons; it was a business that was conducted by individual members, not collectively.

A combination of factors led to the demise of the Killing Crew. The severity of the violence associated with the Killing Crew coupled with the arms dealing attracted the attention of the police. As a result, the police made special efforts to break up this gang by arresting and convicting the leaders, Phillip and Eddie. They were both given lengthy prison sentences for drug dealing. At the same time, other more veteran members began to mature out of the gang. More importantly, the gang's base of operation was being undermined by the city's housing authority who decided that the Martin Homes were to be demolished and the families relocated to other neighborhoods.

With the two leaders in prison and older members leaving the gang, the group's little rascals were not so eager to "drop their rags." That is, they were not willing to give up their affiliation with the gang. They decided to change the name of the gang to the Martin Thugs. The gang went by this name for almost two years until the Martin Homes were completely demolished, and no reports have surfaced to indicate that they still exist.

There are groups of youth that reside in these types of neighborhoods who engage in activities similar to the gangs but are not gang members. They are described as delinquent youth. Throughout the neighborhoods (barrios, projects) these non-gang-affiliated youth use and deal drugs, engage in violent behavior, and commit other crimes. They are able to avoid conflict and coexist with gangs by not identifying themselves as one.

Conclusion

This chapter has emphasized the importance of ecological context in understanding the emergence of youth street gangs in Mexican American communities. In this regard, context must be understood from both a historical and a contemporary framework. In this chapter, an argument has been made that the presence of vice districts in minority communities—a specific form of institutional racism—for decades shapes perceptions, cultural patterns of learning, and opportunities. Moreover, the social isolation and structural inequality experienced during the two decades by poor urban minorities has engendered self-destructive adaptive behaviors (Wilson 1996). Such behaviors include increased welfare dependency, persistent poverty, crime, deviant behaviors, and the growth of an increasing Mexican American underclass. It could be argued that the result is what is controversially referred to as social disorganization—defined as a decrease in conventional social rules of behavior (Sampson and Wilson 1995). Harold Bauder theorizes that external perceptions of these communities are socially constructed in a manner that devalues urban minorities and is reinforced by a dominant cultural ideology (2002).

It is within this context that during the 1990s the Mexican American gangs described in this chapter emerges. Mexican American gangs exhibit as wide a spectrum of gang types that exists among other racial and ethnic groups described in current literature. Moreover, this chapter begins to identify how females are embedded with these gangs and individual gang members. The majority of contemporary Mexican American gangs are involved in illegal activities such as theft, drug dealing, and violence, as are a large portion of the girls. These gangs are more likely to use lethal violence than in the past, although the gangs tend to be highly discriminate in the actual use of these weapons. The gang's organizational hierarchy varies depending on the need for such a structure. Obviously, gangs described as criminal enterprises are more in need of a sophisticated structure than barrio-based gangs. The severity of drug use and abuse varies among the gangs, but all are heavy users of marijuana and alcohol. Most are occasionally users of cocaine, and a minority of mostly older gang members inject heroin. However, almost half of the male sample reported noninjecting heroin use, which has serious implications for future related health and social problems. As will be discussed, these drug use patterns parallel those of their female associates.

The gangs within this context seem to represent a means by which to fulfill an economic need generated by the structural position in society rather than a social need, as was more the case in the past. However, some of the barrio-based gangs may be more social in nature than the more criminal gangs. The resources generated by the gangs, especially through drug sales and markets, are related to their relationships with criminal adults. In cases where the gang is generating high volumes of drug sales and income, adults tend to get involved as either partners or competitors. Competitive adult relationships often result in high-profile violent incidents.

Before the 1970s, the Mexican American gangs existed, but were distinct from those that operate today. These earlier urban gangs were linked multigenerationally, just as the European ethnic gangs described by Williams Foote Whyte (1973) and others. Among the positive benefits of these multigenerational ties was the existence of indigenous social control mechanisms such as extended family members and long-term neighbors. These mechanisms managed to moderate through supervision the extreme behavior of these delinquent groups and gangs including the victimization of intimate-partner violence. However, this generational connectiveness broke down largely as a result of greater economic and urban ecological factors that increasingly marginalized low-income Chicano communities in large Southwestern cities (Moore 1988; Morales 1982; Soja, Morales, and Wolff 1983; Vigil 1988). These processes also created conditions that nurtured the environments in which contemporary Mexican American gangs began to flourish. These are the same economic processes that affected low-income black communities in the Northeast (Wilson 1987, 1996).

What is important about this chapter is that it contributes to our understanding of the context and linkage between types of male gangs and females associated with these gangs. Girls within this social context of persistent poverty and weak community institutions—including the family—are more likely to engage in crime, violence perpetration and victimization, drug abuse, and high-risk sexual behaviors. Chapter 3 discusses how these girls develop a deeper involvement with a street lifestyle as a result of their links to these male street gangs.

Notes

1. The study did include some neighborhoods adjacent to and south of the West Side of the city.

Chapter 3

The Research Process: Acquiring Access, Maintaining Visibility, and Establishing Rapport

The Male Gang Study

The male gang study referred to in Chapter 2 took place from the years 1995 to 1998. I was principal investigator of the study that focused on understanding the relationship between gang violence and illicit drug use. In the study one hundred and sixty adolescent Mexican American male gang members were interviewed in-depth about their life history. The members' average age was eighteen. They were randomly drawn from twenty-seven street gangs located in economically disadvantaged Mexican American communities in San Antonio.

The research was limited to two large geographical areas (the South Side and the West Side) that were identified as major commerce and residency centers for San Antonio's Mexican American population. These areas were also known as having the highest concentration of delinquent behavior and Mexican American gang activity. Due to the delinquent, deviant, criminal, or lower-class nature of some gang activities, it is often difficult to identify gang members and gain information in accurate and reliable ways. Community field-workers on my research team began to acquaint themselves with gang members and community and neighborhood influentials in order to collect data on key gangs and gang activity. In the process, I made sure all field staff made extensive efforts to gain access, entrée, and rapport with these male adolescents. Field staff were trained by myself and other experienced field researchers. Additionally, during the initial phase of the project weekly meetings were held with the field staff where strategies and encountered problems were discussed.

Observational data was collected based on fieldwork in recreational centers, housing projects, downtown areas, gang hangouts, and other public gatherings such as corner stores and parks. Of importance, all efforts were made not to rely on institutional agencies and agents of social control (school officials or police). For a period of ten months, the community researchers went out daily to establish contact, observe gang activities, and develop gang rosters. The rosters of gangs were developed through different information sources. These rosters included the name and street address of each member of the gangs in the research areas. Additionally, the rosters provided gang members' ranks (i.e., OG) and the identities of gang leaders, which avoided selection bias that was a characteristic of earlier research.[1] These rosters were used to obtain the stratified random sample of one hundred and sixty male gang members. This is especially problematic in surveys conducted by law enforcement, which tend to overestimate gang populations. The other major problem with police gang rosters is that of self-selection bias.

Data collected on the male gang sample found them engaged in persistent and serious antisocial behaviors. Crime among the sample was exceptionally high, with 68 percent reporting owning a gun and 56 percent reporting that they had carried it in the previous thirty days. Of those questioned, 82 percent said they had fired a gun in a gang-related fight. Half had sold drugs in the last three months and 56 percent were arrested for a violent crime. Gang members reported participation in various other criminal activities including drug selling and dealing, burglary, auto theft, car jacking, robbery, fencing, and weapon sales (Valdez and Sifaneck 2003). In regards to substance use, exceptionally high levels of lifetime use and current use of illicit drugs such as marijuana (lifetime 98 percent; current 75 percent), cocaine (lifetime 90 percent; current 53 percent), and heroin (lifetime 57 percent, current 26 percent) are reported. They were also observed to be active in high-risk sexual behaviors and engaging in intimate-partner violence.

During the course of conducting the male-gang study, my research team and I began to learn about the girls associated with the lives and activities of the male gang members. It became clear that females were associated with gangs differently than males. More specifically, the females' behavior differed qualitatively from the males in respect to drug use, violence, and sexual behavior. It became apparent that females were experiencing a gender socialization process distinct from the males and it deserved further study.

As noted previously, gaining access and trust of the male gang members required extensive work *in the field* for several years that permitted us to establish ourselves in the community. As a research team, we understood the challenges we would face in attempting to identify a hidden population such as the adolescent gang-associated females. *Hidden populations,* refer to subsets of a population whose membership is not readily distinguished or specified based on existing knowledge and/or for sampling capabilities (Morgan 1996; Valdez and Kaplan 1999; Wiebel 1990). These socially marginal groups have low social visibility often due to stigmatized or illegal behaviors, which are difficult to locate (Fitzgerald 1996; Thompson and Collins 2002; Watters and Biernacki 1989). The aim of the female study was to speak with these adolescent girls in order to obtain an accurate representation of their lives within the context of the male gangs and the larger community. In trying to do this, accessing these adolescent girls proved to be an even bigger challenge given the initial guarded reactions we encountered from inquiries to male gang members about their female counterparts. This was facilitated, however, by implementing specific field and sampling techniques throughout the research process.

The Female Study

The Research Team
Before going into detail about the research design and methodology, it is important to recognize the research team that was working with me to identify, access, and recruit the adolescent females into the research project. First, given that this research was building upon the work done with the male gang members, having a male community field specialist and a project director from the original male study involved in the female research was imperative. Richard, the community field specialist, and John, the project director, were middle-aged men indigenous to the target neighborhoods in San Antonio, Texas. They grew up on the West Side and had extensive contacts in the community. At the time of the present research, they had been working for me for approximately four years. Specifically, Richard had been the primary outreach specialist involved in identifying, gaining access to, and recruiting the male gang sample. In doing this, Richard developed extensive contacts within the target population and, more importantly, among numerous male gangs.

Due to the sensitive nature of this research, combined with the gender composition of participants, it was critical to utilize female community field specialists. At the start of the research, two young females were hired to initiate the fieldwork in the community. The first, Katrina, was a Caucasian female in her late twenties fluent in Spanish. She was a PhD candidate in anthropology at a major university in New Orleans. She had spent several years conducting ethnographic research in Central America. The second, Rosie, was a Mexican American female in her mid-twenties, working on a master's degree at a local private university. Both Katrina and Rosie were actively involved in the recruitment and interviews of the young female adolescents.

In addition to the previously mentioned female staff, a third person was an important member of my research team. Melissa was a high school graduate and mother of four in her late twenties working as a clerk in my office. Similar to Richard, Melissa was born and raised in one of the target neighborhoods and had an extensive family network in this community. During the initial stages of the research, I realized that she had insights about the research focus that provided a deeper understanding of the social context of the lives of these girls. Given this, Melissa became one of the primary interviewers on the study given her ability to establish rapport with participants. Melissa's rapport and that of the other female members of the staff was important in that it enhanced their ability to convey sympathy and understanding without judgment that allowed for the elicitation of more truthful responses. For instance, females often indicated to the interviewers and community outreach specialists that they had discussed subjects with them that they had not discussed with anyone else. Moreover, Melissa was the sole transcriber of all qualitative scenarios included in the life-history questionnaire.

As a male researcher, it was important for me to establish some rapport with these young women. Given the nature and context of the focus of this research, I had to make sure that I felt comfortable enough to interact with them. Conversely, my presence should not make them feel uncomfortable so as to impede their communication with me. After taking these issues into consideration, most of my field contact was done alongside my female research staff. As I have documented, it is not sufficient to depend on the mere introduction by a gatekeeper (Valdez and Kaplan 1999). That is, researchers must prove themselves to be interested and engaged with the population as something more than their scientific and academic objects. This is easier to do when the researcher has a particular interest in the subject matter. After I was seen in the field with my staff, the young women began to feel comfortable enough to talk with me. This rapport allowed me to conduct short, on-the-spot interviews in the field or in the office where they would come for their scheduled interviews. In addition, I established trust and rapport with several young women whom I followed for the duration of the research.

The mixed-gender field-research team approach proved to be invaluable in establishing a presence and gaining entrée. Having Richard conduct fieldwork alongside Katrina and Rosie was an effective strategy. That is, making initial contact with the young women was possible through Richard's access to the male gang adolescents many of whom were boyfriends, brothers, and cousins of the girls to be targeted. During the course of the study, the research team and I maintained high visibility and frequent social contacts within the community to develop or to improve rapport and thereby became immersed into the social world of many San Antonio female adolescents. Overall, our level of involvement contributed to our ability to interpret statements made by these young females.

Acquiring Access

Literature on ethnographic research methods has extensively discussed the important role of gatekeepers in accessing entrée into the world of hidden populations. Gatekeepers serve multiple purposes in the process of conducting research, including identifying potential research sites, facilitating initial contacts with informants and subjects, and providing initial information on the subject matter. In this research, the male gang members were the primary gatekeepers in accessing the young female adolescent population. While my research team and I had limited prior contact with the young women, we did have extensive knowledge of the gangs and gang members from the prior research study.

The first step in acquiring access to this female population was to identify male gang members from distinct gangs with whom Richard had established a very good relationship during the prior study. In doing this, Richard and the female community outreach specialists would then approach the males and discuss the purpose of the present study of gang-affiliated females. The staff would then proceed to ask if there were any young girls that met the eligibility criteria (described later) that hung out with their gang. In practically all the cases, the males indicated there were females hanging out with them. Without getting into the details about how the sample universe was obtained (which will be discussed later in the chapter), the males were then asked to identify any females they personally knew that hung out with the gang and would be willing

to speak to them (research team). In most cases, the males would provide names and contact information (if available) of potential girls.
Initially, we did notice that males were wary of giving out names of girls
with whom they had a familial or personal relationship. Eventually however, almost all the males we spoke with were willing to give information
about some girls associated with their respective gangs. This information
gave the research team a critical starting point from which to contact
potential respondents.

One example of gaining access to female adolescents through a male
gang member gatekeeper was the case of Jaime, a member of the Big
Cholos (see Figure 3.1). Jaime was a small-time dealer for his gang and
most of the girls he knew that hung out with them bought from him.
Upon contacting Jaime, he informed the community outreach specialists
of one young woman who hung out with their gang and with whom he
had a personal relationship in the past, Diana. The young woman eventually put us in contact with Melissa. After agreeing to speak with us,
these two young women referred us to yet another group of girls. In sum,
a total of nineteen girls were identified in this network, several of whom
were associated with other male gangs.

As the example illustrates, getting initial access to these young women
through a male gang-member contact was critical to getting the research
process started. However, once we obtained access to one or two girls in

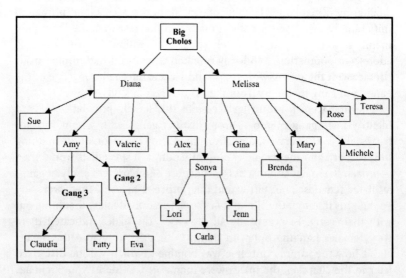

Figure 3.1 Network of Young Women Obtained via Male Gang Gatekeeper

each of the gangs, it became easier to get information on other young women who were associated with each respective gang.

We knew we could not access this population solely on information obtained from the male gang members and the young women they referred us to. This was especially the case given that the girls that were being identified were typically associated with the male gang members through familial or personal relationships. We knew, however, from the previous male research that there were other girls who were identified as those they partied with or girls they grew up with as children. The research team made a concerted effort to gain access to other young women using an alternative approach: street contacts.

Making "on-the-street" contacts proved to be one of the most important strategies in gaining access to this population. Based on knowledge obtained from the initial contact made with the young women, community researchers identified areas in which potential respondents congregate in the community, including downtown malls, bus stops, parks, and convenience stores. Community researchers implemented a field-intensive strategy by frequenting these locations and making contact with young women who appeared to fit the age and ethnic eligibility criteria. Upon approaching young women in the streets, community researchers would identify themselves and attempt to engage the young women in a conversation. If successful in getting her to talk, the community researcher would eventually inquire about the male gangs and whether they were familiar with a specific gang. It was not uncommon for the young girls to be hesitant in speaking about the male gangs, but when the community researchers mentioned names of respective members they knew, the conversation developed.

In general, the process of gaining access to this young adolescent female population required intensive field contact with both male gang members and girls hanging out in the community. As will be described later in this chapter, before including any girl into the study's rosters, she had to be verified by several individuals as being associated with the male gang. Throughout the process of identifying these young women, community-outreach specialists collected as much information as possible as to where they may be located (i.e., addresses, phone numbers, etc.). When visiting homes, our staff often made initial contact with parents or guardians (e.g., grandmothers) and explained the purpose of the research before speaking to the adolescent. In doing this, we established good relationships with these parents, which in turn facilitated our continual contact with the young girl. This helped in securing parental consent, which was required by the university's Institutional Review Board (IRB).

Maintaining Visibility

Researchers attempting to make contact and build rapport with highly exclusive and hidden populations such as the young girls in this research cannot depend on the mere introduction by a gatekeeper or another person. One must work diligently to gain the confidence of the population through simply "being there" and then reinforcing this presence by displaying that they are sincere and can be trusted.

My research team and I maintained contact with all girls identified during the research process for over two years. All project community outreach specialists spent considerable hours working in the streets attempting to identify and locate young women associated with male gangs. After a few months in the field, our presence started to become known out in the community. For instance, on one occasion one of the team's female outreach specialists was walking downtown when she heard someone yell out. "Hey, there goes that girl from the university. Let's go talk to her." A group of four young women proceeded to cross the downtown intersection to meet her. Identified as university researchers, our legitimacy in the community was established among the population.

Our research team knew how important it was to be visible out in the community if we were going to establish trust and rapport with these young girls. On many occasions, the field team met up with previously identified young girls out in the field and invited them for a quick bite to eat. This gesture was greatly appreciated by the girls and was typically a perfect opportunity for the research team to get updates of what was going on in the neighborhood or new leads of potential respondents. One field note illustrates the research team's visibility in the neighborhood:

> We were driving through the San Isidro courts (housing project) looking for a specific street where we were told a young girl lived. When we found the street, we drove down it very slowly to see if we could see anybody. We saw Lisa standing in front of a house with an older lady. We walked toward them and greeted both Lisa and the woman, who turned out to be her mother. To our surprise, Lisa's mother recognized Richard from a few months before when he went looking for another young girl. This obviously helped us out a lot because we had no problems in getting Lisa's mother to sign the consent form.

Thus, once we had accessed the population and maintained a certain degree of visibility in the community, the research team was able to go to the next step of establishing rapport.

Establishing Rapport

Establishing visibility is necessary but it is not sufficient to build trust among the population. The researchers must establish social rapport with the young women, becoming, in some manner, a part of their social networks. After several months of high visibility in the field, the community specialists were more readily able to approach young girls on the streets, on their own turf and on their own terms. We built up enough trust with several young women that they felt comfortable enough to contact us whenever they needed.

The following field note documented by one of the female outreach specialists depicts the trust some of these girls had with the research team members:

> We went over to Stacey's house because she called us all upset because she was getting kicked out of her apartment. When we got there we noticed she had some bruises. She eventually told us that she and her boyfriend had gotten into a fight on Saturday night. She wanted to leave her apartment because she thought he was coming over and she did not want to be there when he got there. She went on to explain that the manager of the apartment complex wanted to kick her out because there had been a lot of "drama" at her place lately and she already had two violations. We ended up taking her to a friend's house and told her to call us if she needed anything.

Other young women appeared to feel comfortable speaking with us and often mentioned that they felt they could talk to us about anything. For instance, Victoria—a seventeen-year-old girl with two young children—lives in one of San Antonio's largest public housing complexes. The following field note demonstrates her level of comfort in discussing things that were happening in her neighborhood:

> Victoria invited us over to her house yesterday. She wanted to talk to us about the problems she was having with the managers at the housing unit. They have not helped her out with anything and she thought they were being racist because she was Mexican. The conversation eventually shifted to the new director at the community agency. Her boyfriend, who is in a gang, is being harassed by some of the agency employees whenever he goes over there.

Establishing rapport with the adolescents was a key strategy, but even more important was making social contact with parents, guardians, and adults in the community. Given the ages of the young adolescent women participating in the study the research team had to seek parental consent for every participant. In doing this, the research team was able to establish rapport and trust with many of these adults. One field note reads:

> Today I went out to look for several of the study subjects with whom we have had little or no contact. I started out looking for Monica, a girl involved with the Big Cholos. No one has been home the couple of times I've been there. Richard said he had gone there once before looking for another girl, Veronica, and that the man there had been pretty rude and didn't want to talk to him. Richard thought that maybe it was Monica's house and Veronica had only given him that address as a contact. So, when I drove up there was a man in a wheelchair in the front yard talking to a teenage boy. I went up to them and asked if this was Monica's house and the man said no, but the boy said that name sounded familiar. I told them I was looking for a girl about fifteen or sixteen years old. The man in the wheelchair asked me if I was sure I wasn't looking for a Veronica, who was his niece. I told him that I thought someone had been looking for a Veronica before at that address as well. Anyway, he told me that Veronica was his niece and he didn't talk to her anymore. He asked me why I was looking for these girls and I explained the project to him. After I did that, he became much more receptive. He said he had a fight with his nephews and nieces awhile ago when they lived there with him and he didn't talk to them anymore. He told me they had all stolen things from him. But, then he said that he had talked to Veronica a few weeks ago and was trying to make amends with her. She had just gotten out of juvenile and she called him to apologize to him. He said she had been in there about five or six months and no one came to visit her the entire time, not even for Christmas. He said he thought she was trying to turn her life around and he was also going to try to meet her halfway.

Eventually, the man turned out to be an important contact for the research team. Besides Veronica, he was crucial in getting us access to several other young women who hung out with his niece.

This rapport and contact usually led to more social interaction between us and the adolescent girls. The more we saw these girls the more we became embedded in their social networks and the closer were the personal emotional ties between the project members and the girls. A sense of mutual commitment to the objectives of the study emerged and with that came a sense of shared ownership. This not only led to making the hidden population more accessible for research but also provided natural validity checks of the girls association with the male gangs as they became selected to participate in the study.

Selecting a Sample of Gang-Associated Female Adolescents: The Research Process

The research utilized a cross-sectional, multimethod design with the sample of Mexican American gang-affiliated females between the ages of fourteen and eighteen years old (see Appendix for details on sampling procedures). The use of quantitative and qualitative data-collection approaches including the use of psychometric measures provided information relevant to the development of culturally specific violence-prevention approaches. The risk-factor variables we studied were derived from a sociocultural model of intimate-partner violence and included examination of the following risk variables:

- *Social/Economic.* Socioeconomic status and familial employment status
- *Family.* Culturally specific family stress and conflict
  History of intimate-partner violence
- *Personal.* Experience of early childhood trauma and violence
  Exposure to and involvement with gang-related violent events
- *Cultural.* Cultural norms and expectations regarding gender role
- *Situational.* Contextual events associated with sexual and intimate-partner violence, including substance use

Eligibility

The females included in this research were recruited from nine specific catchment areas identified as the West Side. The young women needed to be Mexican American; between the ages of fourteen and eighteen; and know of a male in one of the twenty-seven male gangs identified in the previous National Institute Drug Abuse (NIDA) study on drug-related gang violence among Mexican American males.

Overview and Description of Gang-Affiliated Mexican American Adolescent Females

Table 3.1 provides an overview of the characteristics of the sample. The mean age of the girls was 16 years old. Only 62 percent of the gang-affiliated respondents were presently enrolled in school, with a mean education length of 9.6 years. Approximately 30 percent indicated they had been expelled from school at least once. Nine of ten subjects were born in San Antonio, Texas.

Results revealed some distinguishing family characteristics. For instance, only 23 percent of the gang-affiliated girls were living with both parents at the time of the interview. The mean household family size was 5.49 members. Slightly more than half of the sample had lived in public housing. Close to half of the young women reported their parents receiving some form of government assistance. Parents' educational level was an average of 9.8 years for both the mother and father respectively.

Data was collected on childbearing and history of pregnancy. Approximately half reported ever having been pregnant. Twenty-one percent reported having children of which all were living with them.

Table 3.1 Characteristics of Gang-Affiliated Adolescent Females

Variable	%/Mean
Mean age (Standard Deviation [SD])	16.13 (1.57)
Mean years education (SD)	9.62 (1.39)
Ever expelled from school	27
Born in San Antonio	89
Family	
Living with both parents	23
Parents with steady job	78
Parents receiving government assistance	45
Ever lived in public housing	51
Mother's Years Mean Education (SD)	9.82 (2.19)
Father's Years Mean Education (SD)	9.83 (2.41)
Children	
Ever been pregnant	47
Have children	21
Children living with subject	100

Conclusion

This study has presented some specific strategies for conducting research among hidden populations. These strategies address aspects of the research process including acquiring access, maintaining visibility, and establishing rapport. The chapter also discusses how we developed quantitative sampling tactics appropriate for the type of population studied. Underlying these strategies is a fundamental appreciation of the value of the available stock of community "common sense" and the importance of *verstehen*. These strategies may be tempered by a researcher's knowledge of the population, resources, time limitations, and other situation factors.

The strategies we presented in this chapter were developed in the particular social context presented by Mexican American working class life. They will undoubtedly have to be adapted for other ethnic gang members in social contexts. Future research will have to determine whether these strategies provide a basis for formal methodological theory that fits the varying realities of other ethnic groups. For example, the characteristics of Mexican American communities with the central role of the extended family affects the way gatekeepers are used and that gender differences are accessed. Nevertheless, the processes we describe must be entertained if one is working with this type of population. For example, gender differences in the black community will not be the same as in the Mexican American community, but the special characteristics of each community will have to be recognized if representative samples of male and female gang members are to be recruited.

Despite these sophisticated methods, not all of the data we collected is always the whole truth. The stories told often have a spin that makes the person providing the information appear in a positive light. For instance, when asked to describe a fight, the respondent describing the fight is never the one worse off after the encounter. This is what Malcolm Klein calls a "predominant myth" within gangs, which exaggerates many of the behaviors they describe (1995). Particular stories get refined through telling and retelling. Jody Miller states that "these stories become part of the normative structure of gangs, even when they are not consistently enacted in behaviors" (2001). Nonetheless, they become important in that they are providing a reality as seen through their own value system. Another issue that needs to be mentioned is that subjects are predisposed toward giving socially desirable responses if they engaged in high-risk behaviors. Nonetheless, I am reasonably sure that in most cases honest responses were given to the interviewers. But even if they were not entirely true, they reveal enough about the constructed norms and values of the girls' social worlds.

Notes

1. Numerous studies detail the range of gang members from associations based on street-corner friendships to formal membership in complex gang structures. However, these previous studies have not adequately described how their studies have avoided selection bias, which may result in accessing only the more available, verbal, outgoing, or self-promoting gang members.

Chapter 4

Families in a Dangerous Community

Introduction

The role of the family has traditionally been of interest to gang researchers in understanding adolescents' association with street gangs (Moore 1990; Spergel 1995; Vigil 1988; Whyte 1973). It is widely recognized that increases in delinquency and violence among these adolescents may originate in the quality of family relations (Robbins and Szapocznik 2000). Family involvement in gangs and drugs is argued to be a catalyst for adolescent gang membership, especially among Mexican Americans (Adler, Ovando, and Hocevar 1984; Cox 1987; Heller 1966; Morales 1982). Youth street gangs are described as a surrogate family for its members, offering something that the family does not. Among more traditional Mexican Americans the family—nuclear and extended—has been identified as the most influential institution in the culture (Williams 1990). However, many Mexican American families are experiencing cultural and structural changes moving them away from their more conventional characteristics (Erickson 1998; Valdez and Halley 1996). For example, traditional gender roles associated with the Mexican American family are being modified, reflected in differences across generations and classes. Mexican American adolescent girls involved in street-based delinquent groups are often caught between the conservative roles associated with their families and the new gender roles modeled by their peer groups (Horowitz 1983). In this chapter we explore how the family constrains or facilitates involvement in high-risk behaviors.

The Mexican American Family and Gangs

To understand the role of the family in the development of gangs, Joan Moore and James Vigil examine three models used to explain the roots of gang involvement: a social-structure model, a subcultural model, and a psychological model (1989). The social-structure approach indicates that the stresses caused by immigration and poverty impairs traditional family functioning and is one of the main reasons for youth to join gangs. This explanation was first proposed by Frederic Thrasher, who pointed out the weakness of social controls in immigrant neighborhoods in Chicago as the main cause for membership in gangs (1963). The subcultural model was first proposed by Walter Miller to explain how working-class norms help in the development and persistence of gangs (1958). More recently, Vigil describes economically, ecologically, and culturally marginalized families and explains how these multiple marginalizing factors contribute to creating a subculture conducive to the development of gangs (1988). Moore describes the families within the Mexican American community that are characterized by generations of drug use, criminality, incarceration, and street connections as *cholo* families (1994).

The psychological model of gang membership is similar to the intrapersonal/psychotherapeutic approach. In the psychological model, the gang membership is seen as a response to the abusive emotional climate of the household, which generates the need for the "surrogate" family of the gang (Moore 1994). Some argue that male family members have more influence than peers on the decisions of a boy to join a gang (Moore 1994). Others point out the importance of the quality of the emotional climate within the family as a deterrent or a stimulus to adolescents' involvement with gangs (Werner 1983). Instead of being supporters of societal norms and conventional morality, sometimes family members encourage an adolescent's decision to join a gang (Covey, Menard, and Franzese 1992). "Intergenerational closure," as defined by scholars studying African Americans in Chicago, may have a reverse effect on Mexican Americans (Valdez and Sifaneck 2003). This term refers to the level of linkage between adults and children in the community (Sampson, Morenoff, and Earls 1999).

This chapter explores the relationship between the family and the behaviors and attitudes of high-risk Mexican American females by focusing on four major themes among these low-income families: family structure and process; the normalization of drugs, alcohol, and violence in the family; the role of psychosocial factors; and family relationships to institutions.

Family Structure and Process

This chapter explores family structure and process in explaining variations in behaviors among these gang-affiliated Mexican American
females. George Simmel's distinction between group processes (content)
and structural arrangement (form) provided us the analytical mechanism to better understand social life particularly as it was emerging in
modern urban society (1971). Social forms, argued Simmel, "become
combined and hypostatized into larger, institutionalized structures.
These more visible, solid structures—states, labor unions, priesthoods,
family structures, military organizations, communities-represent an
objectification of social forms" (Simmel 1971, emphasis added).
Content, on the other hand, is the interest, purpose, or motive of the
phenomenon or interaction. One of the issues that concerned Simmel
was that social forms often may become liberated from their connection
with practical purposes and become objects of cultivation of their own
right. Men become devoted to them not for some practical advantage but
for their own sake (1971). This is the issue that frames our discussion of
the role of the family and its influence on deviant adolescent behavior.

Previous studies have found that family structure and process characteristics have been correlated with aggression and other serious criminal
behaviors among children and adolescents (Sampson and Lauritsen
1994). Traditionally, the nuclear and extended family structures—with
their clearly defined gender roles often based on a patriarchal hierarchy
system—have been considered ideal in Western society. The extended
family was considered optimal for agrarian society and the nuclear family for industrial society. Many contemporary politically conservative
groups consider the breakup of the nuclear family—largely the result of
high rates of divorce—as the root cause of many social problems, particularly for adolescents. Divorce not only dissolves the union between husband and wife it also breaks up children and parents and separates
families and friends. Existing research does suggest that children living
in broken homes are slightly more likely to engage in aggressive behaviors, drop out of school, and have other behavior problems than children
living in two-parent homes (Farrington and West 1971; McCord 1982;
Rankin 1983).

There have been other studies that have argued that the quality of
family relations (process) is more important than structure (form) in the
emergence or absence of behavioral problems among adolescents
(Donovan, Jessor, and Costa 1988; Jessor and Jessor 1977). For instance,
runaways are forced out of their homes often because of conflicts with

parents and their inability to communicate (Manov and Lowther 1983). Researchers interested in family process often focus on assessing the family's conflict resolution style and other communication characteristics. If the family's relations are beyond resolution, many perceive divorce as a potentially constructive and healthy way of dealing with the situation. An unhappy dysfunctional marriage may be more detrimental to the emotional stability of children than divorce and single-parent families.

However, as Robert Sampson and Janet Lauritsen indicate, studies focusing exclusively on family factors and violence are rare, especially those that focus on adolescents (1994, 25). This is expected, they argue, given that serious violent behaviors are not typically engaged in by youth. Those few studies that do exist on family characteristics and violence usually examine functioning or intervening family processes. What these studies have found is that parental neglect, harsh punishment styles of parents, parental permissive attitudes toward deviance, and marital discord and conflict have been found to be associated with aggression and serious criminality among family members (Sampson and Lauritsen 1994). Also associated with aggression among adolescents is parental criminality and alcoholism (McCord 1982). However, the relationships found between each of these situations and adolescent aggression are generally considered weak and are not consistent across adolescent groups or types of behavior (Glueck and Eleanor 1950).

Another way in which family is associated with aggression and violence is through what is often described as the cycle of violence. That is, it is argued that there is an intergenerational transmission of violence either through childhood abuse by adults or by witnessing violence in the home environment (Kruttschnitt, Ward, and Sheble 1987; Widom 1989). Harold Lewis (1986) and others also reported high rates of childhood victimization among convicted murderers on death row and juvenile murderers as well as in other incarcerated populations. However, Sampson and Lauritsen's review of the research on intergenerational transmission of violence suggests that evidence is "inconclusive and plagued with methodological problems" (1994, 27). They go on to argue that there may be a correlation between experiencing abuse as a child and perpetrating abuse as an adult, however, the magnitude of the relationship is small (1994).

These studies stress that family process is a more important factor than family structure and that more explicit attention be paid to the effects of family functioning on juvenile aggression and its relationship to later violent offending as an adult. In this manner, family process may be a critically important moderating mechanism between macrosocial factors (poverty, unemployment, economic inequality, etc.) and the emergence of violent perpetration and offense among adolescents.

Table 4.1 presents the breakdown of the nuclear family structure of this study's young women. While 54 percent of the respondents lived in a two-parent home in elementary school, by the time they had reached high school, only 29 percent continued to live in a two-parent home. The majority resided in a female-headed household at the time of the study.

Table 4.1 Characteristics of High-Risk Mexican American Families

Variable	Percent
Living with both parents	
Elementary school	54
Middle school	40
High school	29
Current year	25
Living with other relatives	10

The effect that these types of structural changes have on the roles of family members is illustrated by the situation of Maria, a sixteen-year-old girl with an ex-boyfriend in one gang and a fifteen-year-old brother in a rival gang. Their father had recently left. She describes the instability in her home while relating a story of a fight between her boyfriend and her brother's gang:

Maria: Well [my fifteen-year-old brother] got mad because, because I was with my boyfriend, I didn't tell him. He acts like he's my father, you know, since my dad's not there. So we got into a real big fight because of that. They wanted to kick my boyfriend's ass and they had bats and everything.

Interviewer: Who's they?

Maria: My brother and my sister's boyfriend and the guys around there, because where I live there's a lot of gang guys.... My brother and her boyfriend saw him walking me home. That's when they all started fighting and stuff. Just two guys against like thirty guys. But my mom took him out of there so when I got home me and my brother got in a real bad fight. I hit him with a bat.

Interviewer: How bad did you hurt him?

Maria: Well, he pressed charges on me.

In the interview, Maria reveals the resentment she feels for her brother taking on the role of the father figure, especially since he is younger than her. When her brother tries to exercise control over her actions, she reacts with violence.

Debbie, a seventeen-year-old female, describes a fight between her and her half sister. Debbie explains that she feels that she is more loved by the family because Debbie's father was actually married to their mother. In contrast, their mother was never married to her half sister's father and her half sister never knew her own father. Debbie says the following in an interview:

> Like, I had went out in the afternoon and I came back to ask my mom for some money. I used to get SSI checks and my mom had my money. I told her to give me twenty dollars. She was like, "For what?" I told her just give it to me. She was like "No," and then my sister got in on it. She started telling me shit, saying "You leave mom alone, already. God damn, you already take all her fucking money and shit, and you want more money. That money's hers." I go, … "I get it because of [my deceased father]." I told her, "You're just mad because you can't get any [SSI money]." I say, "Shit, like you don't even know your father."

Debbie describes some of the tension between the siblings with different fathers. Her mother never married her sister's father and he was never around. As is often the case with this population, siblings often have different fathers but live in the same household. Also, there is often no male head of household at all, as in Debbie's case, but only the mother and her children. Such a situation creates tensions among families already dealing with difficulties due to their economic problems. The added stress of multiple parents and conflicting familial responsibilities complicates family relations and roles.

Often, due to problems within the family, the young women are forced to leave their homes. While many times it is their choice to leave because they want to live with a boyfriend or another family member, sometimes they are told to leave and not welcomed back. Valerie, seventeen years old, describes such a case due to a fight between her and her stepfather:

> [The fight] was because of me, because I always wanted to go out you know and party. I started drinking and smoking and doing all this stuff. I went back home you know to try to settle down, go back to school and everything. Me and [my stepfather] don't get along cause of things that have happened in the past and everything. I told my mom, "I'm gonna go out and find a job." And I was getting ready and he says, "No you're not gonna go." And I was like, "I'm gonna go, [my mom] told me it was alright. She gave me permission." I was about to leave … and he called me. I was like, "What?" He goes, "You're not going." He started yelling at me.

He got in my face and was turning all red and everything. Then I got mad, you know. I've never hit anybody in my family and I wasn't planning to you know, but he got real close to my face. My mom was like you leave her alone. And he got real close and I thought he was gonna hit me. So, I pushed him and I started crying, I was like, "I'm sorry you know." I thought he was gonna hit me back and I just moved out of the way.... And I told my mom, "I gonna go; there's gonna be too many problems here. I'm gonna give you more problems...." I was like you know, "If it makes you happy that I'm not gonna be here, I rather you be happy with him and me gone...." So I decided to leave and I left. I haven't lived with my mom since.

Valerie clearly expresses her frustration and distress over the situation. She made mistakes and admits them, but feels there is no way to return to her family. She was made to feel that she was the source of her mother and stepfather's problems. She believes that without being around her brothers and sisters will have a chance for a complete family. In the meantime, she has been forced to temporarily move in with a friend. To complicate matters, her friend lives on the other side of town, so Valerie has no actual contact with any of her family or her former social network.

Another young girl that illustrates this *serial residency* pattern is Teresa, who was fourteen years old at the time of her interview. Her mother had been incarcerated for dealing heroin about two years prior to the interview. In those years, Teresa moved from one household to another. Her legal guardian is her grandmother, but she has lived with three different aunts and her mother's friend during that period. She also moved in with her boyfriend, a member of Varrio La Palma during that time. The following sections of an interview describe her problems with her boyfriend, as well as her mobility and her relationship to her extended family members:

[My aunt] didn't throw me out or nothing. But, she wanted me to leave because my ex-boyfriend, he would always hit me. I'd come home with bruises and black eyes.

Interviewer: From a visit with your boyfriend?

Theresa: Yeah. I would stay there like two weeks and then come back all bruised up.

Teresa had an argument with her aunt, who kept insisting that she leave her boyfriend. She ultimately left her aunt's home and subsequently moved back in with her grandmother.

Teresa: My cousin and his friend were at my grandmother's house for the past three days.

Interviewer: Okay so they were staying there?

Teresa: Well my cousin lives there.

Interviewer: So he lives back there with you? ...

Teresa: Yeah. He kind of lives there. Yeah, he doesn't live there 100 percent of the time. Because he sometimes lives with my other uncle.

Interviewer: Is this the aunt and uncle you used to live with?

Teresa: No. It's another one. But, yesterday they kicked him out.

Teresa, now fifteen, is pregnant for the third time and planning to have her baby soon. She is trying to fix up an apartment at her grandmother's house for her and her current boyfriend in an attempt to finally have a home of her own. She talks longingly for the day when her mother is released from prison because her mom is "cool."

One of the more common living arrangements within this group of females is living with the grandparents or a grandmother, usually the mother's mother. These girls often leave their children with their mothers because they are unable to support them, and other times it is because the mother is incarcerated or involved in illegal activities. Numerous girls relate this situation in their interviews. Nancy, a sixteen-year-old girl with a boyfriend in the Invaders gang, states, "I live with my grandparents. And my mom well she isn't really there all the time." Likewise, Melissa, fourteen years old, relates a story about a friend of hers who was sexually assaulted: "[She went] to her grandma. She doesn't live with her mom.... Her mom didn't want her."

One grandmother explains during a field visit how she was fighting for custody of her step-granddaughter because the child's mother was forcing her to sell cocaine:

We have to go to court. We have a notarized document right now giving us custody. [Her mother] is afraid to fight us because she knows we'll tell them what Priscilla told us. I finally got her to tell me what her mother was doing. She was having Priscilla and her brother sell cocaine for her.

This young adolescent female is caught up in a custody case between her mother and grandparents.

Finally, these young women often move in with their boyfriends' families due to pregnancy or other serious problems in their own families.

Lucy is a sixteen-year-old mother of a three-month-old girl. She was living with her gang-involved boyfriend until the baby was born. After the baby was born, her boyfriend became increasingly abusive to her because the baby was not his. She then moved back in with her mother. "Yeah, I'm back with my mom. I used to live with my ex-boyfriend. Not with my baby's dad, my ex-boyfriend."

Like Lucy had, Cecilia lives with her boyfriend. During her interview, she reveals that her mother was never really around and her father was dead. She had lived with her grandmother, but she said there was too much violence there since her cousins and uncles are in the Gangsters, one of the more violent gangs in town. In order to escape that violence, she moved in with her boyfriend but faced a different kind of violence in his home.

> Cecilia: It's like now I want to leave him but I can't. Last night I wanted to leave him so bad because we were fighting. He hit me. I wanted to leave and I got my stuff and I go, "You know what? I'm doing this for myself, not for anybody else." And I go, "I'm doing this for you; I am going because I'm hurting you; you always hurt me; you played me; you do a lot of things to me and I can't take it no more," I go, "Just let me leave." I was getting up with my stuff and he got me by my hair and he threw me on the floor and he goes, "You ain't going nowhere...."
>
> Interviewer: And so, his mom still lives there with him, with ya'll?
>
> Cecilia: Well we recently moved in with his mom. Well, I'm not living there; I stay there.
>
> Interviewer: Right but he lives with his mom?
>
> Cecilia: Yeah.
>
> Interviewer: Was he living by himself before?
>
> Cecilia: He was, he had his own apartment right there on Goliad but he got evicted.
>
> Interviewer: And now he's getting evicted out of there too?
>
> Cecilia: Yeah.

It is interesting that Cecilia differentiates "living" from "staying." Even though she said she has nowhere else to go, she says she does not live at her boyfriend's, but only "stays" there. The fact that she knows no other options forces her to remain in a very dangerous and volatile situation, suffering almost daily abuse from her boyfriend.

Often, because of abuse in the family, these young women move in with their boyfriends in order to get away from the abuse. They have what they see as diminishing opportunities and feel like this is the only way to get away from the abuse at home. Virginia describes how her mother kicked her father out when her mother discovered that he had been sexually abusing Virginia. However, her mother took him back in, so Virginia moved in with her boyfriend's family.

> Interviewer: And then after a certain amount of time went by [your mom] got back together with your dad anyway?
>
> Virginia: Yeah.
>
> Interviewer: What was up with that?
>
> Virginia: I don't know, I didn't really understand. Then when they got together and my dad got back in the house. I left the house and started staying with Daniel and his mom.

A lack of viable options often forces these girls into situations where they have no parental supervision, such as Virginia and Teresa, who lived with a friend's mother for a while. Without any parental supervision or support, these young women tried to find some sense of stability. As a result, they frequently found themselves living with people they barely know, often putting themselves highly at risk for victimization and further abuse.

The Normalization of Violence, Criminal Activities, and Drugs and Alcohol

The following data reveal how the use of drugs and alcohol, violent acts, and criminal behavior have been normalized within the family context and the lives of these young women. Table 4.2 presents the findings related to criminal activities within the family. Over two-thirds (71 percent) of the respondents had at least one family member who was involved in some illegal activities. Almost one-fourth (22 percent) had a father who was involved in illegal activities and 15 percent had a mother involved in them. In addition, over half of the respondents (54 percent) had witnessed their parents physically fight in the home.

With a vast proportion of the respondents reporting violence and illegal activities in the family, many of the young women felt the impact in their everyday lives.

Table 4.2 Family Involvement in Illegal/Violent Activities

Variable	Percent
(One or more) Family members involved in criminal activities	71
Father	22
Mother	15
Brother	21
Sister	6
Ever witnessed parents physically fight	54

Previous studies conducted by this research team revealed a very high frequency of use of 30 marijuana (75 percent), cocaine (53 percent), and heroin (26 percent) use in the previous thirty days among male gang members with whom the studied females were associated. The following data also showed that the sample of females' families involvement in drugs and alcohol was also extremely high, especially when compared to the population at large. Table 4.3 presents the findings related to drug and alcohol use within this population. Eighty-two percent of the respondents had a family member who used drugs. Fathers used the most drugs (42 percent), followed by brothers (38 percent). Of the mothers, 27 percent had used drugs. Sixty-four percent of the respondents lived with someone who had a drinking problem. Of the fathers, 43 percent were identified as having a drinking problem, compared with 21 percent of the mothers.

Table 4.3 Family Involvement in Drugs and Alcohol

Variable	Percent
Had a family member who used drugs	82
Father used drugs	42
Mother used drugs	27
Brother used drugs	38
Sister used drugs	19
Someone in the house who had a drinking problem	64
Father with drinking problem	43
Mother with drinking problem	21
Brother with drinking problem	5
Sister with drinking problem	3

As previously mentioned, substance abuse, especially alcohol, has been proven to be a significant contributor to domestic and intimate-partner violence (National Center for Injury Prevention 2003). The following excerpts from the life-history interviews provide an insight into the group dynamics within the respondents' families. Nancy, who was quoted earlier, relates an incident of domestic violence in her home. She emphasizes the role of alcohol and drugs in this incident, highlighting the injurious effects they can have.

> It was when my dad came home from work. He said that he was going to go out with his friends for a while and they were drinking. And he didn't come home until like the next day at six o'clock in the morning. One of his friends had called him and he got mad because my mom didn't take a message. He didn't know who it was. So then he started arguing with her because he was really drunk and already using drugs. So he just started hitting her. That's when my sister got in and he hit my sister too. So my mom got mad and threw him out. But he came back that same night and stayed with her. He was coked up and drinking.

The anecdote describes an incident of domestic violence that seemed to be the norm within this family and others in this population. The mother threw the father out after he beat her and her daughter, but took him back later that night. Nancy spent time between the houses of her mother and grandmother because her mother was never really around for her. The use of alcohol and drugs within the family seemed to be the catalyst for the violence in this particular incident.

At the time of the interview, Iris was eighteen years old with two children. Her common-law husband had been very abusive to her and she filed assault charges on him the week prior to her interview. She was initially afraid to do so because if he was locked up she feared his gang enemies would come after her and her children and he would not be around to protect them. However, she could not allow her children to be exposed to the violence and drugs in her house anymore. She says:

> His whole life he was living with his grandma because his mom abandoned him, took off. His mom and dad left him there. He lived on the West Side. He would always be outside running the streets ever since he was about six.... His grandma didn't really ask him where he was going. He would just take off. He told me he met his gang friends when he was like seven years old. He got in when he was seven, but they were older than him, they were like fourteen. Some were around his age, but not all of them. He started using drugs at seven. And he didn't really like being a kid. He grew up too fast and his grandma was never there. She would always be doing drugs. His grandma was a prostitute. She would do drugs and didn't care about him, or even her own kids. She would leave them

with relatives. And she didn't care about her kids. She was always in and out of prison. When she was in prison he had to go like to other family members. And one time she had a baby. She was too much into heroin. She even sold her own baby for heroin.

The result of this kind of family background resulted in Iris's boyfriend being addicted to heroin and in and out of prison by the age of nineteen. Iris initially thought that she would be able to change him. But by the time of her interview, she seemed to have given up on him. She was scared for her children and finally took steps to protect them from entering the same cycle their father was in.

Cindy, a fourteen-year-old female gang member, describes how her grandmother, who she lives with, got into a fight with one of Cindy's friends.

> On Thanksgiving some girl named Carmen was sitting outside with Grandmother. She thought she was all bad and everything. She was sitting on my grandma's chair and broke it. My grandma told her to give her money for the chair. Carmen said, "For that raggedy ass chair I ain't gonna give you nothing." My grandma hit her. The girl then hit my grandma like four times over the head. The ambulance had to come for her. [Carmen] was drunk, really, really, really wasted.

The grandmother's manner of dealing with this young woman was to react with violence, which caused Carmen to retaliate with violence of her own. The resolution of differences between these families and friends often seems to center on violence, especially when drugs and alcohol are involved.

Violence within these households is not unusual, as these interviews have shown. What has not been clearly presented is what role drugs and alcohol play in the unfolding of the violent event itself. In the following excerpt, Pearl describes a fight that took place between her two sisters:

Pearl: My sister Rose, right, she sells.

Interviewer: What does she sell?

Pearl: Heroin, coke, and weed. See she thought that my [other] sister, Alice, had gone with everyone else to Houston see my brother Fidel in prison, right. Rose she had left her stuff on top of the entertainment center. She had went to the store real fast to go deliver. My sister Alice was the only one there. And when [Rose] came back everything was missing. She had everything, it was worth like four thousand dollars. My sister was the only one there. So later on that day [Rose] got all drunk. She brought it up because she was depressed. I mean, they took all her stuff. And then she confronted Alice. Alice, she was like, "Well, yeah, I'm not gonna lie. I took it and they started throwing it down, *gacho*." Well, Rose was sitting on this glass table. My sister Alice just got up and she, like, threw the glass table. Rose fell back ... and then Alice got a knife in the [kitchen], ... and she stabbed my sister in the back.

Interviewer: Alice stabbed Rose?

Pearl: Yeah, and they called the cops and everything, and they had took my sister in. My sister Alice.

While this may be one of the more extreme cases, it serves to demonstrate several points. First, the brother, Fidel, was in prison for dealing drugs and Rose was also dealing drugs. Apparently this illegal activity, while maybe not condoned by the family, was at least tolerated. Additionally, once both Rose and Alice were drunk, they confronted each other violently, causing serious injury. Because Alice lives in an environment where her siblings are selling drugs, they are more accessible. In addition, their presence only seems to reinforce that it is okay to use and sell drugs.

While the abuse of drugs by adolescents is problematic, there are other consequences of alcohol and drugs in the family that are even more serious and place these young women at an even greater risk of victimization. The following two examples describe different cases of sexual abuse in the family where alcohol and/or drugs played a role in its inception, persistence, and as a coping mechanism.

I was twelve years old, and it was my mother's boyfriend. He would come in and ... touch me and stuff. I told my mother about it, but she didn't believe me. I kept telling her and she wouldn't ever believe me. It kept going on because we were living with him, at his house, and he kept coming to me. He would make me touch him and go down on him.... I told my mom and she didn't believe me, she was on crack then, and she just let it happen.

Another young woman recalls:

I started using drugs, you know, when I was, when [the sexual abuse] was occurring. I was doing good in school and everything. But, it would get in the way and that's one of my problems. I stopped going to school. I didn't let it get in the way; it was already in the way, you know what I mean? I couldn't handle that. I couldn't handle going to school at the same time. I started having a lot of problems like that.

The first respondent describes a situation where, her mother's boy-friend repeatedly molested her, and due to her mother's addiction to crack, her mother did not stop the abuse. In addition, they were living at his house and because of this, the mother may have been more reluctant to believe her. The mother's crack addiction, while not the cause of the abuse, was surely a factor in its continuation. The second respondent describes how she turned to drugs as a means to deal with the shame and difficulties caused by her father's continual molestation. She relates how she had been doing well in school and other areas of her life before this occurred. In order to deal with this issue she turned to drugs, which helped her handle the pressure of hiding this secret and keeping up appearances.

Mercedes, a fourteen-year-old girl who moved back and forth between various family members including an aunt and her grand-mother, describes an incident where she actually got alcohol from one of her relatives: "We were smoking and everything and then my uncle came with liquor. Presidente (a Mexican brandy) and some other white liquor. We were drinking and drinking ..."

Like the previous example with Rose and Alice, Amanda, a sixteen-year-old adolescent, describes a situation in her family where the con-stant presence of drugs caused continuous problems within the family:

> There was a time when my dad was locked up. It was just my mom and my brothers living there. At the time my brother was selling. And the youngest one was addicted on drugs, so he kept stealing my brother's stuff. My older brother was selling and he just got tired of it. They just started fighting. And my mom just got, she just argued with both of them. She ran off the oldest one.

Her father was already incarcerated for drug dealing and it seems her older brother was following in his path. The mother finally got tired of the violence in her home and made him leave. The presence of drugs in the house had obviously caused much stress and violence already and her mother dealt with it in the most expeditious manner: getting rid of the main source of drugs in the home. Whether this made a significant difference in the home is, unfortunately, unknown. However, the mother clearly believed that the source of the familial stress was her oldest son.

Role of Stress, Family Coping, Ethnic Identity, and Mother-Daughter Relationships in Substance Use

The preceding information has provided a qualitative understanding of the role of substance use in the family among this population. I now turn to a brief analysis of substance use and several identified family-related predictors. Specifically, despite the beyond-risk status of the female adolescents, differences in levels of substance use appear to be related to family process, acculturation stress, and ethnic identity.

Two dependent measures of substance use were utilized for the purposes of this analysis. The measures were derived using a five-point Likert scale indicating how often the respondent had used a selected number of substances. The scale included five responses ranging from zero to four and consisting of the answers: "never," "rarely," "sometimes," "often" (most of the time) and "very often" (all of the time). The first question was how often the respondent had used alcohol and tobacco during the past year. The second was how often the respondent had used marijuana, benzodiazepines (i.e., Rohypnol, Xanax, Valium, and other downers), and cocaine during the past year. These drugs were selected because they were the most widely reported illicit drugs used by the population. The responses to the Likert scale for each of the substances were summed and weighted to derive two separate scales to be used in the analysis: alcohol and tobacco recurrence, and illicit drug (marijuana, benzodiazepines, and cocaine) recurrence. The scores for the alcohol and tobacco scale ranged from zero to eight while that of the illicit drug scale ranged from zero to twelve.

Four psychometric instruments were used as independent variables in this analysis. The first was a twelve-item version of the Multigroup Ethnic Identity Measure (MEIM) (Phinney 2002) that was used to assess two aspects of ethnic identity: the search for ethnic identity—which is a developmental and cognitive component—and affirmation, belonging, and commitment—which is an affective component. The higher the mean score on the total scale, the stronger the respondent's total ethnic identity.

The second independent variable was the Mother-Daughter Relationship Scale (MDRS) (Inazu and Fox 1980), which measures the absence or presence of open communication, uncertainty, and ambiguity in defining an adolescent's relationship with her mother. The MDRS conceptualizes a mother's influence in a combination of direct and indirect influences. Direct influences include the mother's role as information source and social supervisor and indirect influences include her role as a source of socioemotional support and as a role model. Higher scores indicate a more positive, supportive relationship.

The third independent variable was the Family Crisis Oriented Personal Scale (F-COPES) (McCubbin, Larson, and Olsen 1982), which identifies problem solving strategies and behavioral strategies used by families in difficult or problematic situations. The instrument has thirty coping-behavior items that focus on two levels of family interaction: internal family coping patterns—which are the ways in which families internally handle difficulties with other family members—and external coping patterns—which refers to the way the family handles problems that are outside the family but involve family members. Higher scores on the total scale indicate a higher number of successful coping strategies within the family.

Finally, the fourth was the Hispanic Stress Inventory, U.S. Born Version—Family/ Culture Conflict Scale (HSI/CCS), which has been developed as a culturally appropriate assessment of psychosocial stress appraisal (Cervantes, Padilla, and Salgado de Snyder 1991). The scale assesses acculturation, conflict, and stress as related to family relations, communication, and intracultural values. Two scores are obtained from the instrument, a stress-event frequency (SEF) score and a stress-event appraisal (SEA) score.

Means, standard deviations, and range are presented for the two dependent measures of substance use recurrence in Table 4.4. The alcohol and tobacco measure had a mean score of 3.65 (Standard Deviation [SD] = 2.23). Sixty-five percent of the sample reported recurrence of alcohol and tobacco "sometimes to very often" in the past year. Only 7 percent indicated they had not used alcohol or tobacco during this time period. The mean for the illicit drug use measure was 3.81 (SD = 2.97). Almost a quarter (24 percent) of the sample reported frequent (often to very often) recurrence of marijuana, benzodiazepines, and cocaine use in the last year and only 17 percent stated that they had not used any of these substances in the last year.

Table 4.4 Descriptive Statistics for Alcohol and Tobacco Recurrence and Illicit Drug Recurrence for Mexican American Adolescent Females

Substances	Mean	Standard Deviation	Range
Alcohol and Tobacco Recurrence	3.65	2.23	0–8
Illicit Drug Recurrence	3.81	2.97	0–12

Means and standard deviation results for the psychometric scales are presented in Table 4.5. The mean score on the MDRS for the sample was 27.76 (SD = 8.73) and the mean score on the MEIM was 3.09 (SD = 0.568). The F-COPES scale mean score was 99.23 (SD = 14.81). The large standard deviation gives an indication of the variability in the coping strategies these families employ. For the HSI/CCS, the SEF was 4.85 (SD = 2.27) and the SEA mean was 21.83 (SD = 8.26).

Table 4.6 shows the regression analysis results for both the alcohol and tobacco and illicit drug use recurrence scales. Findings for the alcohol and tobacco measure indicate the MDRS as the only independent variable to have significantly predicted the recurrence of these substances among this population of Mexican American adolescent females. That is, in the year previous to the interview, alcohol and tobacco use was lower when the socioemotional support of the mother was higher.

Table 4.5   Means and Standard Deviations for Psychometric Scales

Measure	Mean	Standard Deviations
Mother-Daughter Relationship Scale (MDRS)	27.76	8.73
Multigroup Ethnic Identity Measure (MEIM)	3.09	0.568
Family Crisis Oriented Personal Scales (F-COPES)	99.23	14.81
Hispanic Stress Inventory		
Family/ Conflict Scale (HSI/CCS)		
Stress Event Frequency (SEF)	4.85	2.27
Stress Event Appraisal (SEA)	21.83	8.26

Results for illicit drug use recurrence revealed two independent variables as significantly predicting the use of marijuana, benzodiazepines, and cocaine over the previous year. The first was the family acculturation SEF. That is, as the number of family acculturation stress events increased, the use of marijuana, cocaine, and benzodiazepines also increased. The second significant predictor was the F-COPES, which indicates that the number of the family's problem solving and strategies for managing difficult situations increased, marijuana, cocaine, and benzodiazepine use decreased.

The preceding analysis indicates that positive family relationships and the mother-daughter relationship in particular are protective factors against alcohol and tobacco use. Clearly, the girls in the study who maintained constructive relationships with their mothers as measured by the MDRS used less of these substances. What did prove to be significant in averting illicit drug use was the ability of the immediate family (adults and children) to cope with difficulties, stress, and conflicts, both internally and externally, as measured by the F-COPES. This indicates that the benefits of mother-daughter relationships may be diminished within the larger context of the family in these communities. The families with the inability to develop appropriate coping strategies are more likely to have adolescents frequently using drugs.

Table 4.6 Multiple Regression Analysis of the Effects of the Psychometric Measures on Alcohol and Tobacco and Illicit Drug Use Recurrence

	Alcohol and Tobacco Recurrence	Illicit Drug Recurrence
Predictor Variables	β	β
MDRS	-0.184*	-0.044
F-COPES	0.04	-0.165*
MEIM	0.007	-0.092
HSI		
SEF	-0.002	0.212**
SEA	0.048	0.095
R^2	0.162	0.236

***$p < 0.001$ **$p < 0.01$ *$p < 0.05$ Controlling for: living with parents, parents with a job, living in public housing, receives government assistance, age, expelled from school, and ever arrested.

Family Relationships to Institutions

One thing that truly characterizes the families of these girls is their negative perceptions of and hostility toward secondary institutions such as schools, local governments, criminal justice, and organizational religion. Table 4.7 illustrates the absence of ties these families have to community organizations and institutions in this study.

Table 4.7 Participation in Community Activities

Variable	Family	Respondent
Participated in following during the past year		
Community groups	17	17
Political parties	11	5
Social or Recreational Groups	45	43
Church groups	35	30
Issue-oriented groups	6	2
Attended church regularly growing up	65	63
Parents went to school because respondent		
was having problems	79	
Parents went to school for PTA	25	
Parents went to school for Open House	63	
Parents went to school for athletic events	37	
Parents went to school fairs	30	
Parents went to teacher conferences	57	

As these data indicate, families participated in the year previous to the study in issue-oriented groups least (6 percent) and they participated most in social or recreational groups (45 percent) and organized church activities (35 percent). I would argue that these levels of participation are reflective more of their economic status rather than of their ethnicity or lifestyle. Surprisingly, many had fairly high levels of attending school functions such as PTA meetings, open houses, and parent-teacher conferences. The high rates of parent-teacher conferences may be related to the disciplinary problems of their children rather than to scholarship issues.

As illustrated in the following material, educational achievement was something that was not encouraged or emphasized among these families, which some girls found disappointing. This is expressed in the following interview with Monica, a nineteen-year-old female: "I was absent a lot. Everybody thought I was absent because I didn't want to go to school. But my mom gives us a choice if we wanted to go to school or not. I didn't go. I didn't want to wake up." Monica seems to be indirectly expressing a desire that her mother would have made her go to school rather then leave the decision up to her.

Another discusses how her addiction to heroin discouraged her from attending school: I was hooked on brown [heroin] right. I would do brown, take a shower, get dressed, and everything would be all right. I didn't go to school, right. I would just be selling all day, drinking, smoking, and taking brown all day. I did that for like maybe two months straight." She also describes her boyfriend's school history:

Monica: He dropped out of school when he was fourteen. He stopped going because nobody would take him to school like to register. So he just had to stop going.

Interviewer: Do you know what grade he was in?

Monica: I think the seventh or eighth grade. No one would take him. He had no choice but to stay home and not go to school.

Interviewer: And you've known him for how long, seven years?

Monica: Yeah seven years.

The families in these particular cases did not actively encourage their children to attend school since they maintained the view that the educational system is not only not open to them but also repressive. Many persons outside this culture interpret this behavior as not valuing education. But it is more complicated than it appears. Nonetheless, this disinterest in education inevitably influences the children.

The following excerpts come from a section where the females are asked to discuss their current boyfriend's educational experience.

Interviewer: And is he in school?

Respondent: No.

Interviewer: What's the last grade he finished?

Respondent: I don't know, when I was with him he was in eighth grade, probably like the ninth grade.

Interviewer: Do you know how many years of school he completed?

Respondent: No. Like he went back to school but then he stopped again.

Interviewer: Okay, do you know what grade he finished in school?

Respondent: I don't know.

It was interesting that all of these female respondents were involved in fairly long-term relationships (six months or more) and they had never asked or discussed school with their partners. These excerpts indicate how educational achievement is not valued within this social group.

Parents' disinterest in school was not necessarily an indication of their lack of concern for their children's well-being. Yvette describes that her father was around when she truly needed him but wasn't there for the little things like school. She says: "When I need something you know he'll give it to me, you know. He'll be there and stuff. Like when I get in trouble. Like when I do good in school or something like he won't be there."

She appears to resent the fact that he does not take an interest in her well-being when it comes to things like school. While she still sees a value in her education, her father—at least as far as she can see—does not. He takes little notice of her accomplishments, except when she is in trouble. The message he is sending her is that there is no need to pay attention as long as you are doing well. In order to get any attention from him, she has to be in trouble or need some help.

It is not just school that disinterests these young women and their families but also other institutions, including churches and community services. Marie, a girl in our study, exemplifies this idea by stating, "Just before I went over there I was all ready, I was here and we were trying to figure a way how we were gonna go to our church, to get counseling. But, because my car was broken, we didn't have a ride. We needed to go because when I put him in jail, it was because of domestic violence. So when we went to court, they said in order for them to dismiss it, we needed some type of counseling and we needed proof."

This young woman expresses her disinterest in the actual counseling provided by the church. She stresses that they need proof they attended the court-ordered counseling in order to keep her abusive boyfriend out of jail. She appears to have little use for the services provided to her and uses them only to get what she wants, rather than using them to improve her situation.

It also appears that attending or doing well in school is often looked upon as nonmasculine or not tough. While this may be desirable for some girls, it is not always acceptable within Maria's social networks.

Maria: He hasn't had a girlfriend, like, that many girlfriends.

Interviewer: Okay, that's a good thing too. Minimal exposure.

Maria: He's still a virgin.

Interviewer: That's good. What else? What are his good qualities? Those are it? Those are good ones, right?

Maria: Yeah, he's a school boy. I don't know what I am going to do about Justin. I mean, he's a really good to me, but he's the youngest guy I've ever dated and he's such a school boy.

The term "school boy" is often used within this population to describe someone who regularly attends school and does well in school. According to these two respondents, this is something that is not necessarily desired in a mate. A school boy may contradict the macho image that is desired by these young women when searching for a boyfriend who better fits into their social networks.

The schoolboy argument is further strengthened by the majority of the descriptions of the girls' boyfriends. The majority of the descriptions reflect the statements in the following excerpts:

Respondent: He's not in school anymore, he dropped. They kicked him out of New Horizons, the same school I was going to. They kicked him out and he didn't go back.

Interviewer: How far did he get?

Respondent: Just half of the ninth grade. Because at New Horizons it was all for like freshmans and he, he didn't finish the school year and they kicked him out. He don't go to school but he would've been in probably the tenth.

Interviewer: And how far did he go in school?

Respondent: Seventh grade.

Interviewer: He dropped out in the seventh grade?

Respondent: Yeah, well he got expelled.

Interviewer: What happened?

Respondent: He was too bad, the teachers couldn't handle him.

Most of the descriptions are similar to these, adding credence to the idea that school is not something that is seen as important to this population. Most of the respondents have not completed school nor do they have plans to complete it. Their parents, for the most part, have little involvement in the school, usually limited to the times when the child is in trouble. As a result, rather than expressing an interest and becoming involved in the community schools, parents generally have a fear of the institution and, due to this fear, they do not involve themselves in the everyday activities of their children's education. With little reinforcement from family and peers, the majority of the girls opt to drop out of school. Because of this lack of interest and involvement in community institutions, it is often more acceptable in the young women's social networks to drop out of school rather than continue with their education.

Conclusion

As discussed, Mexican Americans place value on maintaining close relations with nuclear family members as well as the extended family, including aunts, uncles, cousins, and grandparents. Even as family structure breaks down and changes due to the proliferation of divorce, separation, and incarceration in the families of the beyond-risk adolescent females, some attempts are made to maintain these values. However, the roles of members within the *cholo* structure are often ambiguous and often lead to interpersonal conflicts and violence. An example of this is male children taking on the role of an absent parent and attempting to control the behavior of their sisters.

Contributing to risky behavior among the young females is a pattern of serial residency whereby they move from various households within and outside the family. There are varying reasons for this, such as the incarceration of one or more parents, the girl's pregnancy, or the alcohol or drug problem of a parent. Often the girl may have been kicked out of her home or run away from an abusive family member, especially one that is sexually abusive. The girls that leave their families rarely occupy a permanent residence; they often end up living with sympathetic relatives or friends. Many even have lived with the parents of their boyfriends even though both were often under eighteen years of age.

This type of residential instability increases her risk for violence perpetration and victimization, exposing her to predatory adults and high-risk situations where there is excessive drinking and drug use.

The vignettes in this chapter reveal the pervasiveness of alcohol and drugs among the respondents. Most adolescents in the United States are likely to experiment with drugs and/or alcohol at some point in their lives (Johnson, O'Malley, and Bachman 2002). However, compared to the general adolescent population, the rates of the drug and alcohol use of these females are exceedingly high, as are the rates of the drug and alcohol use of the adults with whom they associate. Drugs and alcohol often heighten the likelihood of violence in the home, acting as a catalyst to confrontations and disputes. Additionally, drugs and alcohol often work as a coping mechanism for other problems within the family, often masking what is really wrong. With such high levels of drug use by the respondents and their families, it is not surprising that its effects are so multifaceted.

This research indicates that positive family relationships and, in particular, the mother-daughter relationship are protective factors against alcohol and tobacco use. Clearly, girls who maintained constructive relationships with their mothers, as measured by the MDRS, in these highly volatile social environments used less of these substances. This research provides evidence of the protective function that the mother-daughter relationship has for these high-risk female adolescents, despite the fact that they may be gang affiliated and street oriented. These results are particularly relevant in light of the increased number of single-female-headed households with adolescent daughters found among low-income Hispanics. However, the mother-daughter relationship proved to be less important in reducing marijuana, cocaine, and benzodiazepine use. Seemingly, these illicit drugs are more likely to be associated with the adolescent syndrome of problem behavior and peer-group susceptibility than the use of tobacco and alcohol, substances with relatively high prevalence rates among this age group.

Chapter 5

Risk Behaviors: Delinquency, Violence, Substance Use, and Sexual Relations

Studies have found that gang membership and affiliation has a "facilitation effect on delinquency—that is, youth's participation in delinquency increases dramatically when they join gangs, and declines significantly once they leave their gang" (Miller 2001). Women's involvement in gangs and crime, violence, substance use, and high-risk sexual relations suggest similar trends, but more complex patterns. The difference between male and female gang members is that females commit fewer crimes than their male counterparts, but more than nongang males and females. Moreover, they are involved in less serious or violent crimes than male gang members because they are structurally excluded from male delinquent activities, or possibly decide to exclude themselves. Even though substance use is reportedly higher among girl gang members than girls who are not in gangs, girls in gangs have less of a tendency to use substances than male gang members. Also, there is a wide continuum of drug use among girls associated with gangs, ranging from relatively low use to levels of use that parallel those of men.

More recently there has been increased violence, substance use, and sexual relations among gang and nongang girls. For instance, nationwide studies reveal a steady increase beginning in 1992 in prevalence rates for use of drugs such as marijuana, heroin, inhalants, and cocaine among females (Substance Abuse and Mental Health Services Administration 1996). A recent study conducted by the Office for National Drug Control Policy (ONDCP) found that girls have caught up with boys in illicit drug and alcohol use. Moreover, there are more girls who are new users of substances than boys (Office of National Drug Control Policy 2006). Similarly, the number of adult women and adolescents arrested and incarcerated is growing faster than that of men (U.S. Department of Justice 1995). These crimes tend to be nonviolent and nonproperty offenses for adult women and more related to their legal status as adolescents for young females (Chesney-Lind and Shelden 1997; Joe and Chesney-Lind 1995). However, female adolescent crimes are more likely than those of males to be motivated by interpersonal disputes rather than material gains—instrumental versus expressive violence (Loper and Cornell 1995).

This chapter will focus on the offending behavior (i.e., violence and substance use) and the sexual activity of Mexican American female gang members. The emphasis is on these girls as perpetrators, not necessarily as victims, which will be addressed in Chapter 6. Researchers argue that engaging in these antisocial behaviors is a means by which girls prove their worth to the gang. As Edwardo Portillos states, "Notions of protecting your homeboys, not backing down from a fight, and enacting revenge against those who have challenged you become the ideals of the marginalized Chicana and Mexicana gang members ... [who] positively sanction these ideals" (1999). John Hagedorn and Mary Devitt found that girls may actually fight more than male gang members, but they fight differently, with fewer weapons and lethal consequences (1999). He found that those who most loved to fight had a less male-centered outlook, and those who fought less had more traditional ideals of gender. As David Curry states, discussion of girls' involvement with gangs has tended to go to one extreme or the other (1998). Girls are either portrayed as victims of injury or have been seen as "liberated," degendered gangbangers. Many studies emphasize how gender inequality and patriarchy shape female violence and other criminal behaviors within a street gang culture (Lauritsen, Sampson, and Laub 1991; Miller 1998). They use these experiences to help construct an oppositional femininity. This chapter examines young women's participation in delinquency, violence, sex, and substance use within the context of a Mexican American gang subculture.

High Rates of Delinquency and Violence

Given the existing literature it is not surprising that girls involved in this study were involved in a diverse array of delinquent activities. Table 5.1 provides the prevalence of self-reported delinquency for lifetime and previous-month involvement. The girls were asked if they had ever participated in these activities during the two indicated timeframes. The activities were identified as ranging from minor offenses to more serious crimes. The minor offenses included fighting, drug use, running away from home, curfew violation, shoplifting/theft (fifty dollars or less), vandalism, stealing car parts, breaking and entering, disturbing the peace, and public intoxication. Eleven serious delinquent activities were included: bringing a weapon to school, arson, auto theft, violent acts, armed robbery, unarmed robbery, car jacking, selling weapons, selling drugs, theft (more than fifty dollars) and burglary.

Table 5.1 Prevalence of Self-Reported Delinquency: Lifetime and Previous Month

Delinquent Activity	Lifetime Percentage	Previous Month Percentage (n)
Minor Delinquency		
Fighting	86	43 (55)
Using drugs	94	69 (97)
Running away from home	63	14 (13)
Staying out late without permission	69	57 (59)
Curfew violation	54	26 (21)
Shoplifting / theft ($50 or less)	37	30 (17)
Vandalism	25	40 (15)
Taking car parts	11	29 (5)
Breaking and entering	13	32 (6)
Disturbing the peace	35	60 (32)
Public intoxication	19	43 (12)
Serious Delinquency		
Bringing a weapon to school	12	17 (3)
Arson	6	22 (2)
Auto theft	21	22 (7)
Violent acts (drive-by shooting, rape, assault, beating someone)	39	38 (22)
Armed robbery	5	-
Unarmed robbery	11	18 (3)
Car jacking	18	30 (8)
Selling weapons	11	25 (4)
Selling drugs	38	28 (16)
Theft (more than $50)	21	29 (9)
Burglary	11	24 (4)

In regards to lifetime prevalence, the use of drugs was the activity most widely reported by the young women (94 percent), followed by fighting (86 percent). Nonproperty offenses such as staying out late without permission, running away from home, and curfew violations were reported by more than half the sample, with 69, 63, and 54 percent, respectively. Approximately one-third of the young women reported engaging in shoplifting fifty dollars or less and/or engaging in activities that disturbed the peace. A smaller percentage reported vandalism, taking car parts, breaking and entering, and public intoxication. The two most prevalent forms of serious delinquent acts that young girls engaged in were violent acts (drive-by shooting, assault, and beating someone) and selling drugs. Approximately 21 percent of the sample indicated having ever engaged in theft of something more than fifty dollars and automobile theft. Arson and armed robbery were the least likely reported by the young women, with the remainder of the activities ranging from 11 to 12 percent of the sample.

Similar prevalence trends were observed for engaging in delinquent activity during the previous month. Of interest, however, are the high rates of reported participation in a number of minor delinquent activities. More specifically, six activities were reported by more than 40 percent of those reporting lifetime participation. These delinquent activities included fighting, using drugs, staying out late without permission, vandalism, disturbing the peace, and public intoxication. A similar pattern was observed for the serious activities in which violent acts, car jacking, theft, and selling drugs were the most widely reported during the previous month. Notably, the young women engaged in more serious activities appeared to be more likely to engage in income-generating or instrumental offenses.

Another measure of delinquency included arrest and incarceration history. Close to half of the young women reported having been arrested at least once (see Table 5.2). A more detailed description of the most recent arrest was obtained from the young women. Data revealed theft and assault (most reported as a result of fights) as the most widely reported reasons for their last arrest. Running away or truancy and drug possession followed with 14 and 13 percent, respectively. Seventy three percent of the sample reported ever having been in jail or juvenile detention. A mean of 13.9 was reported as the age of first incarceration with an average of three times. These data clearly indicate that many of the girls had a history of incarceration that occurred after they became affiliated with the gang.

Gang-Affiliated Delinquency and Violence

Gangs can be seen as a representation of a means by which some youths seek to resolve problems presented by their disadvantaged structural position in society and in their community (Campbell 1995). This situation is even more acute for the young females in this study whose situations are compounded by class, race, and gender issues (Horowitz 1983; Moore 1991; Valdez and Halley 1996; Williams 1990). All of the young women in the study were distinctly integrated into the male gangs through their relationships with the male members. Analyses revealed 11.7 as the mean age when these young women first associated with gangs. At the time of the study, 43 percent reported having a boyfriend involved in a gang while an overwhelming 81 percent said they had a good friend in a gang. Others reported having brothers, cousins, and other relatives in a male gang. This association with the male gangs resulted, in many instances, in the girls' participation in delinquent behaviors.

Table 5.2   Arrest and Incarceration History

History	Percentage (Mean)
Ever Been Arrested	49
Most Recent Arrest for:	
Drug Possession	13
Auto Theft	8
Theft	26
Robbery	2
Assault	25
Running Away/Truancy	14
Other Nonviolent Offenses	12
Ever Been in Jail/Juvenile Detention	73
Mean Age of First Time Incarceration	(13.94)
Mean # of Times in Jail/Juvenile Detention	(3.00)

Overall, the young women reported a high frequency of gang-associated illegal activities. Table 5.3 indicates that holding drugs (55 percent), selling drugs (31 percent), and holding weapons (27 percent) were the delinquent activities that the young women most widely reported engaging in during the previous year. Some of the girls told interviewers that they were actually selling drugs, usually to other female close friends or relatives. Other girls frequently "stashed" gang members' drugs (marijuana, coke, or heroin) while they were on the streets doing other business. The girls were some of the few people whom the male gang members trusted, although many girls reported "pinching" drugs for their own use. The girls were also considered a safe haven for hiding the gang's weapons that were often discarded or destroyed after being used. The guys' personal weapons were also held by these girls since the guys were always at risk for being stopped and searched by the police, especially if they were identified as gang members by the police.

Shoplifting was the criminal behavior that was the fourth most prevalent in these girls, but it is the second activity reported as happening "very often." Shoplifting is much more accessible to a wider number of girls (and women) than other criminal acts. This is consistent with published criminal justice literature. While not as frequently reported, other delinquent activities such as carjacking, weapon sales, burglaries, auto theft, and robberies were reported by 12 to 19 percent of the sample.

To get a sense of the young women's level of participation in these male-gang delinquent activities, they were asked how often they engaged in this behavior during the previous year. While the young women reported rarely engaging in most of the activities, a couple of interesting patterns emerged. For instance, "sometimes" was the modal category reported for selling drugs and weapons and for holding drugs and weapons. All such activities are serious and it can be speculated that they generate income for the male gang and possibly for the females themselves. Furthermore, not including selling and holding drugs and weapons, auto theft and robbery (two additional income generators) were two of the most reported activities, occurring "often" during the previous year.

Table 5.3 Frequency of Participation in Male-Gang Delinquent Activities during Previous Year

Activity	Participation in Previous Year (%)	How Often (%)			
		Rarely	Sometimes	Often	Very Often
Selling drugs	31	17	52	18	13
Carjacking	19	48	28	10	14
Burglaries	13	45	40	5	10
Auto theft	14	52	14	24	10
Robbery	12	50	16	28	6
Weapon sales	19	39	46	11	4
Holding drugs	55	32	34	18	16
Holding weapons	27	29	37	12	22
Theft/shoplifting	24	42	28	11	19
Other	12	28	17	39	17

A gang-activity scale was computed, adding the total frequency of each illegal activity based on the Likert scale. A total number of ten illegal activities with the five corresponding Likert scale responses was computed. For example, zero equals no illegal gang activity, and fifteen could indicate several possible illegal activities with varying levels of frequency. This index provided a frequency distribution of zero to twenty-seven. A mean of 4.7 was calculated, with a standard deviation of 6.2, suggesting that many girls participated in several crimes with their gang. This gang activity variable was recoded for analytical purposes and the responses collapsed as follows: 0 (n = 45); 1 (n = 18) and 2 (n = 14); 3 and 4 were combined into one category (n = 17); 5 (n = 12) and 6 (n = 12); those indicating a frequency of illegal gang activity between 7 and 14 were combined (n = 18); those responding 15 through 27 (n = 14) were also combined. Through this recoding, a range of 0 through 7 was created, resulting in a gang activity scale. The gang activity scale was further broken into three groups: none (0, n = 45), low (1–3, n = 49), and high (4–7, n = 56). A reliability analysis calculated an alpha of 0.84, indicating high reliability of this scale.

The degree of participation in male-gang delinquent activities was assessed with two associated measures, using a chi-square analysis. The first cross tabulation examined the level of male-gang delinquent activity (none, low, and high) and the length of affiliation (one to two years, three to four years, and five or more years) (Table 5.4). Results indicated that the level of participation in such activities was significantly associated with the duration of gang affiliation. That is, the young women who had been associated with a male gang for five or more years were more likely to have a high level of participation in the male-gang delinquent activities, as seen in Table 5.4.

Table 5.4 Level of Girls' Participation in Male-Gang Delinquent Activity by Duration of Gang Association

	1–2 years	3–4 years	5 or more years
Level of Participation in Male-Gang Delinquent Activity*		Percentage (n)	
None	46 (21)	26 (12)	21 (12)
Low	33 (15)	39 (18)	28 (16)
High	22 (10)	35 (16)	52 (30)

* p < 0.01

The second analysis, presented in Table 5.5, examined the association between frequency of contact with the male gang in the past year (never, rarely, sometimes, and often) and the level of male-gang delinquent activity participation. A similar relationship was observed in that the young women who reported a high level of participation in male-gang delinquent activity tended to hang out with the gang often. This was in contrast to the young women who reported never hanging out with the gang and not participating in male-gang delinquent activity.

Table 5.5 Level of Girls' Participation in Male-Gang Delinquent Activity by How Often They "Hang Out" with Male Gang

	Never	*Rarely*	*Sometimes*	*Often*
*Level of Participation in Male Gang Delinquent Activity***	*Percentage (n)*			
None	57 (16)	33 (14)	29 (12)	8 (3)
Low	21 (6)	44 (19)	27 (11)	34 (13)
High	21 (6)	23 (10)	44 (18)	58 (22)

** p < 0.001

These results indicated that there were considerable variations in gang-associated girls' participation in delinquency activities.

Fights

Data presented in Table 5.6 reflect the extent and nature of the young women's first-hand participation in physical fights. Ninety-four percent of the sample reported ever being involved in physical fights. The specific types of fights varied in regards to the context in which the violence occurred. For instance, 68 percent of the young women indicated that they had engaged in neighborhood fights at least once. Similarly, 64 percent reported involvement in school fights. More surprisingly, household fights with family members were reported by 81 percent of the young females.

Table 5.7 shows specific characteristics of each young woman's last physical fight collected for each type of fight. Neighborhood (51 percent) and household (42 percent) fights appeared to be the most likely to have involved the subject's or the adversary's use of either alcohol or drugs when compared to school fights. The use of weapons, however, was reported more in household fights with family members and was connected with altercations that were the least likely to have a police response. The qualitative data reveal that weapons in these fights tended to be easily available household items like kitchen utensils rather than more lethal weapons.

Table 5.6 Prevalence of Self-Reported Participation in Violent Physical Fights in the Neighborhood, Home, and School Setting

Types of Fights	Percentage
Ever Engaged in Physical Fight	94
Neighborhood Fights	68
Household Family Fights (excluding intimates)	81
School Fights	64

Table 5.7 Characteristics and Type of Last Physical Fight Respondant Was Involved In

Characteristics	Type of Fight		
	Neighborhood	Household	School
Alcohol/Drugs Involved	51	42	11
Weapon Used	23	33	14
Police Respond	39	24	55

Alcohol, Tobacco, and Illicit Drug Use

In analyzing the data on alcohol and drug use collected from the young women, it is apparent that a high number of them report polydrug use. Table 5.8 shows lifetime, age of onset, and current (past month and forty-eight hours) substance use for the adolescent female population. Data show a wide variation of illegal drug use among the girls. In examining lifetime history of use, the most widely reported illicit drug was marijuana, with 95 percent of the population indicating having used the drug at some point. The second most reported illicit drug was cocaine, with a little more than half of the sample (57 percent) reporting having used it at some time in their lives. Of particular interest was the large proportion (42 percent) of young women who reported having used benzodiazepine, a drug category that includes Rohypnol, popularly known as the "date-rape" drug." Moreover, approximately a quarter of the young women reported use of heroin during their lifetime. Only six percent reported injecting either heroin, cocaine, or speedball. Most of the heroin was used by sniffing, known as noninjecting heroin use.

A similar pattern was observed for current drug use as measured during the previous thirty days. Marijuana (63 percent) and cocaine (35 percent) were the two most frequently reported drugs used during the previous month. The mean number of times marijuana was used during the prior forty-eight hours among the young women was 3.01. The remaining illicit drugs ranged from a high of 21 percent (benzodi-azepines) to 2 percent (crack). In addition to drug prevalence rates, data was collected on past and current alcohol use (see Table 5.8). Most of the sample (94 percent) reported past alcohol use, with an average age at initiation of 13.1 years old. As expected, 62 percent of the subjects reported current alcohol use (previous thirty days).

Table 5.8 Prevalence of Substance Use

Variable	Lifetime use N (%)	Mean Age of First Time Use	Use in last 30 days N (%)	Mean Number of Times Used Drugs in Last 48 Hours (SD)
Alcohol	141 (94)	13.1 (2.1)	93 (62)	1.08 (3.4)
Marijuana/Hashish	142 (95)	12.9 (1.2)	94 (63)	3.01 (11.9)
Crack	14 (9)	15.1 (2.2)	3 (2)	0.01 (0.2)
Acid/Ecstasy	50 (33)	15.6 (1.8)	19 (13)	0.02 (0.1)
Inhalants	42 (28)	13.5 (1.8)	12 (8)	0.08 (0.6)
Benzodiazepines	64 (42)	14.4 (1.5)	31 (21)	0.09 (0.4)
Cocaine only	85 (57)	14.8 (1.6)	53 (35)	0.31 (1.4)
Heroin only	36 (24)	14.7 (2.0)	14 (9)	0.2 (1.5)
Speedball	24 (16)	14.8 (2.1)	7 (5)	0.03 (0.3)
Other opiates	11 (7)	15.6 (1.6)	8 (5)	0.03 (0.3)
Amphetamines	19 (13)	15.3 (2.1)	7 (5)	0.01 (0.1)
Other drugs	14 (9)	14.9 (1.6)	7 (5)	0.00 (0.0)
Tobacco	104 (69)	13.2 (2.0)	80 (53)	4.0 (9.5)

Table 5.8 also shows the age of first use of substances among the female study population. Similar to the previous patterns presented, the young women in this study initiated marijuana use at the early mean age of 12.9 years old. Marijuana was followed by alcohol, tobacco, and

inhalants, at 13.1, 13.2, and 13.5, respectively. Harder drugs such as cocaine, heroin, and speedball were the last illicit drugs used, as illustrated in the table. Compared to national studies, the prevalence and scope of illegal drug use in this population is exceptionally high compared to other adolescent populations.

Table 5.9   Sexual Behavior Characteristics of Sample

Sexual Behavior	Percentage (Mean)
Ever Had Consensual Sex	83
Age of First Sexual Experience	(14 years old)
Mean Number of Sex Partners (in Lifetime)	(3)
Lifetime Pregnancy	47
Full Term Pregnancy	62
Currently have steady boyfriend/husband	74
Mean Age of Partner	(18 years old)
Sexually Active with Partner	71
Sex with Someone Else outside Relationship	17
Infected with STD (in Lifetime)	16

Sexual Behavior

As found in other studies (Erickson 1998; Horowitz 1983), gang-related girls have a much earlier age of onset of sexual intercourse and pregnancy and a higher number of sex partners and births compared to national rates (Braverman and Strasburger 1993). In discussions with these young females, most admitted to having a sexual experience by their early teens; many had become pregnant and approximately one-fourth had given birth. Given the relatively high rate of teenage pregnancy in San Antonio—one of the highest in the nation—this group's high rate of sexual activity is not surprising (San Antonio Metropolitan Health District Director's Office 1997).

As reflected in Table 5.9, an overwhelming 83 percent of the young women reported being sexually active at the time of the study. While the mean age for the first sexual experience was fourteen years old, the girls reported having an average of three sex partners in their lifetimes. The high rate of sexual involvement helps explain the fact that almost half of the girls reported getting pregnant at least once in their lifetime. Among this group only sixty-two percent reported a full-term pregnancy.

In regards to intimate partners, 74 percent indicated they were currently in a steady relationship with a male. The male partners however, were an average of two years older than the girls themselves. Approximately three-quarters of the sample were sexually active with their current partner and 17 percent reported having sexual relations with someone else besides their primary partner. Finally, 16 percent of the young women reported having been infected at some point in their lives with a sexually transmitted disease such as gonorrhea.

The Context of Risky Behavior

The preceding data has provided an overview of the deleterious behaviors in which these young women have engaged. The following documents the context, extent, and nature of these behaviors as a consequence of their exposure to individual gang members. A qualitative typology is presented, which depicts how these young women's connection to a male gang differentially exposes them to patterns of behaviors that result in serious social and health consequences.

Typology

The typology constructed consists of four ideal types of girls based on our data: girlfriends, usually characterized as steady dating partners; hoodrats, generally viewed as neighborhood girls sexually involved with multiple partners (hoodrats was a term that was used by the population to define this group of girls); good girls, long-term, neighborhood-based friends; and relatives. The typology is not static because the girls could possibly move from one type to another over time. Typically, the girls had characteristics of more than one type. For example, some girls (good girls) had grown up with some male gang members and ultimately became girlfriends. A detailed description of each one of the types follows. These ideal types are polythetic in that they are grouped by overall similarity, not necessarily containing girls that are identical on all variables or dimensions (Bailey 1994).

The girlfriend is defined as being a male gang member's current steady partner. Male partners refer to these girls as "my main chick" or *santita* (saint). For some of these girls the girlfriend status is more recent, while for others it has developed into a longer commitment to a partner, often solidified by the birth of a child. Subsequently included in this type are the young wives who are the mothers of the gang member's children. The motherhood identification gives the young woman a new and higher status, as she is no longer referred to as his "girl" but rather as the mother of his baby. Furthermore, these girlfriends and wives are given the same respect by the gang and other individuals associated with them. Respect, among other things, meant that she would not be sexually harassed by the gang members and would be physically protected from others. This type of female was the least involved in day-to-day gang activities.

The second type, identified as a hoodrat, is a girl that within the community has the most disparaging reputation and is perceived as sexually promiscuous, although this may in fact be a false impression. She is often seen hanging out and partying with the guys and is generally viewed as a heavy polydrug and alcohol user. In fact, many people in the community believe that the gang member's access to illicit drugs is what attracts these girls to the gang in the first place. The hoodrat normally does not develop serious emotional relationships with any of the guys, who often refer to her in derogatory terms such as, "bitch," "skank," "player," and "whore." She is not respected by male gang members or by other girls in the neighborhood, and it is difficult to rid herself of her reputation once the community labels her a hoodrat. Nonetheless, it is this type of female who is most involved in the everyday street activities of the gang. Ironically though, involvement in these types of activities, especially crime, does gain the respect of some male gang members. For these young women, the exciting nature of the gang and streets may seem more appealing to them than traditional gender behaviors.

Good girls, the third type in the typology, are the childhood friends of many male gang members. For many of these girls such friendships were developed in the neighborhoods where they grew up. These girls attended the same schools and were usually in the same grade as their male counterparts. In some instances, their parents and/or other relatives interacted with each other. Through the course of time, these childhood friendships developed into relationships based on mutual respect. Most males refer to these girls as "nice girls." Many are not involved in illegal drug use or criminal activities even though they live in the same neighborhoods. Most of the good girls have more conventional lifestyles in comparison to the other types. This conventional good girl type parallels the type found in Joan Moore's work on Mexican American female heroin users (1994).

The final type, relatives, consists of girls who are close kin to gang members, for example, sisters and cousins. Their identification as relatives affords the young women a special status within the network. For instance, if one of these young women has a boyfriend in a gang, she is not only seen as his "main chick" but more importantly as a homeboy's

sister or cousin. Both the good girls and relatives had limited involvement in the male gang member's activities.

This typology allows for the exploration of the extent to which these
females are exposed to high-risk behavior based on key themes. The
activities that proved to be most salient in understanding these women's
roles in the context of the male gang were substance use, delinquency,
and violence (e.g., fights). Although all the girls were associated with
male gangs, the extent of their participation in and exposure to these
four activities was found to be related to negative outcomes.

Substance Use

The girls' substance use previously discussed may quite possibly be linked
to the high rates of use reported by the males. Among the males, daily use
of marijuana is normative behavior. Many of these guys smoke marijuana
when they awake and continue to smoke throughout the day. With such
frequent drug use, it is inevitable that it would spill over to the females.

However, there were distinct patterns of use among and within the
different types of young girls. For instance, girlfriends reported a pattern
that ranged from nonuse to occasional use. Nonuse tended to be most
common among those who had just recently become emotionally
attached to a guy. Since the male members prefer to exclude these new
girls in their gang's activities at the initiation of their relationship, contact with members of the male gang and exposure to illicit drug use is
minimal. Sonic, a member of the Thugs, describes his girlfriend in these
terms: "She's a nice girl and a very smart and high-class girl. She lives
outside the neighborhood. She doesn't do any drugs."

However, there were those girlfriends who reported occasional drug
use, marijuana and cocaine in particular. These females tend to be those
who are involved in a more serious long-term relationship. For instance,
Suzie, a seventeen-year-old girl, reported hanging out with the Big
Cholos (BC) since the age of thirteen. In hanging out with the gang, she
met Marcos, who she has been married to for approximately two years.
She states, "I like to hang out with the guys. We just kick back, smoke
out, and have fun." Similarly, while Mary's long-term boyfriend of five
years doesn't like her hanging out with the BC, she emphasizes that the
gang members "have all become my best friends. I like to hang out with
the guys to drink or get high." Although this type of girlfriend has limited participation in her partner's gang activities, the long-time exposure
to her boyfriend's lifestyle puts her at higher risk for drug use. These
young women often speak of being encouraged to use drugs (usually
marijuana) when they are alone with their boyfriends.

The hoodrats are more frequent users of alcohol and drugs than the other females. Polydrug use and alcohol is a common everyday experience for this type of girl. Some hoodrats fear that if they reject or resist using drugs, they will not be welcomed around the gangs. Rather than being ostracized from the gang, they give in to the various drug-using behaviors. One girl explained how her association with the BC gang influenced her drug use. "I know some guys who will hook us up for free. I like doing drugs. I have done both pot and cocaine and a little bit of heroin. I tried shooting up about three times but I really did not like it." The repercussions of this drug use for these types of girls may sometimes be sexual exploitation and violence. A member of the Thugs says, "[the hoodrats] are all bitches that just get all fucked up and fuck 'em. They get all buzzing." In some instances, these situations lead to girls getting raped. One respondent described how she saw a seventeen-year-old girl from the neighborhood get "gang raped" after a party:

Everyone had been drinking and smoking [weed]. She always wanted to be around the guys. After almost everyone had left, three members of the Nine-Ball Crew (NBC) took her into the back room and 'pulled a train' on her. She was all fucked up. She wanted to do it because she did not fight back. Everyone in the neighborhood knows this happened but she still hangs out with them like nothing.

Apparently, the victim had no ties (i.e., brother, boyfriend, etc.) with any of the members of the NBC. It may have influenced the perpetrators' behavior assuming that there would be limited, if any, consequences.

Good girls' and relatives' exposure to drug and alcohol use was limited, due in large part to being denied access to these substances by male members. However, these young women were occasional users of alcohol and marijuana that they typically obtained from good friends of the male gang, older siblings, or cousins. Drug use among these types of girls seemed to remain at nonabusive levels. That is, their drug use did not lead to problem behavior such as high-risk sexual encounters or physical violence.

It is evident from the data that young women's drug and alcohol use varied depending on their relationship and exposure to the male gang. The females less likely to be at risk for substance use were the good girls and relatives. For girlfriends in long-term relationships with their partners, drug use was a more consistent activity in their lives. Although most girlfriends reported drug and alcohol use as occasional, their potential risk for frequent or heavy use was high. Hoodrats reported more frequent use of drugs and alcohol and were more integrated into the everyday activities of the male gang. Nonetheless, the hoodrats' dependency on the males for drugs and alcohol also made them more likely to be sexually victimized and exploited, although it should be emphasized that all females who use drugs are potentially at risk within this highly volatile environment.

Delinquency

Involvement in delinquent or violent activities varied among the types of girls identified in this study. Hoodrats were more likely to participate in illegal activities in association with male gang members. These females are used to hiding and stashing either weapons or drugs for gang members in locations less vulnerable to police. A member of the Knights states, "If the cops are after us, we make [girls] hold the guns. Everyone knows the police are not going to search the women." Another young girl, Gloria, started hanging out with Nine-Ball Crew in the sixth grade, mostly for protection. By the next year she was hanging out with the guys on a more regular basis. She reported selling and holding drugs along with shoplifting. She also has been witness to more serious violent delinquent behavior:

> We were driving to Military and this car honked at us because we were going slow. The car went past us and Joker got mad, sped up, and bumped her off the side of the road. He put a gun to her head and said, 'what the hell do you think you're doing stupid,' he was going to shoot her but then he took out a hunting knife and carved his initials on her stomach, stabbed her feet and left her there on the side of the road.

Another delinquent activity that frequently involves hoodrats is male gang members using them to lure rival male gang members to locations where they could be assaulted, undetected by authorities. Under the illusion that the female is interested in him, the rival member is taken to a designated place where he is physically attacked. A fourteen-year-old female adolescent described how the members of the Vatos Locos asked her to help them:

> He was from the East Side. They couldn't stand him. He wouldn't go into the courts [public housing]. They hated him because he would talk shit. And then they told me, 'Tell him to walk you home.' I was like 'Hell no!' Then they told me, 'Come on we'll give you ten bucks.' I said all right. I told him, 'Hey could you walk me home?' He said, 'You live in the courts?' 'Yeah.' 'All right I'll walk you through the park.' Okay go for it. I took him

around and made him walk me through the middle of the park. They kicked his ass. I was laughing.

Some hoodrats were involved in more serious activities such as drug dealing and weapon sales. These activities, however, were often done independently of those of the male gang. Similar to males, these females strive to gain economic independence by engaging in such illegal activities. Nonetheless, some females took advantage of opportunities offered by the male gangs to participate in criminal activities. For example, females discussed how they had been involved in "popping a car," or car jacking.

Participation in such illegal activities was nearly absent in the responses of the girlfriends, good girls, and the relatives. There was not much evidence of them being involved in any illegal activities, although there were some relatives who reported having been involved in "holding drugs" for their homeboys. One girl revealed that she was selling for her older brother: "I sell for my brother sometimes. He leaves then he comes back and he will fall asleep. He lets me sell. People will come and shit, I just sell!" Similarly, Carmen's association with the Chicano Boyz has exposed her to many delinquent acts, including selling drugs, carjacking, burglaries, auto theft, robbery, weapon sales, and holding guns and other weapons. She describes a time when she and her boyfriend Eddy went to a guy's house to pick up some money:

> There was this guy that owed Eddy drug money and Eddy is the type of guy that if you don't give him his money he'll get really pissed off and he'll do something bad to you or your family. We went over to the guy's house with four or five of Eddy's friends; they had a lot of weapons, a 44 and other guns and knives. When we got there a little girl answered the door, this guy's daughter. Eddy told the guy that if he didn't give him his money he was going to shoot his little girl. The guy said that he did have the money but not there, Eddy turned and shot the guy in the leg. The guy took off, we never see him anymore but Eddy is looking for him and says that if he finds him he's going to kill him.

These episodes suggest that female criminal involvement is restricted to the hoodrat and, on occasion, some of the other types of girls. The hoodrats' involvement, nonetheless, was distinct from the others. The hoodrats are typically used by male gang members to commit crimes such as holding weapons or drugs or assaulting rival gang members. The hoodrats see these requests as yet another gesture of being welcomed into the male gang. Male gang members involve the girlfriends or relatives in less serious and less aggressive crimes. What is clear is that association with male gangs makes all the types more prone to criminal drug use and delinquent behavior than other females (Chesney-Lind and Shelden 1997).

"What the Fuck, Bitch!" Personal Violent Confrontations in the Community

"Gangs" and "violence" have come to be known synonymously in today's society. Although the young women in this study had no formal affiliation with an established gang (i.e., they were not members), the threat of personal violence was one of many risks they were exposed to in the community. All types of girls appeared to be equally involved in physical fights out in the streets. There was no one type of girl that was immune to this violence. The social context in which these young women lived was conducive to violent confrontations with numerous types of individual's with whom they came in contact during the course of their everyday activities. That is, living in close proximity and hanging out in similar locations (e.g., downtown mall) facilitated the physical fights. Detailed descriptions of the fights were recounted by the majority of the young girls we talked to during their in-depth interviews. The physical fights ranged from pushing and shoving to more severe attacks that resulted in someone getting seriously hurt. A large proportion of these incidents occurred in public and most often with other females. The incidents varied depending on the circumstances surrounding the confrontation and the manner in which the young women perceived and reacted to eminent threats. Three types of fights emerged from the descriptions provided: talking shit / mad dogging, association with male gang, and jealousy.

Talking Shit / Maddoging

The first type of physical violence encountered by these young Mexican American females was associated with other girls engaging in what they identified as "talking shit." Talking shit within this context refers to someone saying insulting things toward another that are perceived as being disrespectful. Talking shit was a widely reported instigating factor for many of the physical fights reported. For instance, Stephanie, an eighteen-year-old girl reported hanging out often with her cousins' male gang. At a popular cruising strip for adolescents, Stephanie became involved in a violent fight one night that could have easily turned fatal. Stephanie describes the incident:

A month ago, I was down Military with the girls and some homeboys. Yeah, we were parked and out there standing. Well, this girl passes by in her car and she's all "You fucking bitch," and talking shit. They were going real slow, cruising. I chased the car and I just went over there and I was like, "What the fuck did you say bitch?" I pulled her out of the car and started kicking her ass. I busted her nose and she was bleeding all right here [motioning with her hand]. They looked like they were like all on heroin, all fucked up and tripping and shit. I know how people are when they're on heroin. My best friend's boyfriend, he's a Tecato—he likes to shoot up a lot and I know the way they are. The other lady went and got a gun from the back of the truck but she couldn't even put the bullets in because she was so fucked up. Then my other friends went around and kicked her ass.

Similarly, Sulema first began associating with The Killing Crew at the age of fourteen because of her brother. At the time of the interview she was sixteen years old and living in public housing with seven other family members. She describes in detail a violent fight in her neighborhood she was involved in:

Well, me and my friends were walking around the neighborhood. There was a lot of girls—they were with their boyfriends and they were trying to act bad or cool. They started telling us stuff and just like looking at us and laughing. We told them stuff back and one of the girls went up to my friend and started telling her stuff. I told her stuff and then like all of us just like started fighting. So one of them, came over to my friend and started saying, "You fucking hoodrat and you little ho and little bitches." I guess because like how we were dressed or something. My friend just like hit her in the back of the head and slapped her. I got one by her hair and like she tripped over like the curve, so like I was hitting her in the face. They were drunk because they were drinking with their boyfriends.

Although in most instances the young women described this lack of respect, there were some cases where talking shit was associated with the spread of rumors within a specific network of friends. "Everybody was telling me that she was talking shit. And everybody was telling her that I was talking shit about her. I didn't want to fight her because she was my best friend."

In addition to talking shit, the young women spoke about the act of "maddogging" as a reason for engaging in physical fights in the community. Maddogging is defined as the act of staring at someone in such a way as to cause intimidation. This appeared to be a very common way in which the physical confrontations occurred in public between two young women who have never seen each other before. Miranda is a nine-teen-year-old young woman who is currently dating a nineteen-year-old male involved in a large and highly organized gang in the neighborhood, Chicana Boyz. She began to associate with this particular male gang at the age of eleven. The following excerpt reflects a young woman's risk of involvement in physical confrontations as a result of what she perceived as a form of disrespect when someone stared her down:

> You know how like people walk up and down in downtown on Saturdays? This girl, every time we pass her she would just stare and I would be like okay, what's the matter? We would just keep on staring. Finally she said, "You know like what the fuck, like what's your problem?" And then my friend goes, "You're over here like maddogging us like if you know us, whatever bitch." She goes, "Well what the fuck, you want something?" Then my friend, she got tired of it and she just went at her. She punched her. When she punched her I went at the other girl and we were just there fighting for about fifteen minutes because people were blocking the area so no one could go through.

Miranda goes on to describe how the police showed up: "We were fighting for about fifteen minutes and then the cops finally got through. When they got through they were hitting people to get through with their sticks and they shoved us on the floor and they handcuffed us. They took her in because she had a knife in her shoes. But they let us go; they just gave us a warning that not to let it happen again. We smoked weed before we went down there."

Association with Male Gang

Association with a male gang was an instigating factor for the second type of physical violence the young women spoke about occurring in their neighborhoods. Although the girls were not gang members themselves, their association with a specific male gang created tensions with other girls associated with rival gangs. Many of these physical confrontations occurred in neutral areas, such as downtown San Antonio, where most adolescents and young adults congregate on the main strip on Friday and Saturday nights.

The following fourteen-year-old girl reported hanging out with a male gang at the early age of eleven. She currently has a boyfriend who is a member of the Invaders. The following details reflect the constant risk of engaging in physical confrontations as a result of their association with male gangs in the community:

I was downtown coming from my grandpa's on a Saturday night. I was by myself. This chick bumped into me so I was like, "Hey watch out, say excuse me or something next time." She started tripping [getting mad]. All of a sudden she goes, "Yeah I know you, you're with the...." All of sudden, I just see her coming with her homegirls. I saw a guy I knew from the gang. He goes, "Hey what's up." I gave him my purse to hold and we just strapped it on. I sort of brought it on to myself because I didn't have to say nothing but I still did. She pushed me, so I just hit her and I threw her to the floor. Then somebody kicked me in my mouth and I was like what, it hurt and I started bleeding. I got up and I went at her and I busted her nose.

Having an extensive network of family and friends involved in a male gang does not make good girls and relatives any less vulnerable to engaging in firsthand physical confrontations. Lucia is a sixteen-year-old girl who started hanging out with her brother's gang, the South Perez Boys, at the age of eleven. She is currently dating a young man in the gang and her brother and cousin are also members. The following incident reflects the violent confrontation she engaged in because of this acquaintanceship:

I was downtown with my friends. We were walking and we saw two of our homeboys. We hugged one of them and his girlfriend saw and got mad. We were just chilling and that girl comes up to us and was talking all this stuff to me. There was cops across the street, but I was like, dang, I didn't want to fight, I didn't want to get arrested. This big tour bus got in the way and I just started beating her up. She was all hurt so they walked her home. So that chick's friend wanted to fight me. We went into an alley and we just started fighting. Then her boyfriend, he's from another gang, he got all mad because I was beating her up. I had this ring on and the diamond had fell off of it so it scratched her face up. She was pulling my hair so I couldn't like hit her. I was banging her head on the floor and she had like a big old gash on her head. So her boyfriend pushes me off of her and then his homeboy kicks me in my mouth. Then like we just see all these cops coming with their nightsticks. Yeah, so everybody gets up. I act like I didn't get into a fight and I walk off. That girl was still there on the ground. I thought they were gonna arrest me because the cops shined the light on us.

There were also good girls, who reported having no familial or romantic ties to male gang members but rather close friendships. Even these young women were exposed to street violence as a result of their association with the male gangs. For instance, at age thirteen Rosa began to hang out with an all-male gang. Her association with this male gang at the age of nineteen is through a close male friend. She describes how this association led to a violent physical fight with a neighborhood girl associated with another local gang:

> This girl who was with the Invaders, she was their ho. I had just moved in the neighborhood and they knew that I had been with Up and Above. She was always saying stuff. I got mad but I really didn't care, I had just moved in there and I didn't want enemies. They knew where I lived and everything. One day I just got tired of it and she was telling me things, cussing at me and I went out there and I said, "Well what, what's up, you want me?" She was like just talking all this shit. Then my dad comes out and says, "You know what, cut all this, the talking, and kick her ass." So I did, I beat her up pretty bad. I just punched her and flipped her over. Then I just started punching her in her face. I got on top of her and I punched and punched and then I banged her against the pole to hang clothes in the back. She tried to hit me. Her boyfriend like, grabbed my arm and pushed me back and I fell to the ground and my dad stepped in and pushed him out of the way. I kept punching her and she was bleeding bad and my wrist are all cut up because of her teeth. So my dad pulled me away.

Jealousy

The final type of physical confrontation was a result of a sense of jealousy associated with a male partner. The jealousy was typically a result of a perceived threat from another woman in the form of staring or talking. As opposed to the other two types of physical confrontations discussed previously, these fights appeared to initiate instantly without much provocation. Such was the case with Jennifer, who at three months pregnant decided to fight her boyfriend's neighbor. "Some girl next door was calling him. I was living there with him and I was three months pregnant. She was calling him, that if he had a cigarette. I went outside and told her why are you asking him for a cigarette? She started telling me off so I went at her but my boyfriend stopped me because I was pregnant. I had a skirt on so I went to go and put my shorts on. I went outside and I just hit her, boom! She fell in the mud and I kicked her."

The following excerpt describes the risk these young women put themselves in either as victims or perpetrators of violence because of jealousy. Maria is an eighteen-year-old mother of one who has been hanging out with Big Cholos since she was thirteen as a result of her cousin's membership. She dropped out of school in her junior year. She states:

> I was downtown with some guy named Joey I was dating. I wasn't with him [as a boyfriend], it was just a guy I messed around with. I saw him

talking with a girl. I got mad. I acted like I didn't care, I was like, whatever. I was acting all hard, like guys just come and go, right. Then I had got mad because he left. "Where the fuck is he?" Then I saw him and I told him that I was gonna beat her up. So, I don't know I just went up to her and she was all scared because like I'm all gangster and she's all like those real nice girls—all nice clothes. I don't know, I just got jealous. I just started beating her up. I can't believe she didn't pull my hair because it's long. She was just holding her purse. She was just covering her face and her head. I was popping her all over. I really didn't feel my pain until after. I was calm and then all my knuckles they're all red they're like, they had like bruises.

In a few cases, young women had to deal with their boyfriends' past relationships, which in many cases led to confrontations. For instance, Jimena is a fifteen-year-old girl being raised by her single mother. The altercation she describes took place because of her boyfriend's past history with girls in the neighborhood:

The boyfriend that I'm with, before he would be like messing around with everybody. He would mess around with all those girls that lived in the courts [public housing]. Well, those girls that he would mess around with, there was one that got mad because she found out that he liked me and not her. He would just mess around with her because of the fun of it. One of those days she went to my house and was trying to talk shit to me. She was all, "Well he's mine." That's when we just got into it, we just started fighting. She like tried to grab me by my hair but I had grabbed her first and she fell on the floor and that's when I started kicking her in her face. She got up and I started banging her right there on the side of my house.

Sexual Relationships

Girls in this gang subculture appeared to be socially categorized by how they related sexually to the gang members. Many of the male gang members were involved sexually with two distinct types: girls with whom they have significant steady relationships and girls with whom they have insignificant, casual sexual relationships. The significant relationships were usually with the girlfriend types. In discussions with the male gang members as part of a parallel study with the males, most reported to be presently involved in an emotional relationship with either a girlfriend or wife, with the relationships ranging in length from two months to several years. In some cases, these commitments have developed into live-in relationships. For example, C. J. is a member of one of the most notorious gangs in San Antonio. C. J.'s common-law wife stated, "We've been together for five years, and we've been living together for two years. We have a little girl, Amber; she's going to be two." C. J. describes the mother of his child as a "nice girl who is pretty smart."

In contrast, insignificant relationships tended to be had with the hoodrat types. For the most part, the relationships the males had with these hoodrats were based primarily on sex and had an absence of any emotional connection. For example, males can be with a hoodrat in a social situation, such as a party, and fellow gang members are allowed to "hit on her." Biggy, a well-known San Antonio gang member, described the difference between his girlfriend and a hoodrat in the following account:

> Biggy: You know there's hoodrats and respectable girls.
>
> Interviewer: What's the difference between a hoodrat and a respectable girl?
>
> Biggy: A respectable girl is like if I had a chick. I liked her a lot and everything. She will be my main chick, and all my boys respect her. Other chicks or whatever, they're just hoodrats and bitches. She's like my bitch, so I don't give a damn about her. I just scrape them or do whatever I want with them. Sometimes I'll be with them and my homeboy comes over. He could start hugging her or kissing her or whatever. That's a hoodrat.

Although the community perceives hoodrats as being "loose" (sexually available), these girls have some very different opinions about their roles. One seventeen-year-old girl, who is perceived to be a hoodrat, describes her reasons for not having a boyfriend: "I don't want a boyfriend because I don't want some guy telling me what to do. And the girls, well, I don't like hanging around them because they are all backstabbing bitches. They see me in my little dresses all dressed up and they just think I am out to steal their guys. They're stupid. I am not even looking at the guys. These girls start yelling at me and start calling me a 'ho.'" Although this girl is a self-identified hoodrat, she did not accept the pejorative connotation associated with the label.

The other two types, although generally identified as good girls and relatives, may in time transition into girlfriend status. For example, good girls can eventually become girlfriends and receive dual respect from the males in the gang. A relative can also become a girlfriend if a relationship is initiated by a male gang member. Usually, the role change from relative to girlfriend occurs within the same gang. This is especially the case when members frequent the residences of homeboys who have younger sisters. For instance, the following field note describes a young girl's transition from her defining status as a relative to girlfriend within the gang: "Missy is sixteen years old and has a brother in The Invaders. Her brother and his friends used to hang out in front of her home. The guys used to come over and smoke weed and drink outside at all times. This is how she met Joey, her brother's best friend, who, according to Missy, was very popular with all the girls." Similarly, a young female describes her relationship with her boyfriend: "I grew up with all of the Gangsters. He was a good friend before he became my boyfriend."

Conversely, some of these good girls, relatives, and girlfriends can eventually be labeled as hoodrats depending on how they relate to the males sexually, that is, if they are seen as engaging in unbounded sex (Horowitz 1983). Girls in this community are constantly negotiating their image within these social boundaries of the "good girl" image. The guys, on the other hand, may have sexual relationships with various types of girls and not be sexually labeled. This sexual double standard often forces these young women into isolation and community stigmatization.

Considering the fact that the majority of the young women in this study were sexually active, contraceptive use was commonly discussed. The girlfriends/wives reported not using condoms with their partners. Many believed that since they were the only partners with whom the males were sexually active, condom use was not necessary. Some reported that if they were to ask their partners to use a condom, the partner would think she was having sex with others. The remaining types (good girls, relatives, and hoodrats) reported more frequent use of condoms during sexual intercourse, although it was not a consistent practice. The failure to use protection was of concern, given the reported practice of multiple sexual partners by male gang members. One sixteen-year-old male stated, "I've cheated on all of them. I really don't care about being faithful. If I see someone I want, I go for it. They find out sometimes, but they always get over it." This statement was reinforced when fifteen-year-old Susie said she stayed with her boyfriend even after she found out he was sleeping with three other girls.

These descriptions clearly indicate how a girl's relationship to male gang members influences her exposure to high-risk sexual behavior. The girlfriends, good girls, and relatives tend to have more stable and significant sexual relationships with male gang members, characterized as continual, long-term, and affectionate. In contrast, the hoodrat is more likely to have multiple sexual relations with various male members. This places her at higher risk for sexually transmitted diseases, unplanned pregnancy, and childbirth than the other types of females. Nonetheless, the girlfriend types are also exposed to STD risks due to their male partners' sexual behavior outside the relationship.

Conclusion

This chapter has presented an overview of the personal risks these adolescent Mexican American females are involved in and exposed to as a result of their association with male gangs. More specifically, this chapter has demonstrated the process of how females associated with male gang members and their activities lead to negative outcomes. The chapter indicates that regardless of their relationship to the gang, all studied females were to some degree prone to substance use, delinquency, personal physical fights, and high-risk sexual behavior, although the hoodrats were clearly the most at risk due to their involvement in gang activities. This finding parallels social-network studies that associate risky behavior with the individual's immediate social relationships and level of relationships, rather than focusing only on the individual's attributes (Friedman et al. 1999). The association of high-risk behavior with increased involvement in gang activities is also supportive of the social facilitation model discussed by Terence Thornberry and his colleagues that focuses on delinquency careers (1993). As they found, gang affiliation among adolescents in this study increased levels of crime, delinquency, and other high-risk behaviors.

What may explain this behavior among Mexican American females is that they seem to have an alternative normative course in regards to delinquent, violent, and sexual behavior. These findings suggest that early sexual activity, reproduction strategies, and limited educational achievement may be recognized as normative within this community, given their perceived opportunities. Similar findings have been suggested for the African Americans who found that the chance to be a mother was a catalyst to change more negative behaviors (Burton 1990; Franklin 1988). Indeed, choices made by these gang-associated females may be the rational one in the face of the limited options and opportunities available to them. In this sense, problems associated with these females must go beyond being viewed as individual problems, but rather seen within the social, cultural, and economic conditions of their environments. Many of these girls are unaware of their vulnerability to high-risk behaviors, often accepting them as part of their daily life. This places young gang-associated females at a relatively higher risk for unplanned pregnancies, HIV/AIDS, and sexually transmitted diseases.

Chapter 6

Sexual and Physical Violent Victimization

As has been discussed in previous chapters, these communities are dangerous places for adolescent females. They become sexual quarry for male adolescents and adults who may be family members, boyfriends, neighbors, or even strangers. The young girls are objectified as prized trophies in this Mexican American, lower-class community where gender is highly associated with sexuality. Just walking down the street, any young girl past puberty will solicit long stares, lewd remarks, and be propositioned by men and boys of all ages. Young girls of ten to twelve years old must learn to manage their lives and behaviors to minimize the risks associated with these predators. Girls in these neighborhoods who are highly susceptible to this sexual and physical violence are those associated with male gangs.

In the previous chapter I described the violence many of these young women engaged in as a result of association with their male gang member counterparts in the community. These data show that over half of these girls have experienced violence (both perpetration and victimization) in their daily lives. In this chapter, I now turn to the issues of violent victimization associated with sex and dating experienced by these girls. However, dating, as it is commonly understood, is not reflective of the relationships that these young people engage in when they are courting in these communities. As previously discussed, violent risk is more common among street gang-affiliated girls than among other girls in these same neighborhoods.

Violent Victimization in the Lives of Girls Affiliated with Gangs

One of the risks in the lives of male gang members and gang-associated females is the violence they are exposed to as both perpetrators and victims. However, there seem to be important gender differences in the underlying dynamics of violence. Jody Miller found evidence of how gender shapes victimization risk for female gang members, emphasizing the relationship of gender inequality and sexual exploitation to victimization (1998). Public concern with girl gang members as perpetrators of violence is based not only on legal and public health ramifications but also on the fact that they are perceived to be violating and challenging traditional notions of femininity (Moore and Hagedorn 2001). There has been an increase in the participation of minority women in gangs (Moore and Hagedorn 2001). Consequently, their risk for exposure to violence, both as victims and as perpetrators, has increased (Esbensen 2000; Moore and Hagedorn 2001).

Research suggests that young women in gangs have disproportionate histories of victimization before gang involvement as compared with nongang-associated females and male gang members (Esbensen, Deschenes, and Winfree 1999; Miller 1998). Girl gang members seem to posses the psychological and social attributes that make them more vulnerable to risk behaviors. Moreover, it has been suggested that such early victimization can be explained by the fact that it is accepted as normative behavior in this social context. Elijah Anderson argues that, "In this context of persistent poverty and deprivation, alienation from broader society's institutions, notably that of criminal justice, is widespread" (1999, 10). There is a street socialization process, described as a *code of the streets*, that emphasizes the development of collective and individual coping strategies that use violence as a means of resolving conflicts. There, youth subcultures as well as adults are involved in street violence, drug use, crime, and confrontational attitudes toward authority.

Stress has also been related to maladaptive health behaviors among different populations (Ironson et al. 1994; Leserman et al. 1997). Some studies suggest a significant association between stressors and risky sexual behavior among different populations. More recently, a study by Jeannette Ickovics and others reports that low-income women with high levels of stress were more likely to engage in sexual relations with a partner at high risk for HIV infection (2002).

Perceived stress and adverse life circumstances (e.g., criminal involvement, familial disruption, economic hardship) have been associated with high-risk sexual behaviors among adolescents (Rotheram-Borus,

Koopman, and Ehrhardt 1991). Higher rates of violence in these environments may also result from the stress associated with coping with conflicts experienced on a day-to-day basis by these adolescent girls in these neighborhoods (Bettie 2000; Martinez 1996). The literature is consistent in identifying personal stress as having a negative impact on adolescent identity formation, school performance, and prosocial behavior (Alva and Jones 1994). Studies on female gang members have found that family disruptions and the stresses generated are one of the major reasons they joined the gang. Notably, among Hispanic adolescent females, stressful family situations surpassed the combined stressors occurring with friends, in school, or in other personal domains.

These adolescent girls have to face not only these social conditions but also the added conflicts that brought by such an age, which is characterized by peer relationships as being more important as well as the need to fit in (Miller 1998). It has been suggested that girls may turn to gangs looking for protection and a place to fit in and feel they belong (Walker-Barnes and Mason 2001; Weiler 1999). But the process leading to girls joining gangs may be more complex than this line of thinking suggests.

While girls may join gangs in part to seek protection from violence, unfortunately, girls in gangs are not exempt from being victims of violence. As Miller suggests, these girls might be just trading unknown risks for known ones (1998). The gang also offers them a place where they feel they belong (Weiler 1999), a sense of protection from the danger of the streets, and the greater opportunity to retaliate when victimization occurs (Molidor 1996). For others, affiliation with street gangs is just part of living in communities where street gangs are acceptable and embedded in the social environment.

Domains of Violence Victimization among Girl Gang Affiliates

Domains of Sexual and Physical Violence: Boyfriend, Family, and Gangs

Adolescent females are prey for male adolescents and older adults in a street culture that promotes hypermasculinity, sexual conquest, sexual aggression, and sexual objectification of women. Many males in this subculture adopt exaggerated masculine posture and are involved in physical abuse and violence and engaged in heavy drinking and drug use. This behavior is reinforced by hip hop and rap music that has had a pervasive influence on urban Hispanic youth. Many of the lyrics of this musical genre promote an oppositional culture centered on a lifestyle expressed through exaggerated clothing styles, tattoos, and body jewelry. Of more concern is that some artists involved in this genre condone violence and crime by promoting a "gangsta" way of life. Moreover, many critics of this musical genre argue that it also promotes hypermasculinity and sexism. As a result, females associated with these gangs are subordinate to these males whose community image is partially based on his ability to control and manipulate his female partner. A consequence of this relationship is that the females are often the subject of sexual exploitation (Cepeda and Valdez 2003; Chesney-Lind and Sheldon 1992; Miller 1998; Miller 1975).

Boyfriends

Most violence experienced by female adolescents is called "dating violence," which means that it occurs between unmarried couples (Sugarman and Hotaling 1989, 5). Research on female violence has found that over the last twenty years, the most common assailant is a man known to the woman, often her intimate partner (Crowell and Burgess 1966). The rate of violent victimization among females ages twelve to nineteen is significantly lower than among females ages twenty to forty-two. The rank order of the major forms of violent victimization among those ages twelve to nineteen is assault, attempted violence, and aggravated assault (Bureau of Justice Statistics 2000). The younger group also had the highest rate of rape victimization, mostly occurring within a dating or semidating relationship.

Conflict with boyfriends is the most significant source of sexual victimization. Geoffrey Hunt and Karen Joe-Laidler note that male gang members have strict assumptions about girls within this subculture (2001). For instance, there seems to be conventional expectations that girls will voluntarily submit to having sex with them. The consequence of defying or resisting this expectation typically involves some form of coercion or violence without any repercussions from the group.

Family

Previous literature (including data presented in Chapter 4) has shown that girl gang members have a varied and complex relationship with their families (Moore and Hagedorn 1996). Some members report strong family ties, others describe violent confrontations or sexual and physical abuse, and others express extreme hatred. Hunt and Joe-Laidler highlight two important relationships for the girls in this study: one is with their mothers and the other is with their fathers (2001). Most of the girls describe generally positive ties with their mothers; others describe conflictual relationships and blame their mothers for problems at home. But overall "they maintain emotional and instrumental ties with their mothers" (Hunt and Joe-Laidler 2001, 378) and they turn primarily to their mothers in times of need. In their relationships with their fathers, alcohol and drug consumption and alcohol-related violence play a much more significant role. The authors stated that their interactions with their fathers are "best characterized as distant, periodic, and strained" (Hunt and Joe-Laidler 2001, 377). A number of authors suggest that family disruptions are a major reason for these girls to run away and seek protection in the gang life (Esbensen, Deschenes, and Winfree 1999; Hunt and Joe-Laidler 2001; Molidor 1996; Walker-Barnes and Mason 2001; Weiler 1999).

There is one aspect of female gang life commonly outlined in research studies—the gang as a refuge for young women who have been victimized at home (Brotherton 1996; Molidor 1996; Moore and Hagedorn 2001; Walker-Barnes and Mason 2001; Wang 2000). As these studies assert, joining a gang can be an attempt to gain autonomy and independence, not only from family oppression, but also from cultural and class constraints. However, as Weiler states, these girls also express very traditional gender role beliefs, aspirations, and expectations, which serve to hold them in abusive relationships (1999). Other studies have also emphasized the more traditional gender roles associated with Hispanic women (Bowleg, Belgrave, and Reisen 2000; West 2001).

Other studies have contended that family process variables are important antecedents in accounting for violent behavior among these adolescents (Sampson and Lauritsen 1994). Many of the families in this study are characterized by intergenerational transmission of drug use and criminal activity and correspond to unconventional or *cholo* (street-oriented) families (Moore 1990). There are other families that are more traditional and correspond to more conventional families. Regardless of the type of family, our findings have found that a subject who grew up in a family in which she experienced physical neglect and, to a lesser extent, strained parental relationships was more associated with violent victimization. The inability of a participant's family to physically provide for her seemed to contribute to the strain she experienced (Agnew et al. 2002). Daniel Santisteban and his colleagues argue that such a condition leads to pernicious patterns of family interactions that underlie the causes of adolescent problems (2003). Growing up in this environment may also result in "negative social capital" that contributes to specific problem behaviors such as violence and drug use (Sampson, Morenoff, and Earls 1999). More specifically, families may expose these girls to sexual violence risks by perpetrators in these family networks.

Gangs

Hunt and Joe-Laidler examine the role of violence in the lives of female gang members in a comparative ethnographic study of ethnic gangs in the San Francisco Bay Area between 1991 and 1993 (2001). Gang initiation rituals are methods by which gangs as a group sexually exploit and mistreat females. In this case, females wanting to join a street gang are "sexed-in," which involves having sex with all the male gang members. The girls who agree to this demand think that it will provide them gang membership and respect from male gang members, but often the opposite occurs. They lose respect from the gang members themselves and other girls associated with the gang. Miller reports that some of these girls who get "sexed in," are so harassed by other girls and guys that they leave the gang (Miller 2001). Gang rape is another form of sexual victimization that is associated with gangs. The girls are frequently in situations where gang members sexually force themselves on the girls. Within this context, especially at parties, girls are often raped after consuming too much alcohol or drugs, many while they are unconscious.

Sexual Victimization

During the course of conducting our fieldwork for the study, my research team reported hearing stories and reports of sexual victimization associated with young girls in the targeted community. As expected, the accounts were typically secondhand knowledge narrated to us by young women who reported hearing about the events. Given the sensitive nature of the theme of sexual victimization for adolescent females, we knew that getting information about it would require the adolescent's strong sense of trust with our interviewers. In order to address the issue with this population, we decided to first ask the young women during their in-depth interview if they knew of any female who had been forced to have sex with members of any male gang. Research has documented that persons are more willing to disclose such experiences if they are asked if they have witnessed or heard of such events. In some instances, this secondhand knowledge may in fact be their own personal experiences. Moreover, during the latter part of the in-depth interview the young women were asked if they had ever been victims of a forced sexual experience. The stories collected during the in-depth interviews revealed the adolescent girls' sexual victimization experiences as associated with their boyfriends and the male gang itself. Although not the focus here, it is important to note and contextualize the young women's experiences, taking into account that a large proportion of them reported being sexually victimized as a child by family members and other adults.

Sexual Victimization by Boyfriends

Reports of sexual victimization at the hands of boyfriends were commonly reported by the young girls. Detailed descriptions of the victimization experiences provided us with a more in-depth understanding of the volatile situational context in which these young girls found themselves in during the course of their lives. For the young women in these communities, the experience of establishing a personal relationship with a male counterpart is not any different than it is for the average adolescent, in that it is a highly anticipated event during a young female's life trajectory. What is unique about this population, however, is the young women's social isolation in what is presented here as a highly violent context, which makes them easily susceptible to sexual victimization by a partner.

There were distinct characteristics that emerged from the narratives regarding their 'sexual victimization at the hands of boyfriends. First, two types of relationships were identified in regards to the length of time the young girl had been in the relationship before the violent incident occurred. The short-term relationships were identified as those where the girl had been with her boyfriend for only a few months before she was victimized. The long-term relationships were those where the couple had been together for a minimum of one year. Although sexual victimization was observed in both short- and long-term relationships, there were subtle but important differences between the two types of relationships. The young women who reported sexual victimization with short-term boyfriends had experiences that were characterized by more physical coercion than the victimization experienced by girls in long-term relationships. That is, throughout the duration of sexual assault in short-term relationships, the young women attempted to fight back, in most cases with no success. For instance, Joanna, a sixteen-year-old girl, recalls:

It was Art, an ex-boyfriend of mine. At the time he was my boyfriend. I had been with him for about a month and a half. We went to his house and were just watching movies. We started kissing and messing around. He wanted to have sex and I told him no. He said yes. I told him no again and he took off my pants. I told him just leave me alone just stop right now. He was holding me down. He said no ... and he put it in. It took about thirty minutes. I started crying and I started telling him no, to get off, and he wouldn't. Finally he got off and he told me, "Why, why don't you want to do it?" I just told him to take me home. After that day we just never talked.

Similarly, sixteen-year-old Tracy had only been with her boyfriend for a few months before he raped her. At the time of the interview, she reported that he eventually became the father of her child. She states, "He was thirteen and I was thirteen. We were in my room and he just started to slap me around and beat me up because he wanted to have sex. He held me down and we had regular sex for a couple of minutes."

There were other instances where the physical coercion was more violent, leading to injuries that resulted in bruises and bleeding. The following is a witness description provided by one of the young girls we interviewed. Alexa, a seventeen-year-old girl who reportedly had a boyfriend in a gang, was at her friend's house when the sexual victimization initiated:

We were like playing video games. He started arguing with her because he wanted to have sex and she didn't because I was there. I was leaving and she goes, "Don't leave." I tried to help her but he just took control of her. He grabbed her and he took her to the room. I heard him say, "You better because I haven't had none for a long time. I always give it to you when you want it." She told him, "No I don't want to; I'm mad at you." I heard her hit him. Then he hit her. He said, "*Pendeja*" [stupid]. They were yelling. I decided to leave. The next day when I was talking to her she was crying saying that he forced her to have oral sex. She said her arms hurt, and they were all bruised up. She said she was bleeding.

In a couple of instances, the young women reported nearly being sexually victimized by males they had just met. As was the case in the incidents described previously, these experiences included excessive physical coercion. At the time of the interview, Diana was fourteen years old and had known her attacker for one month. She recalls:

I had just recently, just met this guy. We were talking but it wasn't a real steady relationship. He seemed nice and friendly but he wanted to have sex right away and I didn't want to. I wanted to wait. He would get mad and he would just say, "Well you're going to give it to me." We were at his house and his parents had left. He was telling me that he wanted to do something with me and I told him no. That was the reason why he wanted me to come over here. I was going to leave and he said, "Well, you made me go all the way over there to go and get you and you didn't want to do nothing with me?" "That's not the reason why, I thought you wanted me to come over here." He said, "Well I got to have some." He just started shoving me and forcing himself on me. I kept pushing him off of me and telling him no, that I wanted to go home. I started crying and he said no that I was going to stay there until he got some. But his parents showed up. I was crying and they asked me what was going on. I told them what happened and his parents took me home.

The long-term relationships were distinct from the short-term ones, given that in the majority of cases there had already been intimacy before the forced sexual experience. What generally emerged then was a distinct sequence of events that occurred before the sexual victimization. First, the young female articulated the fact that she did not want to have sex. Second, the male exposed the female to both physical and verbal coercion, which led to a struggle. Finally, most young females in these relationships reported eventually acquiescing to the sexual victimization. Her eventual giving in was of particular importance; because of it, most of these young women verbalized that they did not feel that their accounts qualified as forced sexual experiences.

One example of a young woman's acquiescence was the case of Julie, a fourteen-year-old female being raised by her grandmother. She describes in detail one of her experiences with her boyfriend:

Well, I was living with my boyfriend at the time. I kept telling him I did-n't want to have sex. He was *terco* [stubborn]. He's all like, 'Come on, come on.' I kept saying 'no.' Finally he grabbed me and had me by the hands. I was like no—and I hit him. He finally like moved his hand away from me and I popped [hit] him. He got off. Well, that got him more mad. After a couple of minutes again, *terco*. He tried once and the second time he succeeded. Well, after it was in I had no choice.

Priscilla had the same experience at the hands of her boyfriend who she had been dating for approximately a year and a half: "He was at my house and nobody was there and it was dark. He tore my blouse and busted all my buttons. He just pushed me on the bed and he just took off his pants and took off mine. He was holding me down—hard. The whole thing was about twenty minutes. After he finished he left my room. My arms were all red and around my eye where he punched me."

As described previously, there were instances where the male perpe-trator resorted to making the young woman feel bad by using verbal and emotional threats. As a consequence, the females tended to give in to the demands. For instance, in Sarah's case the sexual victimization did not entail physical coercion but her boyfriend was able to convince her after constant verbal coercion. She says of the incident: "I did it because, I guess just to make him happy, ... my boyfriend just so he could shut up. We were at his house and I just didn't want to. We were watching TV and he wanted to but I didn't want to. He was just begging and bothering me. He was all being all nice. So I just did it, and I just let him. I just didn't feel like having sex with him that day. I had sex with him before but it was like that day, I guess I already was tired of it."

Another example of the women's acquiescence to the male partner's verbal coercion was Pamela, who was seventeen years old at the time. Pamela recalls the incident she had with her boyfriend of one year:

> He was all grabbing me and everything. I was like no, no I'm not gonna. I mean I wasn't gonna. I didn't want to do it. He told me 'come on, ... I'm not going to talk to you.' He was getting mad. I go, 'well this is going to be the last time I'm gonna do anything with you.' So, I said go for it. That's it; I just did it with him, but I never did it with him again. I regretted it afterwards. Well because I didn't want to do it. Later on he'll be saying, 'Well, I already got her and she was already mine' and I didn't want him to be saying that.

In general, all of the reported sexual victimization at the hands of boyfriends appeared to have occurred in private settings such as parents' homes or the couple's own private residence. Another characteristic of these incidents was that in no case was there mention of the use of weapons. Finally, while in a large majority of the narratives substance use was mentioned—in particular alcohol and marijuana—it is difficult to isolate the effect that substance use had on these incidents.

Sexual Victimization within the Context of the Gang

Evidence revealed that the young women we studied were not only exposed to being sexually victimized by their boyfriends but also by other male gang members. Given the nature of the young women's association with the male gangs, it was not uncommon for many of them to be around the males within the context of "partying" or "kicking back" (i.e., relaxing) as I described in Chapter 5. It was within this "party" context that many of the sexual assaults occurred. The social climate in these parties tended to be wild and chaotic. Altercations, fights, alcohol,

marijuana, and other substance use were common. Such a climate contributes to young women's sexual victimization.

As previously mentioned, parties were the most commonly reported
context in which incidents of sexual assault perpetrated by members of
a male gang occurred. Reports provided by the young women reveal the
nature of the sexual assault that varied among the incidents ranging
from oral sex to vaginal penetration. One example is Roxanne's story;
she is fifteen years old and has been associating with the Varrio La
Paloma gang for two years. Her affiliation with the gang runs deep in
that she has a boyfriend, a cousin, and a good friend in the VLP. The
female friend of whom she spoke, however, does not have the same
degree of affiliation and was more vulnerable to sexual victimization at
the gang's social gathering. According to Roxanne, her friend, Sam, used
to hang out with the gang as often as she did. Roxanne recalls the day of
the assault:

> This happened like about four months ago. I was at a party that the Nine-
> Ball Crew were having for one of the members. He was like my ex-
> boyfriend. I had took my friend Sam. A while back she had been with one
> of the homeboys. At the party there was drinks and weed and everything.
> Well we got high and drunk. Sam wanted to go home already because like
> her mom was gonna get mad at her, right. I go, "Just kick back with us, just
> a little while longer." That's when Robert called her up. She had got in an
> argument with Robert and he told her to come here. Well, she likes him a
> lot so she listens. She went over there and he took her to his car for a while.
>
> When we got home, she had told me that he had made her give him
> head [oral sex]. If not that he would beat the shit out of her in front of
> everybody. He told her, "You know I want you to go down on me or I'm
> gonna beat you up."

Roxanne went on to explain that Sam eventually told her brother—
who was a member of the VLP—about the incident. Although the Nine-
Ball Crew and the VLP were "not at war" at the time, it was reported that
Sam's brother was intent on revenging the incident.

Although Sam was sexually assaulted by only one male, a number of
the respondents reported young girls being victimized by groups of
males. One such example was provided by Fabiola, a nineteen-year-old
young woman who at the time of her interview reported being married
to a twenty-year-old member of the Gangsters. Fabiola describes how
members of her husband's gang sexually assaulted one of her friends she
took to a party:

We were at a big party at my husband's friend's house. They said invite anybody you want but make sure they're not rival gangs. I invited all my friends—like seven of us. We all went together and were drinking and doing drugs and partying. It was to the point where we were really drunk. My friend Crystal was a virgin at that time. She was real pretty and she had long hair. She knew the guys because she would hang out with us. All the guys wanted to be with her. Then I realized, where did she go. I started asking like, "Hey where's Crystal?"

She was in the backyard and there was about twenty guys all doing it with her. They were taking turns and she was drunk; she didn't know what she was doing and at that time. She had lost it. She was just laying there and they were doing it with her. They were just lined up. I was like, "No, get up" and the guys were laughing at her.

The incident turned worse when, according to Fabiola, one of the guys inserted a foreign object in Crystal's vagina. Fabiola recalls seeing blood everywhere. Nobody wanted to take the responsibility of taking her to the hospital. Fabiola and several other girls reportedly took her to the hospital claiming they did not know what had happened. There were no charges pressed against anyone and Fabiola did not see Crystal as often after the incident. Fabiola says that she complained to her husband about what his homeboys had done. However, his response was, "That's why she shouldn't have opened her legs." The incident reveals the risk these girls are exposed to even though they have been associating with the male gang for a period of time—in this case three years.

Vulnerability was often determined by the young women's relationship to the male gang. Gloria Ana was seventeen years old and the girlfriend of one of the leaders of the criminally oriented VLP gang. Gloria Ana describes:

We were all kicking back at a party. At first she was acting like if she didn't want to have sex with any of the guys. But then the bitch got all fucked up. I guess they put something in her drink. They got her all fucked up and they just threw a train on her. I left for a while, but I got back and there was a big old line. I went in there because I thought it was one of my girlfriends. I was like, "Who the fuck is in there?" I saw her legs up and I was like, "Nah it's cool, not one of my friends." But she was a ho from another gang. She should have never stayed there. I mean she knew [what would happen]. So they did a train on her. About fifteen guys were there. Not all the guys went for it.

She was drunk, and they had given her acid. She was probably wired on cocaine too. She's a flake; she's a ho; I think that was the first [time]. She was just a pussy that was there. Like they don't treat all girls like that. I guess the guys were already fucked up.

Gloria Ana's story is only one example where the respondent justifies another girl's sexual assault. What emerges in her account is the distinction between the types of women presented in a previous chapter. In a sense, it is the streetwise (i.e., *cholas*) and those that have strong intimate relationships with members (i.e., wives/girlfriends) who avoid being sexual victims by monitoring one another's behavior and moderating their alcohol and drug use. Girls who are not part of this protective network and unfamiliar with the consequences of excessive substance use are targeted by the males. Young girls unable to control their alcohol and drug consumption thus are perceived as losing respect within this subculture and are considered *hos*.

Rationalization of Behaviors

As a result of the negative status of some of the young women who were attacked, female witnesses to these assaults often articulate some form of rationalization in regards to the males' behavior. That is, the blame for the sexual assault was in some occasions attributed to the female victim herself. For instance, Destiny, the fifteen-year-old girlfriend of a member of the Chicano Boyz—one of the largest and more organized gangs in the community—rationalizes the young males' behavior in assaulting a young female. She states: "We were all at a party and everybody was drinking. She got really, really drunk and she was messing around with all the guys. She was flirting, sitting on top of them, kissing them and stuff. Then she went to a room with one guy. He came out and told his friend something. Then another guy went in. The guys just kept coming in and out. If she hadn't been so drunk, I don't think she would have done it. In the morning she was crying a lot." When asked if anyone attempted to stop the assault, Destiny responded: "Yeah, a lot of the girls tried to stop it. We weren't high. The guys, they don't let us drink. They don't let us smoke. They say it's wrong because we're a girl. That girl, everybody considered her a ho. You got your queens but then you got your queen ho's who have sex with a lot of the guys."

Another example was that given by Luisa, who also has a boyfriend in the Chicano Boyz. She says:

> This happened at a party to one of our friends. They got her real drunk to where she didn't realize what she was doing. The next thing you know, they take her upstairs to supposedly use the bathroom. I just see guys going up there and I realized what they were up to.

She was not actually raped because she probably knew what she was doing. I heard she had five guys at a time. I know she had left the place crying and holding her ripped blouse.

Similar to other stories, at no time did anyone, including the other girls, try and stop this girl from being gang raped. At one point in the interview, Luisa states, "She probably knew what she was doing." In fact, there is almost tacit approval of the males' behavior in that there are no negative comments made about the perpetrators. Again—as was the case in many stories—the victim was high on marijuana, cocaine, xanax, and alcohol.

In a sense, Destiny's and Luisa's descriptions of the sexual assault reflect a sense of normalcy regarding young women's sexual victimization by males in the gang context. This was constantly exemplified by the rationalization of the males' behavior and the blaming of the victim, which are ideas that may be attributed to the expected gender roles that have been internalized by females in these communities.

Substance Use

As has been demonstrated up to this point, the use of alcohol and drugs is a constant factor in the sexual victimization situations. However, it is not clear to what extent drugs and alcohol play in the behavior of these persons and whether substance consumption is a circumstantial factor that leads to victimization. What is clear is that the use of substances was present in almost all of the sexual victimization cases.

Almost all reports of the young females' sexual victimization include alcohol. The following is an example of how alcohol consumption led to the "gang rape" of Nicole's seventeen-year-old female friend. Nicole says she has been affiliated with the male gang since the age of thirteen, through her older brother's membership. She recalls how interfering with the assault was deemed as "disrespecting the gang":

Everybody in that little apartment was drunk. They drank two bottles of vodka. She just got done having sex with one guy and then other guys came. They're like, "She's drunk; let's do her." She's saying, "No, leave me alone." I was like, "You'll need to leave her alone because she's my best friend, leave her alone." So this homeboy tells me, "You need to go to the bathroom. I don't want you to see this." I'm like, "No, that's my best friend." And he goes, "I'm going to have to kick your ass, I'm going to have to beat you up if you don't go in there because you're disrespecting my gang." So then I went in the bathroom. All I hear is her screaming. I can't do nothing because they're holding the door from the outside. I'm sitting in there for like an hour. I come out and she's crying and crying. So we just left.

In contrast to previous examples, Nicole attempted to prevent the sexual assault but was unable to do anything. The young female's liquor consumption contributed to her victimization. In addition, the alcohol could have also played an important role in the males' behavior.

Elisa, an eighteen-year-old girl, recalls how one of her friends was sexually assaulted by several members of a rival gang. According to Elisa, her friend just wanted to party and get high:

My friend was at a party. She invited us to go to a party but the guys there I didn't know. I was telling her not to go and you know just to go with us somewhere. She didn't want to, because she says that she knew them. My friend was that type of girl who would go with anybody you know if they had drugs and things like that. She left with them and she told me that when she was there, that she was drinking and getting high and everything. There were other girls that were there too, they were like telling her to get all high [on marijuana and cocaine]. She told me that this guy started talking to her. She said she was talking to him and that she was high that all she remembered was that all these guys were like forcing her to do things. One guy told her if she didn't that they were gonna do all this like stuff to her. She was just scared.

Elisa reported seeing her the next day when she told her what had happened to her. She asked Elisa to take her to Planned Parenthood so that she could get a checkup. Apparently, the results indicated that the young woman had contracted an STD during the assault.

Overall, the sexual victimization of these young women within the context of hanging out with male gang members is representative of the constant risk they are exposed to in this community. For the most part, the reports of these rapes came through two sources: the respondent as a witness to the account or the respondent as informed about the incident by the victim. Nonetheless, all the stories described to us reflected very similar circumstances in which the sexual victimization that occurred resulted in extreme negative social and health consequences for the young women.

Physical Victimization

Physical Victimization by a Boyfriend

One of the primary focuses of this research was to understand the social phenomenon associated with intimate-partner violence among this population of adolescent gang-affiliated adolescents. Numerous stories were narrated to us by the young women while others were documented out in the field by the research team as they conducted their fieldwork. The girls' physical fights with their male partners varied in terms of characteristics including such things as extent of injuries, weapons, bystanders, substance use, police presence, etc. Most research on intimate-partner violence only describes to the reader the women's experiences of the events from the perspective of the researcher. What is missing from this type of research is the perspective of the victim herself. Thus, here I present detailed descriptive accounts of physical fights between young women and their boyfriends or husbands from the perspectives of the young women themselves. Specifics regarding the social processes associated with the physical victimization will be addressed in Chapter 7.

In general, the nature of the violence inflicted upon the young women varied from pulling hair and slapping to more extreme acts where bruising or the drawing of blood was evident. Yvonne is sixteen years old and is currently living with her older sister. She moved out of her parent's house a few years ago because of the problems she had with her father, who she says drank excessively. After running away several times to her boyfriend's apartment, she finally decided to move in with her sister. Yvonne had been with her boyfriend for approximately one and a half years before the violent confrontation occurred. The subject of the fight was that he accused her of talking to another male. She recalls:

> One day, I had went to his house. One of my [female] friends had told him that I was talking to this guy named Diego who was my friend. I would always call him up for advice about me and my boyfriend. Well, she ended up telling him something else. That day at his house he told me about it and he got mad. He thought I was messing around or something. I was laying down next to him with my arm around him and he told me to get off of him. He got my purse and threw it outside the house and told me to leave. I'm like—he's just tripping. I was just in shock. He was so mad. I never thought he would do that to me.

Yvonne goes on:

> He grabbed my hair. I was in shock so I didn't do nothing. He was dragging me to go outside through the door but I didn't. He was just talking, saying for me to get out of his house. He pushed me and I went back to bed laying down. I was just crying. He got on top of me and spit in my face and called me a bitch. He then started kicking me to get off. So I got mad when he was kicking me. I just got up and I go, "All right, I'm leaving." He got in my way in the door and I was like, "What, you throw my

purse outside and you do all this." I just hit him in the back of his head and in his stomach, so he would get out of my way.

According to Yvonne, after the incident, she decided to stay with him and talk things out. She mentioned that he started crying and apologizing for what he had just done. Since this was the first time he had ever done something like this, Yvonne reportedly stayed in the relationship after the violent incident.

For Cindy, the nature of the physical victimization and her injuries were more serious. At the time we spoke with Cindy, she was fifteen years old. She was living in public housing with her forty-three-year-old mother and her two siblings. Her parents separated when she was in middle school and, according to Cindy, many of the confrontations were attributed to her father's drinking problems. Cindy had only been going out with her boyfriend for two months when the violent confrontation with him ensued. At the young age of fifteen she had to deal with the emotions that came along with her boyfriend having a child with another woman. She says:

> Me and my boyfriend got in an argument because he said I was playing him. We had been going out for like about two months already and his last girlfriend told him that I was dating another guy. He went to my house and told me, "Who the fuck are you talking to?" I go, "Well, why are you still talking to that other bitch." He goes, "Because she has my baby." I told him, "You don't have to be with me anymore." That's when he pushed me. I go, "Well I don't want to fucking be with you." He slapped me and I started crying. Nobody was home, so like my brother couldn't beat the shit out of him. I don't know I just slapped him. He then punched me in my eye and gave me a black eye.

After the incident, Cindy confessed she was afraid her mom would find out about it. She knew he had a short temper and could sometimes get violent. In order to avoid any further problems she told her mom she had gotten into a fight. Nonetheless, she was still feeling bad about the entire ordeal as she stated, "I just did not know. If it were a girl I would have beat the shit out of her then and there. I don't know, I was like so shocked. I was crying all that day." Cindy was one of the few young women who ended the relationship soon after the incident occurred. "I broke up with him and he came over and was saying, I can't live without you. My big brother David told him what the fuck he was doing here. I told my brother, tell him to leave, tell him to leave." Eventually, Cindy found out that he had cheated on her while they were together and that he was expecting another child with a second female.

The two preceding narratives are examples of incidents that took place in a private setting where witnesses or bystanders were not present. There were, however, a number of physical violent confrontations between the young women and their boyfriends that took place in more public settings, including parties, downtown streets, respective neighborhoods, etc. Adela is a seventeen-year-old mother of three currently living with an adult relative. The incident she describes occurred with her boyfriend of two years, who is the father of one of her children:

I had gone out with Alonso. We had gone to a party. I was kind of like talking shit to him and his friends. I guess they like didn't like it. Well he took me to the party but for some reason he didn't want to me to go where everybody else was. I didn't even know nobody. So I said okay fine I'm gonna leave and I went to the store down the street and called a taxi. I saw some girls I knew and they said they were going to the party. I was already drunk so I went back with them. I ended up back with Alonso. So at the end of the night we went to his friend's house in the courts. We were all drunk and his friends were around. I started talking shit again, so he hit me real hard in my face and then I don't know what happened, I guess I was like out for a while. He just hit me one time real hard in my face and it just—my eye opened up and there was blood everywhere. I just called the taxi and I told them to come and pick me up and they picked me up and they took me to my dad's house.

Although Adela received medical attention after the incident, she reportedly did not press any charges, even though her father was pressuring her to do so. Moreover, Adela was with Alonso for another year—in which several other violent incidents with him occurred—before she broke off the relationship.

A similar scenario occurred with Valerie, a nineteen-year-old mother of one. She lives with her single mother but indicated having her boyfriend frequently spend the night at the house. Valerie expressed her concern for her boyfriend's alcohol and marijuana use, which brings forth his violent character. She recalls the most recent physical fight they had while hanging out in their public housing complex:

We were at the courts. I was yelling at him in front of his friends and I was threatening him. The wife of one of his homeboys was telling me that he was cheating on me. I was telling him, 'You know you just wait until we get to the house. I'm gonna take everything and put your shit on the street.'

I was just embarrassing him in front of his friends. He took me like around the building and he started hitting me. I was hitting him back. He just got me and he threw me to like the hood of a car and started banging my head. I was just screaming and kicking. I guess he was scared that someone was gonna call the cops so he told his friends he was gonna take me home. He was driving and I looked at him and I was cussing him out. I punched him in the face. Then he turned around and did the same to me. I was yelling, "Okay, okay!" I was so—you know I was drinking that night and I was real pissed off. I said you know what, "I'm gonna kill you." So I got the steering wheel while he was driving and I was just trying to you know crash the car. We got to his mom's house and he punched me in my face again. Then I started bleeding. I just started running to a pay phone to call my mom. He got in the car and was driving beside me and saying he was all sorry. "I didn't mean to make you bleed or anything."

Valerie had been with her boyfriend for a little over a year when the preceding incident happened. In discussions with her, she attributes much of his violence toward her as a consequence of his marijuana use. Although she reportedly broke it off with him that evening, a few days later she was back with him.

Stories abounded in which the young women described the serious injuries that resulted from their physical victimization at the hands of their boyfriends. Another example was that of Sabrina, a sixteen-year-old female affiliated with one of the largest male gangs in the community. Although she has only been with her boyfriend for approximately seven months, she says she is really in love with him. During her interview, she tells us how her eighteen-year-old boyfriend has been in and out of jail. She recalls the specific detail of the last violent confrontation she had with him:

He was doing community service at the Southside Community Center. He doesn't like black people because I think something happened to him while he was locked up. So—he's real jealous; he doesn't like for me to talk to other guys. That day he was cleaning up the gym. There was all these black guys playing. I'm standing there and some guy comes up to me. "So you're having a good time?" I'm looking around like, "Oh my god I know you ain't talking to me." So then he's like, "What are you doing?" "I'm with my boyfriend." I said it out loud so my boyfriend could hear. So my boyfriend sees me and he gives me this look like you know I'm gonna beat your ass when we get home. He came over and says, "What have I told you about that." He's like, "Come on, we're going home." We got home and he got all my stuff and he threw them outside.

Sabrina explains how he was really upset about the incident and told her he was going to leave because he did not want to be with her. She recalls how she tried to physically restrain him from leaving the house:

He was really gonna go. I didn't want him to go and get in trouble because of me. He losses his temper quick and he'll react without even thinking. He tried to smack me around. But I would not let him leave. He started throwing things around. I was afraid he might have gone and done something stupid out on the streets. So I was just trying to keep him there at the house. He started punching the walls and he elbowed me in the face. He hit me in the face, yeah he hit me right here [pointing to her upper right cheek]. He split all this open. That's why I got this scar here.

I didn't feel it and then I was like, "Why don't you just stop!" He's like, "Babe you're bleeding; I'm so sorry." He grabs me and drags me to our room and sits me down on the bed. I'm like it's just a cut and he's like no you're gonna need stitches.

Sabrina goes on describing the scene at the time. She recounts how he was very apologetic for the next ten minutes and repeated that he loved her. She told him that she was sorry and was not worried about her face. All she could think about was the fact that she did not want him to leave. She says, "I'm like, please don't leave." She reveals that she did not get any medical attention, which may have been one of the reasons she was left with the scar. She also indicated that she told her parents she accidentally hit her face on a dresser while playing around with her boyfriend. She was afraid he would be sent back to jail if she reported it. Sabrina did not end the relationship. She emphasizes her feeling toward him: "He's real caring and I love him a lot."

Most young women in this research revealed that they had been victims of their boyfriends' physical abuse at some point. With a few exceptions, most of the females remained in the violent relationships after the described incident. Many stories reflected the danger the young women exposed themselves to by not reporting the abuse in order to not jeopardize their relationships. Furthermore, in almost all cases the girls were overpowered by the men, and succumbed to the abuse rather than risk further physical harm.

Physical Victimization at the Hands of the Family

In addition to being victims of physical victimization at the hands of a boyfriend, the young women in these communities also had to deal with violent confrontations with family members. Typically, these events occurred within the private context of the household, making the situation even more volatile. Here, I present case studies of several young women's experiences with family violence as collected and documented in project field notes written by the field team and and as told by young women themselves.

Similar to the physical victimization these girls were exposed to with their boyfriends, the incidents of family violence varied in regard to the extent of injury and weapons used. Typically, the young girl's violent confrontation was with a blood relative. An example is Brandy, who at the time she was recruited for the study was sixteen years old. She was living with her grandmother, aunt, and two cousins in a three-bedroom home. Brandy was a key gatekeeper in our study and often visited our field office. One day she contacted one of our female field staff because she wanted to talk. The field note reads:

> Upon arriving at Brandy's residence, she told me that she had just had a big fight with her cousin. She said that the fight started because of an argument they had over some food. I could not tell the total extent of her injuries because it was dark and we were sitting in my car. She said that he was cooking some meat to eat and that he was also [inviting] his friends. Brandy told him that he was not going to cook meat that did not belong to him [Brandy had purchased the meat]. She was also upset because his hands were dirty and that he was handling all of the meat. After words were exchanged, he pushed her and then she pushed him back. She then pushed him again and that's when he cut her in the arm with the knife he had been cutting the meat with. She grabbed a vase and hit him on the head. He then started to hit her with his fists and tried to choke her. The fight then went to the front porch and finally to the street. At that point, Brandy said that she racked him in the groin and hit him in the nose with her hand. It was then that some of her neighbors started to try and break up the fight. One of the neighbors called the police and when they arrived they arrested her cousin.

The field note goes on to read that her cousin spent the night in jail but was released the next day. This whole situation, of course, caused further problems with her aunt, who was her cousin's mom. To make matters worse, the next day Brandy got into another physical confrontation with her sister-in-law, as the following field note reveals:

> According to Brandy, after we left her off at home last night, her sister-in-law arrived and asked her if she would watch her kids while her and her friend Leo went to the carnival. Brandy told her no because she was going to go out again. An argument started but it wasn't until Leo started to interfere that Brandy told him that it was none of his business. Leo then told Brandy that he had heard that she was telling people that he was a fag. Leo then told Barbara "that she was nothing but a ho." That he heard

that she was walking around the carnival with her low cut blouse and her G-string bikini panties. Then the sister-in-law started to get involved in the argument also. Barbara then said she can't remember exactly who threw the first punch but both her sister-in-law and Leo started to hit and kick her. A big fight erupted in the living room. A lamp and a television were broken.

Several incidents involved physical confrontations with nonfamily members living in the household. In most cases, the person was usually the mother's live-in boyfriend, as was the case with Victoria. Victoria is the eighteen-year-old mother of a three-year-old girl, who tells us about living in one of the largest public housing complexes in the city with her mother and her mother's boyfriend. The following field note describes the details of the physical confrontation Victoria engaged in while at home one day:

We were going down the street and we saw Victoria walking into the corner store. We waited for her to get an update on how she is doing. She told us about how she got into a fight with her mother's boyfriend on Monday. She said that he was talking shit to her all day about how she always yelled at her daughter and how she should stop yelling at her all the time. Victoria said she told him it was none of his business how she disciplined her child, Roseanne was hers and she could do what she wanted to do. She said that he was all in her face and yelling at her and she just went into her room and slammed the door and ignored him.

When her mother got home she said that he started in on her again. Victoria started yelling at him. He started telling her that he wanted her out of his house. Victoria said he had no right to throw her out of the house and then her mother started in and said maybe it would be best if she did go. They were yelling at each other so much and the boyfriend said he was going to call the police. He went to the phone and started to call the police and at that point, Victoria said she just went up and hit him in the face. She started hitting on him. He was yelling and started throwing things around the house and breaking her mother's vases and glasses and things. She said he picked up a big clock off the wall and hit her mother over the head with it. Victoria said that at that point she started hitting him even more because he was hitting her mom. She said he went up to her and hit her in the face. She said she barely even felt it because he hit her like a girl. She said she was so angry that she just kept hitting him. Somehow she stopped hitting him and then her sister told her that her eye was all red. Victoria said when he hit her he hit her in the eye and the inner eye was all red.

Victoria took off and went to her father's house and told him that her mother's boyfriend had hit her and her father came back with her to her house with a bat. When they got there, the police were already there and Victoria said her dad took off because if the police saw him they would take him back in [there was a warrant for his arrest]. So he took off and Victoria went back and was yelling and cussing at the boyfriend. The police made her get into the car because she wouldn't calm down, she was still trying to hit the boyfriend. They told her they were going to take her in if she didn't calm down and she finally did. She took off to her father's house and hasn't been home since.

One week later we found out that Victoria was still at her father's house. Apparently, her mother told her she could never move back in to her house. She later told us that she was happy to be moving in with her father because he pays more attention to her than her mother. This however, did not last. A couple of weeks after the incident at her mother's house, Victoria got into yet another fight: this time with her father. The field note reads:

On Tuesday, Victoria said she was at home and her father was fighting with his girlfriend, who is pregnant. She said he wasn't really hitting her, he was shaking her and grabbing her and yelling at her. She saw all of this going on and told her father he shouldn't hit her when she's pregnant. She said he was drunk and "on his shit" [heroin] and was all messed up. She went up to him and was telling him to stop hitting her and trying to stop him. When she got into it, he accidentally hit her on her face. She did not want any more problems and tried to settle down after that.

The last time we spoke with Victoria, she told one of our field staff that she was going to try to live more peacefully with her father and his girlfriend. She apparently gets along with his girlfriend and is trying to help out around the house. She also was seriously looking for a job. It was obvious, however, that Victoria was still in a difficult situation as far as both of her parents' respective romantic relationships and her father's heroin problem.

There were several accounts of the studied girls getting into physical fights with their mothers. In most of these cases, the violence did not escalate to the point of someone getting seriously injured. There were a few, however, that reported such serious fights. For example Amanda, a fifteen-year-old girl living with her parents and siblings, was petite in size but pretty tough when it came to attitude. Amanda recalls the fight she had with her mother:

My mom would always complain about the way I would dress. She said I would dress like a boy and so like now I dress like you know in skirts. Now she's always *que pinché puta* [fucking whore]. My friends and I are up at all hours so she's always fucking calling me *puta* [whore]. That day I was stoned so I got mad. She started saying *puta, puta*. I told her, "You know what, why in the fuck are you always calling me *puta*? I'm sick and tired of you calling me a *puta*." I got her fucking TV and broke it.

I pushed her. We were just like in each other's face and she hit me. Then I hit her. My mom's big. She's a big lady. She got me like "boom, boom!" She threw me against the wall and she hit me three times, she hit me good. I hit her and kicked her in her stomach. I was bleeding, I don't know maybe when she hit me against the wall. Later we saw there was blood all over.

This was apparently not the first time Amanda had gotten into a fight with her mother. There appeared to be physical confrontations almost on a daily basis in this household.

While the violence experienced with family members was reported to occur slightly less often than violence with their boyfriends, it does reflect the violent nature of the girls' home environments. Contrary to the violent victimization by boyfriends, which revolved around intimate personal relationships, violence with family members was associated with common types of disagreements that arise in most homes. The difference, however, is that for these families, attempts to resolve differences often escalate into violence.

Conclusion

This chapter clearly describes the sexual and physical dangers associated with gang life for girls. The girls experience an extensive amount of violence in their lives, whether in relationships with their boyfriends, in association with the gang, or with their families. Even within this street-based subculture women are expected to adhere to traditional gender roles. Many of the risks they faced within this highly volatile environment were gender specific. For instance, women were often sexually or physically victimized by men because they violated gender-based expectations. Each was expected to act "like a woman" and to acquiesce to every demand imposed by her boyfriend. A common expectation among this subculture seemed to be the conventional one that girls should voluntarily submit to having sex at the demand of their partners. Family-based violence also was often described to have been based on some form of gender expectation. The consequence of defying or resisting such an expectation typically involved some form of coercion or violence without any normative repercussions either from other males or from the majority of the victimized females themselves.

One of the major findings of this chapter is how young women internalize the sexist norms and values specifically imposed on them by men. How else would you explain the lack of identification and empathy of women with those women being brutally victimized by the men in their lives? Young women who are gang raped at parties are perceived by other women as deserving of what they get. The rape victims had violated the ideological expectation of femininity in that they were unable to practice restraint from excessive drug and alcohol use and from sex. As Hunt and his colleagues' research finds, overindulgence was not respectable behavior for female gang members (2000). In order to maintain respect, women used a number of strategies to regulate and control behavior. One tactic was that women who were not worthy of respect were demonized as hos and stigmatized. They somehow violated expectations of their gender and therefore were not offered the protection of other females or males.

The good girls and girls accepted by the gang, although protected from more public victimization, were still vulnerable to more routine victimization at the hands of boyfriends in more private settings. Nonetheless, the patriarchal ideology of the larger society imposes the cultural norm of "connectiveness" to males for Mexican American women, which contributes to their subordination (Amaro 1995). The emotional need for connectiveness with men creates a situation in which women tolerate abuse in order to maintain a relationship. Such a behavior was exhibited numerous times in the examples provided in this chapter.

Structurally, the impact of the larger community on the studied women's views of themselves affected their perception of victimization at the hands of their boyfriends. Similar to what was found by Miller (2001), I found that these women drew upon the same cultural framework found in the larger society with regard to the negative characterization of women, including victim-blaming. In order to gain some respite from traditional gender roles, they had to assume the roles of the oppressor. Nonetheless, taking on these roles within the social space of the gang did not protect them from either sexual or physical violence. All these women were exposed to this violence; they differed only by degrees. Collectively, all these women must survive in an ethnic community that continues to impose clearly defined gender and class barriers on young women.

Chapter 7

The Situational Context of Dating Violence

Studies have examined intimate violence between spouses (or stable or semistable common-law relationships) and adolescents involved in conventional courtship and dating relationships. Many of these studies, along with what has been presented in previous chapters here, have identified the etiology of partner violence as embedded in socially structured gender inequalities that emerge in these relationships (McFarlane et al. 2004; Miller and White 2003; Watts and Zimmerman 2002; Amaro 1995). Limited attention, however, has been paid to adolescent delinquints involved in less clearly defined and short-term dating relationships living in economically marginalized urban communities, as is the case with the studied population.

Previous studies have not focused on circumstances surrounding the violent incidents themselves within adolescent dating relationships or even within those of adults in either dating or more permanent relationships. Understanding the situational level processes that instigate the violent act among these high-risk adolescents is a major focus of this chapter. Such processes are defined as "those factors outside the individual that influence the initiation, unfolding or outcome of a violent event," (Sampson and Lauritsen 1994, 30). These situational processes are defined as microlevel since they usually are concerned with face-to-face street encounters in everyday life. Microlevel processes are important in that they suggest mechanisms and properties that can contribute to a deeper understanding of violence. These microlevel explanations are expected to be more important in subcultures (and societies) that are less "institutionally complete" (Valdez 1993, 193). As James Short states: "Microlevel processes probably are more important to the explanation of the behavior of gang members, individually and collectively, than they are for young people who are involved in more formally and effectively structured, adult-sponsored institutions" (Short 1985). The situational approach is highly appropriate for examining dating violence among females involved in street gangs and marginalized and segmented from the majority society.

Situating Partner and Dating Violence

An extensive amount of research has focused on the issue of intimate-partner violence among adults (Amaro et al. 1990; Kaufman, Kantor, and Jasinski 1998; McFarlane et al. 2004; Watts and Zimmerman 2002). Much of this research has focused on the etiology of the violence and on predictors of such violence aimed at developing appropriate prevention and intervention strategies. During the last few decades, however, a body of literature has emerged that is focused on partner violence among adolescents, which has been referred to as "dating violence" (Miller and White 2003; O'Keefe 1997; Malik, Sorenson, and Aneshensel 1997; Silverman et al. 2001; O'Keefe and Treister 1998; Molidor and Tolman 1998; Giordano et al. 1999; Makepeace 1986; Sugarman and Hotaling 1997). Dating violence refers to a distinct situation of "the perpetration or threat of an act of physical violence by at least one member of an unmarried dyad within the context of the dating process" (Sugarman and Hotaling 1989, 5). A generalization from this literature is that differences in adult versus adolescent partner violence are due to the nature of adolescence as a developmental stage. Adolescents are less apt to have acquired the social and psychological skills at their age to successfully negotiate partner relationships and other peer interactions.

A major finding in adult partner violence relevant to adolescents is that the rate of violence perpetration across gender is similar (Miller and White 2003; Straus and Gelles 1990). Furthermore, men and women involved in partner violence often have a common psychological profile. Some, however, suggest that females engage in more female-perpetrated and nonreciprocal violence—as measured by the Conflict Tactics Scale (CTS) (1995). However, as she and many others acknowledge, the CTS does not adequately measure factors such as severity of injuries and other emotional and physical harm. Moreover, the nature of the violence that is perpetrated by females tends to be more trivial and less serious and occurs in reaction to their male partners' aggression (O'Keefe 1997; Giordano et al. 1999). A criticism of this research is that it minimizes the female participant's interpretation, motivations, and intentions compared to men (Dobash et al. 1992). More importantly, the studies do not consider the situational characteristics that are outside the psychology of the individuals involved.

Many findings regarding adult partner violence are generalized to extend to adolescent dating violence, with some notable differences. For example, Shaista Malik and her colleagues' study of an ethnically diverse high-school-aged population in Long Beach, California, found female subjects were more often the perpetrators of intimate-partner violence than their male counterparts, but no gender distinction was made as for victimization (1997). This female-to-male violence perpetration has been documented in other adolescent dating studies (Gray and Foshee 1997; Morse 1995; Breslin, Riggs, and O'Leary 1990; Riggs, O'Leary, and Breslin 1990; Stets and Henderson 1991). Maura O'Keefe discovered that there were higher rates of violence perpetration by African American and Hispanic female adolescents than by white female adolescents (1997). These findings reveal that there may be differences in the nature of dating violence due to race, ethnicity, and class, which is a subject that will be expanded upon in this chapter. Another difference between adults and adolescents regarding intimate-partner violence is the nature of the relationship between the couples. Couples with more of an emotional commitment, shared time and activities, but in perceived commitment had increased levels of conflict and dating-violence perpetration and victimization (Hanley and O'Neill 1997; O'Keefe 1997). Also, perception of the relationship seemed to differ between males and females, with the former often less invested emotionally than the latter.

Studies have also focused on identifying risk factors for dating violence (O'Keefe 1997; Malik, Sorenson, and Aneshensel 1997; Molidor and Tolman 1998). This research has found that exposure to different types of violence is the strongest predictor of dating-relationship violence. For instance, exposure to family violence along with weapons and violent injury in the community were important factors in explaining dating violence among a sample of high school students (Malik, Sorenson, and Aneshensel 1997). Furthermore, in a sample of urban high school students, being a victim of violence, justifying or accepting dating violence, being in a relationship that includes violence, and alcohol and drug use were all predictors for perpetrating dating violence for both males and females.

Of interest to this chapter is research that focuses on motives for the perpetration of dating violence. O'Keefe found anger, jealousy, and control as important motives for partner violence (1997). However, control was a much stronger motive for men than for women, whose primary motive was anger or self-defense. Maura O'Keefe and Laura Treister (1998), and Richard Felson and Steven Messner (2000), argue that control is associated with the partner that has the most coercive power. This is usually the male, who can actually execute a physical threat. Men minimize female-perpetuated violence and are not concerned with its physical repercussions.

While all of the previously mentioned research has had an important impact in understanding adolescent dating violence and its implications, the nature of the survey methods utilized yield important limitations. One important limitation is that most of the surveys were taken from school-based populations, and therefore captured more conventional adolescents. Given that the high school drop-out rate may be as high as 50 percent in some poor inner-city schools, these surveys exclude adolescents who may be more at risk for violent victimization and perpetration. This is especially the case for those adolescents engaged in sexual relations, chronic drug use, criminality, and street gangs. Jody Miller and Norman White's study is one of the few that focuses on a high-risk population (2003). The authors recruited African American adolescents living in a distressed urban community from a local community agency and from alternative schools. This study provides rich, contextualized data that is significantly different from that provided by most studies on school-based surveys.

Finally, some scholars have used a gender framework in examining dating violence (DeKeseredy and Schwartz 1998; Dobash et al. 1992; Miller and White 2003). In Miller and White's qualitative study, they use "sex as a category rather than as a social structure and meaning system to provide a contextual examination of the nature, circumstances, and meanings of adolescent dating violence" (2003, 1241). Miller and White suggest that the meanings and consequences of dating violence differed for females and males and could be attributed to gender inequalities associated with hegemonic masculinity (2003). In this chapter I explore gender dynamics associated with adolescent dating violence by providing an analysis of the context in which the violence emerges.

As I have argued, what is missing from dating-violence literature are studies that focus on violence victimization and perpetration among adolescents involved in more marginalized, less clearly structured, and stigmatized youth subcultures such as street gangs. In this social environment, young males and females are involved in less normative or conventional relationships (i.e., traditional boyfriend-girlfriend relationships) expected at this life stage. For instance, as has been described, many at this young age are involved in common-law relationships with children and living together with their parent. These types of relationships are seldom found in more middle-class communities that adhere to a moral prescription for timing of sex, marriage, childbearing, and the avoidance of criminal and other delinquent behavior (Jencks 1990; Erickson 1998).

In the case of gang-associated youth, that comprise the subjects of this book, one would expect the violent behaviors that characterize gangs would extend to their interpersonal sexual relationships. Craig Palmer and Christopher Tilley found that female gang members had a greater average of recent sex partners than nongang girls (1995). Sexuality between male and female gang members has also been linked to rape and gang initiation. Further, the gang members' association with drug and alcohol use compared to that of other youth may increase the risks for violence among this population since research shows that young females are increasingly becoming victimized by males who use drugs and alcohol (Daghestani 1988; Gorney 1989; Walker 1984).

In this chapter I examine the gendered power dynamics that influence the violent behaviors between couples. Understanding this context is important, in that the analysis focuses on how an individual's interpretation of behaviors within a particular setting shapes situational processes. Specifically, because I use a grounded-theory approach, the qualitative analysis focuses on microlevel processes by examining the event and how variations in the precursors of the incident, progression of the argument, and interaction between actors influence the violent outcomes.

Precursors: Variations of Gendered Power Dynamics

Three general precursors emerged as motives for the initiation of arguments among the adolescent couples studied: jealousy, control, and disrespect. Conceptually, the precursors identified in this analysis can be seen as variants of "power" as defined by the gender roles characteristic of this population. Nonetheless, for the purposes of this analysis, distinctions will be made between the three identified precursors. The first, jealousy, is behavior and feeling that is motivated by the perceived threat that another person's affection toward one's partner is being supplemented by a rival. Jealousy in this study is limited to the idea of one partner either suspecting or knowing that their partner is sexually interested in or actually involved with another person. Jealousy may also emerge if a partner is suspected of or has been observed having physical sexual contact with another including touching, kissing, hugging, etc. Control refers to a situation in which one partner is trying to dominate and dictate the behavior of the other. This may be done either through direct physical force or through sociopsychological manipulation. When a partner refuses to comply with the other's attempt to control or dictate his or her behavior an argument may ensue. The precursor situation of disrespect implies that one of the partners has demonstrated a lack of good will, esteem, or deference to the other partner through behavior, symbolic gesture, or language. What is important here is that one party has perceived the other as engaging in behavior that is disrespectful.

Progression of Violent Social Interaction

Instigation: Verbal and Nonverbal

Instigation refers to behaviors (either verbal or nonverbal) that provoke or contribute to the progression of an argument and resultant violence. Some instigators may be more direct than others; nonetheless, they must in some way provoke the other person. Verbal provocations include both words or statements that are negatively interpreted by the partner and open verbal defiance. Words may be an outright "diss" or be complaining, nagging, and whining. Nonverbal instigations refer to visible physical behaviors. Examples of nonverbal communication that may provoke or escalate an argument to a physical "fight" (assault) are facial expressions, laughing, purposely ignoring someone, etc. Each verbal or nonverbal occurrence that escalated the argument was considered an act of instigation.

Each incident reported by the adolescent females was analyzed to find patterns of instigation. We attempted to identify the initiator of the incident (the aggressor), the point at which the arguments became physically violent, and how the physical confrontation ended. Individual acts of instigation were identified based on the story of the fight as told by the female respondent. The recounts of these physical fights were analyzed line by line and then each individual act cited was ordered and recoded in a type of instigation.

Progression from an Argument to a Physically Violent Confrontation

An argument that leads to a physical confrontation may evolve through multiple acts of instigation—either verbal or nonverbal—and finally to the termination of the interaction. As stated earlier, each of the fights described in this analysis was categorized by three distinct precursors.

The progression of the argument depends on the precursor and the acts of instigation involved. Some precursors may be more confrontational and direct than others.

For a better understanding of how an argument progresses from a precursor through acts of instigation to a physical confrontation, an example is provided. Figure 7.1 illustrates how an argument triggered by jealousy (a precursor) progresses into multiple instigations and results in a physical violent confrontation.

Figure 7.1 Jealousy (Precursor) and Acts of Instigation

1st Act of Verbal Instigation: He says, "My friends told me they saw you talking to some guy at school today."

2nd Act of Verbal Instigation: She says, "I wasn't talking to anybody, your friends are lying."

3rd Act of Verbal Instigation: He screams, "Don't lie to me. You're a ho!"

1st Act of Physical Confrontation: He slaps her across the face.

2nd Act of Physical Confrontation: She pushes him away from her.

3rd Act of Physical Confrontation: He grabs her violently by the arm.

4th and Final Act of Physical Confrontation: She pushes him away from her and storms off.

As represented in Figure 7.1, the argument does not only consist of physical violent confrontations or assaults but rather progressed from verbal instigations.

Physical Violent Confrontation

Violent confrontation refers to the physical behavior used to harm another person or to attempt to control a person. Further, violence is defined as a physical confrontation carried out with the intent to cause pain or injury to another. It does not include nonphysical, psychologically aggressive behavior as other researchers acknowledge as part of their definitions of dating violence (see Archer and Browne 1989; Carlson 1987). Our analysis also differentiates the degree of injuries that results from acts of violence. Violent behavior can range from pushing, grabbing, slapping, and hair pulling to more aggressive acts such as an attack with a weapon or another object. The first set of behaviors are referred to as "common couple violence" (Hamberger and Guse 2002).

Physical injuries consist of nonlethal injuries such as soreness, scratches, and bruises in the case of minor violent incidents. More serious incidents are those that require medical attention and hospitalization like severe cuts resulting from knife wounds. Once the first physical contact occurs, the incidents are categorized as violent confrontations. The incidents used in this study may consist of a single violent confrontation or a series of them either directed solely from the offender to the victim or an exchange of violence between both parties. The fight here is seen as a process in a particular situation.

Jealousy

As described previously, jealousy in this context refers to a perceived or real threat of another supplementing the affection of one's partner in a dating relationship. The threat is usually reinforced by behavior, which can vary from flirting, kissing, or hugging to speaking to someone the partner perceives as a threat to the relationship. The following example is characteristic of an argument that arose over jealousy and eventually led to a physical confrontation. Ruby is a fifteen-year-old girl who grew up in a violent household with an alcoholic father involved in criminal activities. She lives with her mother who is regularly physically victimized by her new male partner. Ruby has a history of physical fights, including an arrest record for an assault that occurred at school. The following describes the progression of Ruby's argument with her jealous boyfriend when his ex-girlfriend told him that Ruby was cheating on him:

> He went to my house. He told me that if I was looking at somebody else. I go "no." My phone rang and it was some dude named Gabriel. My boyfriend said, "Who the fuck was that, why the fuck are you talking to other dudes?" I told him why the hell are you talking to your ex-chick. And he said, "Because I can." I then told him, "Well what the hell I can't talk to my other friends." He goes "How the hell do I know they're your friends." I said, "Well they're my friends; can't you even trust me?" He then said, "Well sometimes I don't even know if I could trust you." All I could say was, "Well you know what, if you don't want to be with me anymore just tell me." He goes, "What, you just want to break up with me already? If you don't want to be with me it's all right." And that's when like, he opened the gate and he pushed me.

Ruby went on to describe how after the initial push, the argument escalated into a physical violent confrontation with more pushing and slapping by both parties. According to Ruby, her own physical retaliation to her boyfriend's aggression angered him and he began hitting her with his fist, resulting in a black eye.

While the precursor to this argument was jealousy, the primary act of instigation in this circumstance was a male friend (Gabriel) calling during the argument that had already ensued. This instigation reinforced her boyfriend's perception that she was seeing someone behind his back. In this particular situation the phone call transformed the nature of the argument into a physically violent confrontation. Furthermore, while Ruby's pushing and shoving toward her boyfriend may be seen as a form of retaliation or self-defense it seemed to have exacerbated the seriousness of the violence. This scenario was common of other male-initiated violent situations over jealousy that occurred while both partners were alone.

There were incidents where the confrontation occurred in public in the presence of known others. For instance, Melissa is an eighteen-year-old mother of one. She lives with her mother, sister, and her sister's two children. Melissa at the time of the interview was thinking of moving in with her boyfriend. She describes him as having "a bad temper with a short fuse." The following illustrates the extent to which his jealousy drove him to physically assault Melissa one day:

> I had went out with my best [female] friend. [her boyfriend] started calling and calling my house. I wasn't there so he decided to come and wait at my house. I called and my mom told me he was outside sitting in his car. She told me, "Don't come right now until he leaves because you are going to argue." But I thought we wouldn't. When I got there he went up to the car to see if there was any other guys in there. There were two guys who were my best friend's boyfriend and someone else. He saw I was sitting in the back with them.
>
> He thought something right away. We walked up to my sidewalk and started arguing. I told him, "You know what, I don't want to hear this; just go home and we'll fight about it another day. My friends are here; just go away." He's like, "No, you're coming with me." He grabbed my arm and told me to get inside the car. I was like, "No I'm not going to." He's all, "No get in the car." He opened the door and pushed me in. We were just basically arguing, but he got mad and started pulling my hair. I was trying to get away from him. He just kept driving, pulling my hair, and screaming at me. I was crying.

What may have contributed to her boyfriend's aggressive behavior was that the incident occurred in a public place.

Most of the female-initiated arguments in the data were associated with the precursor of jealousy. Amanda, a fifteen-year-old female described an argument she had with her eighteen-year-old boyfriend. She was seven months pregnant with his child when she became suspicious that he was "cheating" on her:

> My friend and I were already going to leave because [my boyfriend] wasn't there [at his place]. I was already getting out of the apartments when I saw him coming. I saw two cars of girls pulling up right there, too. I was like, what? And he goes yeah this and that [explaining the situation to her]. I go, "Whatever, I'm splitting. I don't need you anyway. You can have them."
>
> And he got all mad. He goes, "What did you say?" He came over and got me by my hair. He was telling me, "What did you say?" I yelled, "Leave me alone or I'll call the cops on you. I don't care." He then told me, "You ain't gonna call nobody." He slapped me ... and pushed me into the fence. I fell. His friends were all there. They were telling him to behave, "You're going too far." I was crying a lot. He then says, "I'm sorry, do you forgive me? I don't want to hit you, but it's you; you get me mad."

Again in this situation, Amanda's indirect accusation that her boyfriend was being unfaithful developed into a physical confrontation when she threatened to leave him. According to Amanda, this was not the first time her boyfriend had become physical with her but was one of many in a string of violent confrontations. In this particular situation, the fact that there were third parties present quite possibly may have served as a deterrent for Amanda's boyfriend to exert more serious injuries.

Contrary to the preceding examples, there were cases in which jealousy, the precursor to the argument, was based upon actual events that occurred rather than on perceptions of situations on the part of partners. For instance, in the following narrative the young female witnesses her boyfriend "making out" with, or embracing and kissing, another girl at a party they both were attending. Jasmine states: "He was just going off [flirting] with these girls at a party. He was kissing them on the cheek. I turned around and the next thing I see him making out with [a bisexual stripper]." The flirtation and signs of sexual affection toward another female incited this argument. According to Jasmine, after witnessing the flirtation she retaliated by engaging in similar behavior in order to aggravate him and make him jealous. She explains: "So I'm thinking to myself, like, 'You want to play a game, fine! I'll play a game.' We went back to another apartment. [The bisexual girl and I] were in the restroom rolling up some weed. I was like, 'I saw you kiss my man.' And she goes, 'What?' And I go, 'That's cool; that's fine.' So, I started messing around with her, kissing her. I started making hickies on her neck so I could piss him off." Jasmine's boyfriend became suspicious of what was happening in the bathroom. Jasmine relates what happened next: "He starts knocking on the [bathroom] door and says, 'What are you doing? Get the fuck out!' I wouldn't get out of the bathroom. Then, 'boom,' he busted in and sees us messing around. Just to get back at him, I go, 'How do you like it motherfucker? If you want to fuck around with a bitch then I'm gonna mess around with her too.' So he slaps me, right? So, like I always do I looked around. I grabbed a blow dryer and threw it at him."

According to Jasmine, her boyfriend managed to get her out of the apartment despite her physical resistance. Once outside, he shoved her in the front seat and she hit him with the car door as she closed it. When they arrived home, the argument was still going, and Jasmine describes grabbing a knife and attempting to stab him. As he tried to take the knife from her she reached for the blade and cut her hand seriously enough to require multiple stitches. As did many other females, Jasmine reports that this incident was one of many.

Similarly, seventeen-year-old Lucrecia describes how she caught her eighteen-year-old boyfriend with some neighborhood "little girls." According to Lucrecia, she caught him trying to cheat on her because, she thought, it would get her back for seeing someone else:

> I was pregnant at the time with my son. I was asleep at night. He was up drinking and doing cocaine. He had taken some kind of pills. I think Valiums. I wasn't gonna be up babysitting him, so I went ahead and I went to sleep. I wake up and it's like four o'clock in the morning and he is not there. I go outside of the apartment complex and I'm looking around. So I look and well there he is all wasted. He and his friend are talking to two little girls from around the neighborhood. Those girls know that we have kids.
>
> He's there like trying to hug and kiss one. I started running towards the girl because she knew that was my boyfriend. My boyfriend's all drunk. He gets me, pushes me towards the ground. I was pregnant at the time. I went crazy. I got this stick and tried to hit him. His mom was trying to stop us. I told him I was gonna pack my stuff and leave. I told him he would never see his daughter or his kid on the way. He started going crazy. He was grabbing me by my arms holding me against the wall so I wouldn't leave. He grabbed me by my face, telling me that he loves me. I don't know why he was hitting me if he was the one screwing up.

In this situation, Lucrecia's jealousy was based on her boyfriend's actions that she happened to have witnessed. Even though this particular couple was cohabitating in the boyfriend's parents' home, their prior history of "cheating" on each other appeared to be the reasoning behind much of their mutual jealousy and lack of trust. Although Lucrecia expressed, "I've caught him cheating so many times," she appears to justify his actions by saying, "If he's gonna hit me or something it's for a reason." Furthermore, the physical confrontation in this example may have been exacerbated by the boyfriend's degree of intoxication.

The following case illustrates alcohol as influencing the male-initi-ated confrontation. Celina, the sixteen-year-old female we talked to, was staying at a girlfriend's house that was frequented by male friends, who often came over to party. She recounts her boyfriend's reaction when he found out where she was staying:

> "He was drunk and he started arguing with me [over the phone]. He went to go and pick me up. There were guys there and they were drinking. He thought I was messing around with them. One of them was in my room. [My boyfriend] came in and got all mad and pushed me. Then, I slapped him back. He didn't try to hit me."

The female's boyfriend, who she described as drunk, assumed that she was "cheating" on him because she was "hanging out" with other males. The series of verbal instigations over the phone and in person led to a physical violent confrontation.

Control

The second type of precursor to dating violence was that of control. Control refers to a tendency or compulsion to direct the behavior of or limit the independence or autonomy of a partner, resulting in a power struggle. Males were more likely to attempt and establish control over their female partners' behavior. Margarita, a sixteen-year-old female describes how her male partner became violent when she informed him of her decision to terminate the relationship: "At first he would never hit me or nothing. Then, like if I didn't want to have sex with him he would get mad. He would hit me and force me to have sex. If not he would get very angry." Margarita went on to explain that because of this behavior, she decided she was going to leave him:

> We were at his house, I decided I wanted to leave him [and told him]. When I was walking out he came running after me. He told me I wasn't going to leave him. I told him I was. He got mad and knocked me down and started banging my head on the concrete and choking me. He told me if I was going to leave him I was going to be dead.

The next day he showed up [at night] and he told me that he didn't want me to leave him. He pulled a gun to my head. He had one bullet in there. He turned the trigger and he shot it. [Nothing happened.] He was drunk. He fell asleep in the car [in front of my house]. I called the cops.

In this situation, Margarita was attempting to leave the abusive relationship. However, upon verbalizing her intentions to him, the physical violence and threatening behavior worsened, as evident in the narrative. In this incident, the boyfriend's coercive power to control Margarita upon her decision to end the relationship progressed from verbal threats to physical violence and ultimately to the very serious aggressive act of attempting to shoot her.

Control goes beyond forcing one's will on individuals in specific situations; instead it is part of a larger set of behaviors. Several instances revealed a dominant male partner wanting to dictate behavior in nearly all aspects of his girlfriend's life. Sandra's story illustrates this type of male-initiated control. She explains the most recent encounter with the man who is her ex-boyfriend and the father of her child:

It was around eleven thirty, I had just got off the bus. I was calling my mom to pick [my daughter and me] up at the pay phone and he saw us. He started screaming and telling me, "You're a slut, what are you doing out on the street?" He slapped me. I had the baby in my hands. I told him to leave me alone, I was gonna call the cops. I was trying to press 911. His friends got out of the car. They didn't do nothing to pull him away. I told him to leave me alone; I had my little girl with me. He's all, "So, she's my kid too." He swung at me but he hit [the child]. She fell to the floor. I got mad. I tried to get the phone to hit him in the head with it, but he grabbed it and hit me. I grabbed her and took off running to Church's [a fast-food restaurant]. I started banging on the thing [door] and they opened it. The guys came outside running after him from Church's and he took off. I called the ambulance and the cops.

Sandra explains how, while they are no longer together, her ex-boyfriend continues to attempt to impose his control over her. She states: "I guess he still thinks in his head that I'm still with him and that I belong to him since I have his kid. I belong to him and I'm only his. He happened to see me, and he just started telling me, 'Why are you with him [the new boyfriend]? He's a punk. You don't belong with him; you're mine.'

In this particular incident, the precursor of control was the primary motive for the violent social interaction between Sandra and her ex-boyfriend. While no longer seeing Sandra, the adolescent male attempted to exert his power and control over her by demanding to know why she was out. The physical violence was initiated immediately with a slap and a hit to both Sandra and her daughter. The violence escalated with Sandra attempting to defend herself by using the phone as a weapon, but in turn was victimized with it given the male's physical strength. In this situation, the control Sandra' s ex-boyfriend appears to be imposing is influenced by the fact that they have a daughter together. The daughter may explain the male's own justification for the physical violence. Finally, contrary to findings associated with the precursor of jealousy, the public nature of the incident may have further provoked the situation. That is, according to Sandra, at the time of the violent confrontation her ex-boyfriend was in the presence of male friends and two unidentified girls who shouted insults at her.

Findings also revealed female perpetrated violence was often associated with the precursor of control. For these females, however, this violence was distinct in that their motivations were associated more with emotional, rather than behavioral, control.

Araceli is a seventeen-year-old female whose family can be identified as *cholo*. As mentioned, these types of Mexican American families are characterized by generations of drug use, criminality, incarceration, and street connections among its members (Moore 1994). Araceli recounts the most recent argument with her boyfriend: "I started yelling at him because I bought him something for Valentine's. He said he was gonna buy this thing for me. I'm like, 'Where is it?' He didn't even buy it for me. I was like, 'Where's my fucking thing? Why didn't you give it to me?' I was hitting him in his stomach. Then I hit him on his face. I was just hitting him. I was mad. He grabbed my arms. I started kicking him. Then his brother pulled me back. His brother just held me back. He was bleeding from his mouth and his eye had a bruise. I think I broke one of his ribs." For Araceli, the fact that her boyfriend did not exchange gifts with her for Valentine's Day was the primary factor that motivated her to verbally instigate the argument. For an adolescent female in this type of relationship, the romanticism and emotional commitment often generates expectations that there will be an exchange of gifts such as teddy bears, flowers, and jewelry, which symbolize the importance of the relationship. Not receiving a Valentine's Day present from her boyfriend was perceived as a lack of commitment and confronting him about it was a form of emotional control.

Disrespect

Arguments initiated over disrespect are the most likely to occur in public or in the presence of others. This can often make the confrontations more volatile because the partner that is disrespected needs to "save face"—they need to maintain their image and identity in front of outsiders (Goffman 1959). Among the population studied, the most common confrontations associated with the precursor of disrespect were initiated by the females. For instance, Susana's experience illustrates how the disrespect she felt when she found out that her boyfriend of four years had been "playing her" led to an argument: "A week ago he was pushing me away from him [emotionally]. I would tell him, 'If you want me to leave, just let me know. Don't play me; don't hurt me; don't do nothing.' I go, 'You should be mature enough to know when to let go and when not to.' He was just, like ignoring me all the time and pushing me away until I got tired of it. When Susana decided she was going to leave him, the violence ensued. She says:

> I told him, "I'm leaving." I told him, "I'm going with my cousin just to get away from everything, and if I like it over there, I'm gonna stay over there." I was telling him. He was ignoring me, you know? I got all my stuff together. I went downstairs to use the phone. He threw the phone and pushed me. He told me, I wasn't gonna leave him. I told him. "I don't want to be with you." If he didn't leave me alone I was gonna call the cops. He took the phone off the hook. That's when he hit me. He threw me on the floor. He kicked my leg. His brother came in and his brother and him almost got into it because he hit me.

The precursor to the incident was motivated by Susana's boyfriend's lack of interest as demonstrated by his behavior (pushing her away and ignoring her). For Susana, this negative response toward her incited her verbal instigations. Susana acted upon her threat of leaving after her boyfriend ignored her. Her continued verbal instigations and actions were eventually counteracted by the physical violence of her boyfriend.

Other forms of disrespect could be characterized as intentional. Most of these cases appeared to happen when the individuals involved were reportly intoxicated. The following incident illustrates Rosa's confession of her sexual infidelity to her boyfriend while they were high on prescription pills at his parents' home. She says: "We were on Xanax, and I told him. Then he hit me [in the face]. I started calling [his parents] because he was going to hit me again. I kept calling them. His mom came in and started pushing him. She pushed him away and stopped him. I was walking out and his mom went and got me. She sat me down. She told me. 'Don't go near him.' She fixed up my eye. Later on that night he called me. He started crying and stuff. He's saying that he didn't realize what happened." The fact that they were under the influence of a controlled substance contributed to the physical altercation.

Other forms of disrespect reported by the female participants were less intentional. The following narrative illustrates a form of unintentional disrespect while under the influence. Tamara, a seventeen-year-old female, describes an argument that took place with her boyfriend Adam: "We went to a party together. I was drunk and he was a little tipsy. It was like two o'clock in the morning and we were all messed up. I had accidentally called him Joey, which is my ex. My other boyfriend before him. He was like, 'What?' I was like, 'Joey.' So, he hit me real hard in my face and it just busted my eye open. I started talking shit to him. I started kicking him and stuff. I know I kicked him out of the truck. Then he dragged me out of the truck. I was like scratching him by his face and stuff." The public context of the incident in which the misidentification occurred created an environment in which Tamara's boyfriend had to react, and in this situation violently, to the disrespect. Tamara's insistence in referring to him as "Joey" only instigated the interaction, which progressed into a violent confrontation that resulted in a serious injury. Given the medical attention Tamara required, the incident was reported to the police and charges were filed—but it was only one of a few violent confrontations in which the law was involved. Interestingly, Tamara dropped the charges, telling us that she had not wanted to have further altercations with Adam.

Cindy, a seventeen-year-old female, describes her relationship with her boyfriend and his constant demand for respect. According to Cindy, arguments are usually associated with her style of dress:

> Like he doesn't like when I get smart at him with a remark. He wants it to go his way but he won't see it my way. And he doesn't like it when I talk to him wrong. He feels that I disrespect him a lot. The last argument that we had he got upset because of my clothing. I'm the type of person who likes to fashion. Since I'm his girlfriend he feels that he thinks I show too much cleavage but I don't. I'm always covering up; at least, I wear a bra. And he thinks that I'm showing too much leg. He hates it when a guy looks at me.
>
> One day I was wearing a shirt and showing a little cleavage. He was telling me why don't I put something else over it? And why do you always have to wear stuff like that? He said I like to get the attention from other guys. And I'm like, "Shut up. If you don't like what I wear then why don't you buy me my clothes. I don't want to hear you say you don't like my clothes." I said, "This is how I was dressing right before we met and now you're telling me that you don't like it." He goes, "Well, now that you're

with me respect what I say." We started arguing. He then pushed me and started to call me names like you fucking bitch, you slut, you dress like a whore and all this stuff. So I slapped him and then he grabbed me and slapped me.

The female's interpretation of the style of dress as fashionable contrasted with that of the male, who viewed the style as sexually provocative and degrading. This incident illustrates how gendered values influence the interpretation and meaning of a specific behavior differently between genders—in this case, style of dress.

Conclusion

In this chapter I have attempted to understand the situational processes between the gang-affiliated females and their dating partners that contribute to the escalation of an argument to a physical violent confrontation. The chapter's unique contribution to the literature is that it focuses on dating violence among participants living in "dangerous" communities who are beyond risk or involved in delinquent activities (Miller and White 2003, 1244). Identifying situational precursors and instigations has allowed me to discover how gender expectations (social roles) shape the interpretation of a partner's behavior and gestures and escalate the argument into a violent confrontation. The data illustrate how the context (private or public) and the role of third parties attenuate or exacerbate the unfolding and outcome of the violent incident. Revealed is how differences in these microlevel interaction chains produce distinct variants in the ensuing violent events.

The chapter's findings suggest that even though these high-risk females seem to experience mostly common couple violence (less serious), they seem to have a higher prevalence level of violence than among more conventional groups. They may also be more vulnerable to more severe violent experiences than other female adolescents are but they are less likely to be victims of chronic battering than adults in the general population.

Urban youth street gangs vary in their organizational structure but most maintain a patriarchal hierarchy. Young women associated with these gangs—regardless of the nature of the association—have a subordinate role and often are the subject of sexual exploitation (Chesney-Lind and Sheldon 1992; Miller 1998; Miller 1975). The data presented in this study show how more intimate or personalized violence is triggered within the context of situations framed by gender. For instance, when these young women attempted to exercise independence in their relationships in such ways as going out with friends, the males often interpreted it as their losing control over the girls. Not being able to dominate their female partners challenged the socially structured male hierarchy, particularly within the male gang subculture with clearly defined gender roles. The chapter also showed the repercussions associated with girls who chose to contest the gender expectations of their environment and express or exercise their own agency.

Even jealousy on the part of the adolescent females studied may be interpreted as influenced by gender issues as it reveals the importance they place on their relationships. Hortensia Amaro discusses how lower-class minority females tend to place greater importance on the maintenance of relationships than do males (1995). She claims "that women's sense of personhood is grounded in the motivation to make and enhance relationships to others" (Amaro 1995). Given this, females in this study were more likely to demonstratively react to what they perceive as a threat to an emotional relationship or connection. For the women, this was often based on witnessed behavior (e.g., their partner flirting with another woman) or validated behavior, as opposed to men, whose jealousy was often based on suspicion.

This type of violence on the part of women is often interpreted as emotional or expressive as opposed to the men's violence, which is more rational or instrumental. The disruption of this connection is perceived not only as a loss of a relationship but also as something closer to total loss of self. Here we agree with Miller and White that this interpretation undermines the girl's more instrumental goals of challenging the inequalities of the relationship (2003).

Perceived disrespect as a precursor to violence is more embedded in situated activities and social context. Most situated factors are those outside the individual that influence the initiation, unfolding, or outcome of the event. In this regard, the individual's perception of disrespect is influenced by the values imposed by the cultural context of the neighborhood and community where residents are relatively confined to the local environment (Bauder 2002). But issues of disrespect are also associated with a youth subculture that is involved in street violence, drug use, crime, and confrontational attitudes toward authority. Specifically, the gang subculture is a consequence of a street socialization processes, often described as a "code of the streets," which emphasizes the development of collective and individual coping strategies that uses violence as a means of resolving conflicts (Vigil 1998; Anderson 1999).

When an individual in an intimate relationship perceives that he or she is disrespected by the other, the individual often responds in an aggressive and violent manner. As our data have shown, this is often the case when the disrespect takes place in a public setting and there is a "loss of face." The partner that has been disrespected will often attempt to "save face" (Goffman 1959), mostly because of the audience in the setting. In other words, the individual is engaging in a kind of damage control in order to protect his or her public image. However, violence with disrespect as a precursor evolves differently based on gender.

As shown in these data, men may be likely to physically react in public to what they interpret as disrespect, but they seem to be constrained in escalating the violence beyond pushing and grabbing because of the norm that men should not hit females. Miller and White found a similar normative structure among African American dating couples (2003). However, such constraints seem to break down when female-perpetrated violence gets out of control. In our study, bystanders associated with the female, such as friends or family, tended to deter the violence, but if they were associated with the male, they tended to escalate it. Females (and in some cases males) were more likely to have more serious injuries when fights took place in private with no third parties present especially if the female responded in self-defense to the male aggressor. Male-perpetrated violence instigated by the precursor of control was more likely to result in more serious injuries than other precursors.

This chapter has provided insight on how an argument may escalate through identifiable instigators into either a series of violent acts or one violent act that ends the incident. The data indicate that by prolonging the duration of the physical violent confrontation couples are susceptible to more serious injuries. This may be related to gender role socialization differences in communication and conflict-resolution styles. These differences result in males being more likely to use physical dominance and females being more likely to use verbal persuasion (Charlesworth and Dzur 1987). Nonetheless, as Harriet Douglas found, when an individual verbally attacks his or her partner with aims to diminish self-esteem, create feelings of vulnerability, and activate fears of rejection and abandonment, violence is often provoked (1991). Among this subculture of gang-related youth where norms governing interpersonal and institutional relationships are weak, the use of violence against women is more severe, especially because of the existence of these highly structured gender expectations.

Half of the incidents studied occurred while at least one of the parties was using drugs or alcohol. Males were commonly reported to have been drinking beer and using marijuana, cocaine, prescription pills, or some combination prior to the violent incident. But it was not uncommon for the female to have reported being "buzzed," or slightly high. As previously stated, it is difficult to isolate the effect that substance use has on partner violence in this subgroup of highly marginalized adolescents where using drugs and alcohol is normalized. There are many other social factors, as discussed throughout the chapter, that seem more salient in their contribution to this type of violence such as the role of third parties and whether the space is private or public. Nonetheless, these findings allow us to state that when either of the parties is "completely wasted" (high level of intoxication) the incident will have more serious consequences, especially for the female, given the gender dynamics discussed earlier.

Generally, the forms of partner violence described are less serious but more consistent than those found among adults. However, given this population's social and situational context, this violence may easily escalate and result in more severe consequences.

Chapter 8

Explaining Intimate-Partner Violence: Family, Drugs, and Psychosocial Factors

Introduction

The previous chapters have provided a primarily qualitative in-depth description of community, family, and individual-level factors that put the young women of the study beyond risk in that they are already engaged in substance use, delinquency, sexual and physical violence, and other health and social consequences. In this final chapter I explore distinct predictors in the victimization and perpetration of intimate-partner violence among the sample of young Mexican American females. This is done by presenting quantitative multilevel analyses models that will shed some light on developing a comprehensive understanding of intimate-partner violence. Specifically, the analysis will explore the role of the family, substance use, and psychosocial factors as important variables in explaining intimate-partner violence as measured by the Conflict Tactic Scale.

Conflict Tactics Scale: Measure of Intimate-Partner Violence

The Conflict Tactics Scale (CTS) is currently the most widely used measure of intimate-partner violence (Newton, Connelly, and Landsverk 2001; Cascardi et al. 1999; Strauss and Corbin 1990). The CTS is designed to measure both the extent to which partners in a dating, cohabitating, or marital relationship engage in psychological and physical attacks on each other and the extent of use of reasoning or negotiation to deal with conflicts (Straus et al. 1996). The CTS consists of five scales: negotiation, psychological aggression, physical assault, sexual coercion, and injury. The internal reliability of the CTS ranges from 0.79 to 0.95 and the scale's overall internal consistency coefficient is 0.79 (Molidor and Tolman 1998; Straus et al. 1996).

For the present analysis, participants were asked to report lifetime frequencies of any past dating violence and violence in their most recent or current dating relationships. All subscales except negotiation were used. Results—as well as alphas[1]—for each of the measures are reported separately for victimization and aggression. Subscale scores were treated as categorical variables in the analyses. For psychological aggression and physical assault, in both high-risk and low-risk groups, scores were dichotomized to determine whether a participant ever or never experienced psychological aggression or physical assault (yes/no). The "yes" answers were divided into two categories: high levels (above-average scores) and low levels (below-average scores) of violence. In multivariate analyses, scores for the physical assault question were collapsed into three categories: none, low level, and high level. For the sexual coercion question, scores were dichotomized to determine whether participants ever or never experienced sexual coercion (yes/no). For the injury question, subscale scores were dichotomized as whether the participant ever or never experienced injury.

Family Structure and Process

Although not the only factor, the family, as discussed previously, is believed to play a pivotal role in the evolution of behavioral problems among contemporary adolescents and young adults. Some researchers even argue that differences in family relations may be more important than even psychopathological factors in distinguishing levels of adolescents' behavioral problems such as acting out, unwillingness to follow rules, early sexual involvement, and chronic drug and alcohol use.

Previous studies have found that family process characteristics have been correlated with aggression and other serious criminal behaviors among children and adolescents (Sampson and Lauritsen 1994). These studies argued that quality of family relations (or processes) are more important than structure in emergence or absence of behavioral problems among adolescents (see Chapter 4).

We will explore the influence of family characteristics on violent offending and victimization among the studied group of Mexican

American females. Joan Moore, in her discussions on Mexican American families, identifies two major types (1990). She describes the first as "conventional"; the family adheres to more traditional characteristics associated with Mexican American families (Alvirez, Bean, and Willams 1981; Williams 1990). Moore identifies families more associated with the street life of the barrio such as addicts, criminals, and gang members as "unconventional," or *cholo* families, as discussed earlier in this book. We expect that the gang-affiliated females more associated with the *cholo* families have participated in more aggressive and violent behavior more so than those from conventional families.

Family Process Variables

Family process variables were focused on measuring the familys' involvement in criminality, substance use, and family violence. Two predictors focused on participants' relatives' participation in criminal activities: the participants were asked whether they had relatives who participated in criminal activity (yes/no). Also they were asked if they had close family relatives who participated in criminal activities, coded into parents or siblings (1) versus others (0). Family substance use was measured using a variable (yes/no) to signify having a relative with a drinking or drug problem at some time during the participants' childhood. Three family violence measures were used and coded (into yes/no), including whether the participant had a sibling involved in a violent relationship, parents involved in serious arguments, or parents involved in physical fights. Lastly, a parental involvement index was created that ranged from zero to five. The five items asked about the respondents' parents' participation in school activities including whether they were involved in PTA meetings, open house, athletic events, school fairs, and teacher conferences. The index was further coded into high (0 = 3 to 5 events) and low (1 = 0 to 2 events) participation.

Family Process Variables and CTS Analysis

Table 8.1 reports the percentage and frequency (n) of the family process predictor variables. Thirty percent of the high-risk participants had relatives who participated in criminal activities. More than 61 percent of these relatives were part of the participant's nuclear family. Thirty-six percent had a relative with a drinking problem and 18 percent had a relative with a drug problem. Eighty-four percent of the group had a violent relationship with a sibling. Half of the participants' parents engaged in physical fights and 34 percent had serious arguments. The predictors also included a low-parental-involvement variable.

Findings for the perpetration and victimization models of the family process predictors among the adolescent female group are presented in Table 8.2. High levels of physical assault perpetration were weakly related to having a relative with a drinking problem and low parental involvement. The sexual coercion model explains that low parental involvement and not having a close relative who participates in criminal activities are significant predictors, as are parents who do not engage in physical fights and relatives with drinking problems.

Perpetration of injury was weakly but positively related to having a relative with a drug problem, a relative who participates in criminal activities, and parents with low levels of involvement. Having a relative with a drug problem was significantly and positively related to the perpetration of psychological aggression. In addition, psychological aggression was weakly related to having a close relative who participates in criminal activities.

Table 8.1   Family Process Predictor Variables

Variable	Percentage (n)
Any relative with criminal activities	30 (45)
Close family relatives with criminal activities (% of any relatives)	61 (91)
Relative with a drinking problem	36 (54)
Relative with a drug problem	18 (27)
Sibling with a violent relationship	84 (126)
Parents who participated in serious arguments	34 (51)
Parents who participated in physical fights	55 (83)
Low parental involvement	60 (90)

For victimization, the analysis of the family process predictors produced physical assault as the best predictor for these girls. High levels of physical assault victimization were significantly and positively related to having a relative with a drug problem and low parental involvement. Trends were also seen for whether a participant had or did not have a relative who participated in criminal activities. Victimization of sexual coercion was associated with low parental involvement, and having a relative involved in criminal activities. Interestingly, if the young woman had a close relative (e.g., sibling or parent) who was involved in criminal activities the relationship was inversed, in that she would be less likely to be a victim of sexual coercion.

Table 8.2 Estimates and Odds Ratios ( ) of the Effects of Family Process Variables on the Perpetration and Victimization of Violent Outcomes

Family Process Predictors	Perpetration					Victimization				
	Psychological Aggression	Physical Assault[1] High	Low	Sexual Coercion	Injury	Psychological Aggression	Physical Assault[1] High	Low	Sexual Coercion	Injury
Relative with criminal activities	-.717+ (.488)				.684+ (1.98)		.947+ (.388)		.939* (2.55)	.894+ (2.44)
Close relative with criminal activities		-.960* (.383)	-.690+ (.501)	-.881+ (2.41)	-.992* (.371)	-.831* (.436)				
Relative with a drinking problem	.840+ (.432)	.628+ (1.87)								
Relative with a drug problem	1.06** (2.89)	8.96+ (2.45)	.982* (2.67)	1.34* (.260)						
Sibling with a violent relationship	.751+ (2.11)									
Parents with serious arguments										
Parents with physical fights	-.623+ (.536)	.798* (2.22)	.599+ (1.82)							
Low parental involvement	.698+ (.498)			1.34** (.261)	.812* (2.25)					
Model R^2	.090	.138		.124	.101	.075	.160		.114	.081

Note. Standardized estimates *** p < .00. ** p< .01. * p < .05. + p < .15
[1] For the predictor Physical Assault, the categories were high and low or none

Injury victimization was explained by having a relative who participated in criminal activities and a sibling in a violent relationship. A negative and weak relationship was observed between injury victimization and having a close relative involved with criminal activities. Psychological-aggression was the least effective in explaining violent victimization. Having a relative with a drug problem and not having a close relative involved with criminal activities meant a greater likelihood of being a victim of psychological aggression.

Substance Use

Adolescent girls who abuse substances are more likely to engage in violent behavior (Dougherty 1999). For instance, existing research suggests that substance use is a major correlate of intimate-partner violence. Many studies have found that alcohol plays a prominent role in incidents of intimate-partner violence and is implicated more than the use of other substances (Fishbein and Pease 1996; McNeece and DiNitto 1998). The role illicit drugs play in intimate-partner violence is not as clear. Some studies find higher levels of serious physical assault when the perpetrator uses illicit drugs (see Fishbein and Pease 1996), while others find no direct relationship between the serious assault and drug use (see Singleton and Grady 1996). In general, there appears to be a disinhibition effect associated with the use of alcohol or drugs, which promotes violence. It should be noted that there is virtually no information on substance use and adolescent girls as perpetrators of intimate-partner violence because the problem has been considered almost exclusively a problem of young males (Harway and Liss 1999).

Family members play a crucial role in the presence of substance use and violence as well as in their prevention. Research has consistently found that living in a nonnuclear, disrupted family contributes to adolescent problematic behaviors including violence and drug use (Ellickson and Hays 1992; Ellickson, Collins, and Bell 1999; Ellickson and McGuigan 2000). However, research has also found that female adolescents raised by single mothers consider their mothers significant and enduring sources of support (Gavin and Furman 1996; Furman and Buhrmester 1992). Consistent with the centrality of family for Hispanic populations, Hispanic adolescents identify stressful family situations and poor communication with parents as being the most difficult life events occurring since entering high school (Kobus and Reyes 2000; Alva and Jones 1994; Alva 1995). Notably among Hispanic adolescent females, stressful family situations have more negative impact than the combined stressors occurring with friends, in school, or in other personal domains. Family members, especially mothers, have been identified as those most frequently sought to provide support and help cope with the stress Hispanic adolescents experience (Kobus and Reyes 2000). Here I focus on determining the relationship of illicit drug and alcohol use to sexual and intimate-partner violence among the gang-affiliated Mexican American females and their gang-member partners or relatives.

Substance Use Variables

The alcohol and illegal drug use independent variable was created using a composite measure of thirteen substances, including alcohol. These substances were coded as "1" if the respondent used it or "0" if they did not use it in the last thirty days. Whether a participant had ever been arrested was chosen as one of the substance use related indicators. It was assumed that a large proportion of arrests in the studied population were drug related or were indirectly related to drugs. Being expelled from school was also chosen as an indicator. The San Antonio Independent School District (SAISD) Code of Student Conduct expulsion policy cites specific substance-related behaviors as grounds for mandatory or discretionary expulsion (San Antonio Independent School District 2002). Mandatory expulsion occurs when the student "engages in behavior related to an alcohol or drug offense that could be punishable as a felony" (Article 91) and discretionary expulsion occurs when the student sells, gives, possesses, or uses either drugs (Article 93) or alcohol (Article 94). It was believed that many of the reported expulsions were directly or indirectly related to the violation of the substance provisions of the code. Also included in the study was whether the respondent lived only with her mother (single-female-headed household). This variable was chosen as a social predictor because of the importance of the relationship between an adolescent female and her mother and because of the impact of living in a nonnuclear, disrupted family on adolescent females.

Substance Use Variables and CTS Analysis

Table 8.3 presents the percentage and frequency distributions of substance use related predictor variables for the female associates of gangs. Over two-thirds of the group used alcohol or drugs frequently when socializing. About one-fifth had used alcohol in the past forty-eight hours and over half in the previous thirty days. An even higher percentage (66 percent) had used illicit drugs in the previous thirty days. Over half of the group had gotten into trouble from drinking or drug use.

About half of the group reported having been under the influence of substances in their last fight and had a boyfriend who had both a high-risk drug use index and had been arrested. Over two-fifths of the sample used substances while alone and almost as high a proportion were involved in selling illicit drugs. Almost one-fourth of the group reported the use of heroin at some point in their lives and had been on substances the last time they had sex. They had frequently gotten into trouble because of these substances, but continued to be involved in drug sales as well as fights and sexual encounters where substances were used.

In Table 8.4, the effects of substance use related variables on the perpetration and victimization of sexual and intimate-partner violence for young females are displayed. The models as a whole performed well in predicting the perpetration and victimization of violence in this group. This indicates, in general, that substance-related variables make a significant contribution to understanding the problem of sexual and intimate-partner violence in the lives of these gang-affiliated young women.

Table 8.3 Substance-Related Predictor Variables

Variable	Percentage (n)
In the last violent gang incident, the people who fought were drinking or on drugs when fight happened	49 (73)
Used alcohol in the last 48 hours	20 (30)
Ever used heroin by itself	24 (36)
Drink alcohol and/or use drugs while alone	41 (62)
Gotten in trouble because of drinking or drug use	57 (86)
Use alcohol or drugs frequently when socializing	69 (103)
Involved in selling drugs	38 (57)
On drugs/alcohol when they last had sex	23 (35)
Ever arrested	49 (74)
Used alcohol in the last 30 days	51 (77)
Used illegal drugs in the last 30 days	66 (99)
Boyfriend drug-use risk index	49 (73)

The use of heroin was the strongest predictor in the perpetration of high levels of physical assault. Also influencing the perpetration of high levels of physical assault were the presence of substance use in the last fight the participant had been in, her use of alcohol in the previous forty-eight hours, whether she had ever been arrested, and her boyfriend's drug-use risk index score. For the perpetration of low levels of physical assault, whether the participant had gotten in trouble for substance use was the key variable. The model predicting victimization of both high

Table 8.4 Estimates and Odds Ratios ( ) of Effects of Substance-Related Variables on The Perpetration and Victimization of Violent Outcomes

Family Process Predictors	Perpetration					Victimization				
	Psychological Aggression	Physical Assault[1] High	Physical Assault[1] Low	Sexual Coercion	Injury	Psychological Aggression	Physical Assault[1] High	Physical Assault[1] Low	Sexual Coercion	Injury
In the last violent gang incident, the people who fought drinking or on drugs when fight happened		.990[+-] (.371)	1.28* (.277)	.848* (2.33)			1.16+ (.312)			
Used alcohol in the last 48 hours		1.34+ (.250)			1.41** (4.10)			1.79* (.167)		.772+ (2.16)
Ever used heroine by itself		1.68* (.186)			.831+ (2.30)		2.30*** (.101)			.745+ (2.11)
Drink alcohol &/or use drugs by yourself, alone								-1.96** (7.11)		
Gotten in trouble from drinking or drug use			-1.71** (5.54)		.857* (2.36)					.710+ (2.03)
Use alcohol or drugs frequently, when socializing	.740+ (2.10)			1.49*** (4.43)			1.13+ (.323)	1.04+ (.355)	1.55** (4.73)	

(continued)

Table 8.4 Estimates and Odds Ratios ( ) of Effects of Substance-Related Variables on The Perpetration and Victimization of Violent Outcomes *(continued)*

Family Process Predictors	Perpetration					Victimization				
	Psychological Aggression	Physical Assault¹		Sexual Coercion	Injury	Psychological Aggression	Physical Assault¹		Sexual Coercion	Injury
		High	Low				High	Low		
Involved in selling drugs	-1.47*** (.231)						-1.18* (3.27)	-1.33* (3.76)	-.832+ (.435)	
On drugs/alcohol when they last had sex						-.740+ (.477)	-1.06+ (2.89)			
Have been arrested	.709+ (2.03)		.773+ (.462)	.600+ (1.82)	.815* (2.26)		1.09* (.338)	.915+ (.401)		.834* (2.32)
Used alcohol in the last 30 days										.801+ (2.23)
Used illegal drugs in the last 30 days						-1.02+ (.359)				
Boyfriend drug use risk	.623+ (.536)		-.824+ (2.28)					-.750+ (2.12)		
Model R²	.230	.396		.173	.288	.142	.388		.199	.270

Note. Standardized estimates *** *p* < .00. ** *p* < .01. * *p* < .05. + *p* < .15
¹ *For the predictor Physical Assault, the categories were high and low or none*

and low levels of physical assault showed similar pathways. Again the use of heroin was the strongest predictor and having been arrested was also significant for victimization of high levels of physical assault. The variable substance use involvement in the last fight the participant had been in was a weak predictor. In contrast to the perpetration model, victimization of both high and low levels of physical assault was related to involvement with the selling of drugs. The participant's use of substances frequently while socializing was weakly related to both levels of victimization of physical assault and the participant's use of substances while she was alone was significantly related only to low levels. This pathway was not indicated in the perpetration model.

Similar to physical assault, injury showed common and distinctive pathways for perpetration and victimization of sexual and intimate-partner violence. A strong, positive influence of the participant having ever been arrested could be seen. Perpetration of injury was strongly influenced by alcohol use in the last forty-eight hours and victimization of injury a weaker influence of the same variable. Getting in trouble because of substance use functioned similarly. Whether the subject had ever used heroin was weakly related to both the victimization and perpetration of injury. The differences between the models were in the positive and significant relationship of the use of substances in the participant's last fight for the perpetration of injury, which could not be seen in the victimization of injury model. A weak relationship between the use of alcohol in the previous thirty days and injury victimization was observed that did not appear in the injury model perpetration.

In the perpetration and victimization of sexual coercion models, frequent use of substances while socializing was seen as a highly significant predictor. The difference between perpetration and victimization of sexual coercion was less important in the models. For perpetration, the participant's history of having been arrested had a weak positive effect, while for victimization of sexual coercion, her selling of drugs had a weak negative effect.

The perpetration of psychological aggression was negatively associated with the young girl being on drugs or alcohol during the previous sexual encounter. However, weak positive effects were observed for substance use when socializing and the boyfriend's drug-use risk index. The reasons for such aggressive behavior could be many, as described in the earlier chapter on the situational factors influencing the instigation of violence. Victimization of psychological aggression was weakly associated with the use of substances the last time the participant had sex, and the use of illegal drugs in the previous thirty days.

Childhood Trauma, Psychological Distress, and Intimate-Partner Violence

The experience of severe childhood trauma has been implicated in the development of significant psychological distress and later-life. This is similarly found among Hispanics even though they are often portrayed as having a family-centered culture. Chronic and severe trauma during a period in which coping skills are acquired, when assumptions about the self and the world are formed, can have severe implications for the social and psychological maturation of children (Briere 1992). The interrelationship between psychological development and trauma has been evidenced by victims of abuse who exhibit an array of psychological and emotional problems in adulthood. It is believed that repetitive trauma can damage the individual's sense of self and cause severe identity problems. Experiences of chronic trauma in children are hypothesized to cause severe changes in emotional and somatic states that may be enduring (Herman 1993).

Revictimization is the experience of both childhood sexual abuse and sexual or physical abuse as an adult. A number of studies have recently confirmed this relationship (see Irwin 1999). In one study it was found that 56 percent of female victims of childhood sexual abuse had also encountered unwanted sexual contact in adulthood (Wyatt, Guthrie, and Notgrass 1992). Charles Whitfield and his colleagues, in a study of over eight thousand participants, found that the risk of victimization or perpetration of intimate-partner violence doubled if violent childhood experiences were reported (2003). In another study of intimate-partner violence, depression was strongly associated with victimization and perpetration of intimate-partner violence among women and men (Anderson 2002). This is an important finding in that few previous studies addressed the issue of gender symmetry in the perpetration and victimization of partner violence. Finally, Jacqueline Golding, in a meta-analysis of over forty intimate-partner violence research studies, found that intimate-partner violence increased the risk of mental health problems (1999).

Another study found that the characteristics of abuse have a significant impact on adult psychopathology (Wind and Silvern 1994). This study of 259 female university staff members indicated that the severity of abuse was linked to unfavorable outcomes in adult psychological functioning. The dimensions of duration, frequency, and emotional significance of abuse were connected with adult mental dysfunction. Empirical evidence suggests that women who have experienced sexual abuse are more vulnerable to adult sexual victimization and intimate-partner violence. John Briere notes that a clinical sample of women with a history of childhood sexual abuse were physically assaulted at a higher rate (49 percent) than women who had not been sexually victimized as children (18 percent) (1984). A more recent study, utilizing a community-based sample, found that women who were sexually abused as children were more likely to experience sexual victimization and/or to be abused by an intimate partner than a studied sample of women who were not abused. Child maltreatment and abuse have recently been found to be a significant risk factor for dating violence among adolescents (Wolfe et al. 2001). In summary, among adults, research is clear that early childhood trauma, revictimization, "intimate-partner violence," and mental heath problems are strongly correlated, although causal pathways appear less well studied.

While the study of childhood trauma and its impact on adult development have gained much research attention over the past two decades, very little is known regarding the psychological and social consequences of childhood trauma among Mexican Americans, and even less is known about the impact on adolescents and their development. In this study, we investigate the relationship between reported childhood trauma—both physical and emotional—and its relationship to mental health problems (depression), family and cultural stress, and intimate-partner violence among the adolescent females.

Childhood trauma was considered important in this analysis as it is represented in the literature as an etiologic factor in the development of many individual emotional, behavioral, and personality problems. This variable might be considered temporally distal while the two additional psychological variables could be considered proximal and related to recently appraised stress and current feeling of psychological distress and depression. In addition, we were interested to know how predictive these variables would be along with the Plutchick Feelings & Acts of Violence (PFAV) measure for violence propensity of three dimensions of intimate-partner violence—physical assault, psychological assault, and injury. Logistic regression analyses examine violence perpetration and, as with other logistic regressions conducted for this study, two control variables—age and family income status (Aid to Families with Dependent Children [AFDC])—were first entered into the equation.

Psychosocial Variables

This analysis used standardized questionnaire data taken from the Childhood Trauma Questionnaire (CTQ). Current levels of psychological distress were measured by the Center for Epidemiologic Studies Scale

(CES-D) and violence measures included the Plutchik PFAV scale and the Strauss Conflict Tactic Scale (CTS-2).

Childhood Trauma Questionnaire (CTQ)

The CTQ is a self-report measure consisting of twenty-eight items. The scale is a Likert with five points that has been validated on both adolescent and adult populations. There are five subscales: physical abuse/neglect, emotional abuse/neglect, and sexual abuse. Internal consistency reliability estimates for each subscale were calculated and found to be satisfactory for both populations. The high-risk CTQ scales for emotional abuse (alpha = 0.818), physical abuse (0.874), sexual abuse (0.930), and emotional neglect (0.851) had a high reliability. A moderate reliability was found on the physical neglect scale (0.540). A similar pattern was observed for the low-risk scales with emotional abuse (alpha = 0.787), physical abuse (0.743), sexual abuse (0.917), and emotional neglect (0.834) having high reliability and a moderate alpha for physical neglect scale (0.393).

Plutchick Feelings and Acts of Violence Scale (PFAV)

The PFAV is a self-report standardized questionnaire intended to measure the risk of engaging in violence based on past violent behavior, use of weapons, and feelings of anger (Plutchik and van Praag 1990). Measurement of these factors is based on eleven items with a four-point Likert scale ranging from "never" to "very often" and a twelve-item with a "yes/no" response category. Reliability for the PFAV in this study was 0.85.

Center for Epidemiological Studies Depression Scale (CESD)

The CESD is a twenty-item scale designed for self-reporting depression symptoms. Respondents are asked to supply the frequency of various emotions they experienced during the week prior to the administration of the instrument. This instrument has been validated among many different populations, including Hispanics and adolescents (Radloff 1991). Reliability for this sample was found to be satisfactory (alpha = 0.89).

Psychosocial Variables and CTS Analysis

As seen in Table 8.5, the females had rates of intimate-partner violence, both as victims and perpetrators. Among the young females, nearly 40 percent reported being involved in an intimate-partner relationship where they experienced physical assault. They also were classified as having higher rates of family stress, feelings of violence, and depression, as well as reporting much higher rates of various types of childhood trauma and abuse.

Table 8.5 Perpetration and Victimization Dimensions and Psychological Predictor Variables

Variables	Percentage (n)
Perpetration	
Psychological Aggression[1]	65 (96)
Physical Assault High	46 (65)
Low	34 (48)
None	21 (30)
Sexual Coercion	48 (68)
Injury	45 (63)
Victimization	
Psychological Aggression[1]	58 (85)
Physical Assault High	39 (56)
Low	33 (47)
None	29 (41)
Sexual Coercion	62 (88)
Injury	45 (63)
Predictors	
PFAV	81 (121)
Family Stress	57 (85)
Physical Abuse	27 (40)
Sexual Abuse	35 (52)
Emotional Abuse	33 (49)
Emotional Neglect	21 (31)
Physical Neglect	30 (44)
High Levels of Depression	70 (104)

[1] For the psychological-aggression predictor, the categories were high and low or none

Unique patterns of predictors were found for the perpetration of violence variable. As seen in Table 8.6, the psychological variables were most predictive of the perpetration of physical assault. CES-D depression was a significant predictor, as was family stress and cultural conflict from the Hispanic Stress Inventory. Family stress was also a significant predictor of low levels of physical assault. The single most important predictive psychological variable was family stress. Perpetration of sexual coercion was not predicted by the psychological variables in the logistic regression model. The psychological variables did not predict perpetration of physical injury related to intimate-partner violence. For the violent-victimization dimension, logistic regression analysis was again conducted for the three dimensions of intimate-partner violence.

Table 8.6 Estimates and Expected Beta (Exp. B) of Effects of Psychometric Variables on the Perpetration and Victimization of Violent Outcomes

Family Process Predictors	Perpetration					Victimization				
	Psychological Aggression	Physical Assault[1] High	Low	Sexual Coercion	Injury	Psychological Aggression	Physical Assault[1] High	Low	Sexual Coercion	Injury
High Levels of Depression		1.42** (.240)					1.41** (.243)			.938* (2.55)
Emotional Abuse						.854+ (2.35)				
Sexual Abuse										
Physical Abuse						-1.39*** (.247)	1.56* (4.76)	2.432*** (11.38)		
Emotional Neglect										
Physical Neglect										.948* (2.58)
Family Stress	.679+ (1.97)	1.32* (.267)	1.615** (.199)		.671+ (1.95)		1.04* (.352)	1.08* (.338)		
Feelings & Acts of Violence								.933+ (.393)		.814+ (2.25)
Model R^2	.083	.335			.103					

Note. Standardized estimates *** $p < .00$. ** $p < .01$. * $p < .05$. + $p < .15$. controlling for age and grade in school

[1] For the predictor Physical Assault, the categories were high and low or none

Only high levels of emotional abuse and physical abuse were found to be significant predictors for psychological aggression.

High levels of CES-D depression, physical abuse, and family stress were significant predictors of high levles of physical assault victimization. Low levels of physical assault were predicted by physical abuse, family stress, and risk of engaging in violence (PFAV). None of the psychological variables in the logistic regression analysis predicted sexual coercion victimization. Injury was predicted by CES-D depression, physical neglect, and PFAV.

Conclusions

Family Process

One of the important findings from this analysis is that gang-affiliated females experience high levels of intimate-partner violence. More specifically, on a structural level, high-risk girls' families correspond to Moore's *cholo*, or street-oriented, family in which family members not only engaged in illicit activity but also failed to control their children. Although not presented here, over half of these girls were born to women under twenty years old. Their families tended to live in unconventional settings with persons other than their parents, nearly half of the girls were on some form of federal assistance, and most of the girls lived in households where more than three adults resided and more than five persons, including children, lived. Typically, this meant that the participants were either living with grandparents, other relatives, or friends in overcrowded homes in a serial residential pattern, that is, they moved from one household to another. These social and ecological conditions contributed to the higher-risk behaviors and negative outcomes experienced by these girls.

The process predictable variables used in the analysis are comprised of a constellation of factors associated with Moore's description of *cholo* families. These variables include subjects' relatives involved in criminal activities, family drug and alcohol problems, witnessing parents in physical fights, and violent relationships with siblings and others. This group of young women had high frequencies on these variables, especially compared to the general population of adolescent females. The variable that proved to be more consistent across the different dimensions of perpetration was low parental involvement, a process variable found to be important in other adolescent studies (see Jessor and Jessor 1977; Santisteban et al. 1996). The only statistically significant variable in the subjects' perpetration was whether they had a relative with a drug problem. This is consistent with previous studies that demonstrate the vulnerability of adolescents with parents with substance abuse problems (Barrera, Li, and Chassin 1993).

Significant predictors of victimization—especially for physical assault, sexual coercion, and psychological aggression—were slightly more numerous. As expected, those variables that indicated serious "family process" problems were more predictive of violent dimensions. A strong predictor for two of the violent victimization measures was low parental involvement. This is consistent with earlier studies that found parental neglect in the form of either lack of supervision or personal involvement in daily life associated with aggression among adolescents (Loeber and Stouthamer-Loeber 1986).

Substance Use

The use of substances forms an important part of the lives of the girls in general. As we have seen in the model, predicting victimization of psychological aggression is associated with the temporary nonuse of substances both in general and in sexual encounters. There seems to be much psychological peer pressure on the girls to use drugs or suffer the psychological consequences. Studies of Mexican American adolescent marijuana use in San Antonio have contributed to the theory of peer susceptibility to explain those who initiate use and those who do not (Codina et al. 1998). This process of peer pressure is consistent with our finding that these San Antonio girls frequently got into trouble because of these substances, but still continued to be involved in drug sales and substance use that leads to fights and sexual encounters.

This substance-related maladaptive behavior pattern suggests that for many of these girls, a serious substance abuse problem exists that is, in almost all cases, neither diagnosed nor treated. The finding that one quarter of the sample used heroin evidences this. In addition, 38 percent were involved in selling drugs and almost 49 percent had boyfriends who used heroin and/or cocaine.

Our findings point to a number of specific pathways in which substance use led to the outcomes of sexual and intimate-partner violence. In predicting both high and low levels of the perpetration of physical assault, alcohol use in the previous thirty days provided the principle pathway. However, the effect was weak and maladaptive behavior played a more important role in explaining physical assault. The role of alcohol in predicting victimization was even more pervasive, as it functioned as a significant predictor across all dimensions of violence, with the exception of sexual coercion.

While the use of alcohol was not associated with sexual coercion, the use of drugs in the previous thirty days was the principle pathway to perpetration of sexual coercion. This perpetration of sexual coercion involved the subject's frequent use of substances while socializing. This variable was also the main significant predictor for the victimization of sexual assault. Substances were involved in almost half of the last violent gang fights engaged in by the girls. This variable was significantly and positively related to the prediction of injury. However, as with several other drug variables, the effect was paradoxical in other violence outcomes. Negative associations with the perpetration and victimization of physical assault were observed. The use of heroin was negatively associated with perpetration and victimization of physical assault although it had a positive impact with the perpetration and victimization of injury. The paradoxical effect of heroin seems to be related to both its pharmacological and "economic-compulsive" and "systemic" effects (Goldstein 1985). In certain situations the depressive pharmacological effect of this opioid drug would inhibit physical assault and tend to make the user avoid situations of physical assault. However, in a situation where avoidance behavior may not be possible (for example, when one is compulsively in search of money for drugs or is dealing in drugs), injury will probably be more likely to occur (Goldstein 1985).

Childhood Trauma, Psychological Distress, and Intimate-Partner Violence

The psychosocial measures demonstrate that Mexican American adolescent females affiliated with delinquent youth gangs show significant early childhood physical, emotional, and sexual trauma. Furthermore, the young girls showed other patterns of disturbance in the functioning of their families in their adolescence, and in their abilities to reduce and cope with conflict related to cultural dynamics (stress). They were also much more prone to report a variety of psychological symptomatology at the time of the study. The young females reported high levels of affective symptoms of depression, stress, general irritability, feelings of sadness, and frequent tearfulness and crying. In addition to the actual experience and unresolved conflicts related to early childhood trauma, current family dysfunction, culturally based stress, and psychological symptoms during the adolescent years are likely to have negative consequences on healthy and age-appropriate adolescent development. Such females, gone untreated, will likely continue to experience poor peer relationships, continued family conflicts, and cultural identity conflict as they move into early adulthood. As noted in our review of the study many of the young females will go on to have unhealthy relationships involving revictimization and intimate-partner violence.

Consistent with existing literature, the young females demonstrated a very strong relationship between early childhood abuse and trauma and adolescent experience with intimate-partner violence. This "revictimization" phenomenon as reported by investigators (see Golding 1999) also appeared to occur in younger Mexican American females in our findings. For the sample of females in this book the psychological variables were also predictive of involvement in intimate-partner violence during their adolescence.

Of particular interest are the specific ways in which perpetration and victimization of violence are predicted. The results of this study suggest that physical abuse in early childhood may result in young women seeking out partners who are both psychologically aggressive (verbally hostile, insulting, and degrading) as well as partners who are physically abusive. Family-systems theorists explain these phenomena by suggesting that children learn and adapt to abusive parents and may have few other frames of reference with which to enter into new relationships during adolescence and adulthood (Henggeler et al. 1993). The data from this study suggests that females who were physically abused in childhood might have unconsciously sought destructive intimate-partner relationships.

Furthermore, these results indicate that the perpetration of violence among the sample of females was best predicted by family stress and high levels of depression in adolescence and not by early childhood trauma or abuse. As a result, psychological distress and family-related stressors placed these gang-affiliated females at greater risk for perpetrating physical assault and violence in intimate-partner relationships. This is an important distinction as few studies have actually examined the relationship between perpetration and victimization and intimate partner violence.

Notes

1. Psychological aggression: alpha for perpetrator = 0.78; alpha for victim = 0.80
    Physical assault: alpha for perpetrator = 0.82; alpha for victim = 0.91
    Sexual coercion: alpha for perpetrator = 0.78; alpha for victim = 0.65
    Injury: alpha for perpetrator = 0.72; alpha for victim = 0.71

Chapter 9

Conclusion

In this book I have used a multilevel approach to better understand the nature and extent of intimate violence in a highly susceptible segment of the American population, urban minority gang-associated adolescent females. Findings reveal that females residing in this social environment fail to internalize conventional norms, values, expectations, and behaviors. Instead, they develop norms and values that are adaptive to the social-structural conditions of their communities that further increase their probability of engaging in high-risk behaviors such as sexual and physical violence. What I have emphasized is that in this social setting—isolated from the larger, fragile institutional order—resolving conflicts with violence has become normative. Such circumstances place the adolescent girls *beyond risk* for behaviors that have more deleterious consequences than for other females in more conventional social environments.

Institutional Completeness

The behavior described throughout this book occurs within a community characterized by low levels of "institutional completeness" in entities such as the economy, family, education, and government. San Antonio's West Side is a community lacking in strong extended families, residential stability, home ownership, jobs, and functional schools. Furthermore, there is weak governmental representation and services and capital investments in these neighborhoods. These institutions are what comprise the social fabric of most communities and their absence in the West Side contributes to social disorganization and the lack of a community structure and the community's sense of identification. The environment interacts with historical processes that stem from belief systems, lifestyles, symbols, and practices of this group. This creates a social environment where risk behaviors as described in this book are modeled, reproduced, and reinforced by the subjects of this study.

The absence of viable institutions in the West Side during the last two decades has coincided with the economic restructuring that transformed the job market and reduced pools of low-wage labor available to unskilled Mexican American workers. During this period, the city became the second poorest in the nation, with nearly a quarter of its population living in poverty. Having a job did not necessarily mean you were able to escape poverty, as over a quarter of the population employed remained below the poverty line. These economic changes exacerbated the inequality and, as a by-product, exacerbated poverty, joblessness, and welfare dependency in these urban minority neighborhoods. As an adaptation to these structural realities, certain segments of low-income minority communities chose to participate in sectors of the informal economy, including participation in street gangs.

For most teenagers in mainstream society, school is a major topic of conversation because it is the core of their social networks. However, for the young women in this study—whose networks involve male gang members who are often older, unemployed dropouts—school is not the center of their activities. This is the case for their relationships to other institutions as well. It seems that institutions are only dealt with among this population when there is problem. The institutions are not seen as resources that can assist them in their lives, as they are provided by the middle class. For instance, their relationships with the public schools often result in reprimands from school authorities, court appearances, and possible fines and incarceration. For parents, no news from the schools about their children is interpreted as good news. This is just the opposite of what is expected by middle-class parents who consider finishing high school an essential earmark of their child's education.

The families' role in the lives of these girls is distinct from those in other Hispanic groups. It has generally been argued that the Mexican American family protects its members through its support structure and close-knit family systems and community networks. The behavior of these adolescent females' families reveal how they attempt to fulfill their family obligations; they are seriously hindered, however, by drug and alcohol abuse, incarceration, scarce resources, and lack of institutional support. In these volatile situations, family members' frustration and anger often leads to interpersonal violence, which puts the young women at risk for victimization and perpetration.

In light of these violent behaviors, practitioners may be inclined to pay less attention to these seemingly dysfunctional families and, in the process, limit the positive contribution that families can have on problematic behavior. However, the findings of this study indicate that even within these families there are values that can be nurtured that will promote prosocial behaviors among problematic female adolescents. For instance, one of the most intriguing findings in this book is the importance of the quality of the specific mother-daughter relationship as mediating violent outcomes. The quality of the mother-daughter relationship is associated with the risk of being a victim of psychological and physical violence and the experience of injury from such violence. Without good quality relationships with their mothers, adolescent females are found to develop identities that employ alternative coping mechanisms that lead to antisocial behaviors. This finding supports research indicating that a supportive mother-daughter relationship plays a critical positive role in managing risk factors for the adolescent female (Debold et al. 1999).

Personal and Peer Risk Networks

As was previously indicated, this population's behaviors occur within an impoverished community context where resources are scarce and institutions such as the family provide limited support for conventional life trajectories. This is further magnified given that these females' relationships with peers and intimate partners facilitate the levels of involvement in antisocial behaviors. First, however, I need to reiterate that these young women are involved in day-to-day behaviors that place them at-risk. This is evident in the prevalence of self-reported delinquency, substance use, and early sexual behaviors. These behaviors are compounded by the negative influences male gang members have on these adolescent females. The risk behaviors and negative consequences are not merely the result of individual characteristics, but are primarily determined by the young women's embeddedness in a structure of peer relationships. The social networks of these females can be clearly designated as "risk networks" insofar as they function to support and facilitate their high-risk behavior. These risk networks work to normalize violence in the lives of these young women and tend to isolate them from secondary community institutions such as schools, local governments, and the church.

The risk networks create an environment by which norms and values are internalized that are more consistent with a street-oriented youth culture that increases their probability of involvement in antisocial behaviors. This subculture also includes elements of traditional and conventional Mexican American values and mores. Paradoxically, this cultural context plays a role in the acceptance of a high level of physical and sexual violence in these young adolescent females' relationships. Moreover, the street subculture and lifestyle of the gang peer network is compounded by the class and gender constraints that exacerbate the pressures and risks these young women experience.

Gender Roles as the Etiology of Violence

While a major finding of the book is that the etiology of female adolescent violence perpetration and victimization is multidimensional, gender inequality reinforced by patriarchal ideology emerges as the dominant source of these adolescent females' negative experiences. Females often become the victim of violence when they transgress traditional female gender roles.

As presented in this book, regardless of their relationship to the gang, all the females were prone to some degree of risk. The most predominant risk emerging from the analysis of these women were associated with sexual behavior. The girls who were sexually bound to a steady partner were still exposed to sexually transmitted diseases and infections because of their partners' multiple sexual relationships and high-risk drug use, such as the injection of heroin. Moreover, increased partner intimacy experienced by these girls increased their social isolation, which is associated with intimate-partner violence. Additionally, girls in the study involved in close relationships were more likely than girls who were not to have unprotected sex, become pregnant, and experience full-term pregnancy.

The girls in the study who were not sexually attached, on the other hand, were more open about their sexuality and more likely to have casual, multiple, and serial sexual partners. Also, these women were more likely to be openly involved in urban gang activities like committing violent offenses, criminality, and substance and alcohol use. This makes them vulnerable to sexual and violent victimization, court involvement, drug dependency, and other negative social and health consequences. The social cost of this behavior results in their stigmatization and marginalization by the other types of young females, male gang members, and the community.

One of the intriguing findings from this study is how traditional gender roles associated with Mexican American culture are being influenced by the behavior of these females. The sexually attached girls accept and portray the images and roles of passivity and submissiveness associated with traditional gender roles. Other girls subtly challenge these gender roles by renegotiating their sexuality while rejecting passivity and submissiveness similar to what has been described by Ruth Horowitz (1983). The girls who were not sexually attached to a particular male gang member—known as hoodrats—on the other hand, openly challenge these more traditional gender roles. Thus, the behavior of these girls may be creating a new social identity for women that goes beyond the traditional "good girl"/"bad girl" dichotomy associated with Mexican American gender roles. The unbounded sexual behavior and independence of these young women may be transforming more traditional gender roles.

The high-risk behaviors of these Mexican American females can be seen as falling outside of normative order. Young female adolescents are expected to adhere to a moral prescription for the timing of sex, marriage, and childbearing and to avoid criminal and other delinquent behavior. Middle-class-based norms also demand certain levels of education that, in turn, delay the appropriate age for reproduction until the twenties and early thirties. Other value-laden norms are that adolescents and even adults should not engage in delinquent activity, use illicit drugs, or consume excessive amounts of alcohol. Clearly, the females described in this book do not follow this middle-class American script (Jencks 1990).

Beyond Risk

As discussed in the introduction, "beyond-risk girls" refers to those adolescents who are already engaged in behaviors such as drug use, crime, having sex with multiple partners, and violence. Common risk and protective factors include individual (psychological disposition, attitudes, values), peers, family (norms, activities), school (bonding, performance), community, and society. Social scientists who are engaged in prevention and intervention research develop both universal and selective programs to deter adolescents from antisocial behaviors. The universal programs are aimed at all segments of the population, while the selective programs are at greater-than-average risk for risk behaviors. But as I have emphasized in this book, the girls in this study are already highly involved in street-based activities in risk networks that put them beyond these categories.

A major reason for these girls' behavior is that they are engaged in personal relationships with gang members, friends (male and female), acquaintances, and family members who are involved in behaviors such as fighting, drug use, and having sex with multiple partners. Moreover, in the absence of prosocial adults and institutions (i.e., families, schools, churches, civic governments, etc.) there are few adolescents that can neutralize these negative influences by controlling with whom they associate and under what circumstance. As a result, young girls in these neighborhoods are continuously exposed to high-risk situations and dangers, which are exacerbated when associating with male street gangs. This is why I consider these girls to be beyond risk.

Furthermore, the analyses of these violent scenarios have provided us a glimpse of the nature of situational intimate-partner violence and its meaning for adolescent females in high-risk, street-oriented environments. The etiology of such violence arises from the social-structural context of persistent poverty and gender inequality—factors that in turn shape participants' attitudes and behavior. These social-structural factors are different from most other studies that focus on more prosocial adolescent populations where violence is less normalized. Situational factors consistently interact with the social-structural context, influencing the initiation, unfolding, or outcome of a violent event. However, even though actors are affected by these structures and situations with a certain commonality, they retain their individuality, making their behavior never fully predictable. The degree of unpredictability among adolescents may be what distinguishes adolescent partner violence from that of adults. Nonetheless, this analysis has identified some common precursors to a physical confrontation and some behaviors that instigate this behavior in nontraditional dating relationships. In this regard, these findings may be used to develop culturally appropriate prevention and intervention for high-risk Hispanic females.

In closing, this study implicitly links the joining of a gang to a basic social process of gaining autonomy and independence, not only from family oppression, but also from cultural and class constraints. Yet previous literature is at odds to explain why these girls also express strongly traditional gender-role beliefs, aspirations, and expectations, especially since they hold the females in violent relationships with males (Williams 1990; Weiler 1999). One explanation is that these adolescent females are involved in a process of "paradoxical autonomy." This concept has been proposed to explain the behavior of older Mexican American females that use drugs intravenously. The paradox is rooted in the fact that traditional gender roles are rapidly changing among Mexican Americans. More and more Mexican American women do not expect to be supported by a man. Similar findings have been reported for African American young females (Burton 1990; Franklin 1988). In this socially ambiguous situation, these young females find their own ways to become more autonomous, but at the same time also experience their lives as difficult. This autonomy is paradoxical because it increases their risk for affiliating with a gang and therefore being exposed to the violence that they were seeking to overcome. In this dynamic situation, traditional gender roles can provide a strategic advantage for these females on a short-term basis. The challenge presented by the results of this research is to design future interventions in violence prevention that target the critical links of this process of paradoxical autonomy. Designing services to improve mother-daughter family relations of these females is one recommendation. Training in new gender roles that retain elements of the respect and *familismo* of traditional roles, but without the prescriptions of male dominance and female submissiveness, is another possibility.

Appendix

Overview of Existing Sampling Methods

Under the rubric of snowball sampling, other related methods include adaptive sampling and respondent-driven sampling. For example, adaptive sampling involves procedures linking the selection of units in the sample to specific adaptations made from observations during the process of sample recruitment (Thompson and Seber 1996; Van Meter 1990). Moreover, Steven Thompson and Linda Collins state that even traditional sampling approaches that incorporate oversampling "do not allow the investigator to take advantage of new information about potential sources of study participants, which may emerge as the investigator begins sampling and, through increased contact with the population" (2002, 558). This adaptive sampling method is especially suited for increasing sample representation of a hidden population to obtain less biased estimates of population characteristics (Frank and Snijders 1994).

Similarly, respondent-driven sampling uses various types of incentives to encourage study subjects to recruit other potential respondents (Heckathorn 1997). Potential subjects are generated through a nominating procedure in which, for example, they are asked to provide the first name or "street" name of individuals with targeted characteristics. Respondent-driven sampling helps to increase recruitment when sufficient representation of subjects with desired characteristics cannot be achieved through conventional outreach methods (Thompson and Seber 1996). Drawbacks, however, to these individualized sampling techniques include not obtaining parameters of representation. Moreover, the potential for selection bias frequently exists thereby limiting the validity and representation of the sample (Berk and Ray 1982; Kaplan, Korf, and Sterk 1987; Winship and Mare 1992). To illustrate, snowball samples may be biased toward the more cooperative subjects agreeing to participate, which results in "masking," that is, protecting others by not referring them (Heckathorn 1997) and overemphasizing social-network cohesiveness (Griffiths et al. 1993).

However, most ethnographic approaches used to recruit respondents do lead to some type of bias in the sense that the more widely known individuals are overrepresented, even in the initial sample (Snijders 1992). To minimize the drawbacks of selection bias, Avelardo Valdez and Charles Kaplan (1999) and John Watters and Patrick Biernacki (1989) have made various recommendations and suggestions. For example, Valdez and Kaplan have outlined four techniques to reduce selection bias and to acquire extensive information on gangs: (1) avoid institutional references, (2) maintain high visibility with the target population, (3) make frequent social contacts within the target community, and (4) use community gatekeepers, of which we followed for this study. Similarly, Watters and Biernacki have employed "targeted sampling" techniques (Braunstein 1993), mapping a specific target population to ensure representation of subjects from different areas and subgroups.

Study Sampling Process: Developing a Roster of Young Women

Young women were identified, recruited, and interviewed through a combination of adaptive sampling methods, which I will now explore in greater detail. These multidimensional approaches combined field-intensive outreach and recruitment with various elements of snowball-based methods to increase sample representation and were used in diverse ways to compile a roster of 519 gang-affiliated females connected to 27 male gangs.

A "universe" or "roster" of 519 names of girls associated with 27 gangs was generated based on the field-intensive methods described at the beginning of this chapter. The following discusses how the roster of these gang-affiliated young women was developed to achieve a sample size of one hundred and fifty.

To generate a roster of names of gang-affiliated females associated with the known 27 gangs, community field-workers approached known male gang members and/or their female gang affiliates to discuss the purpose of the present study. Determining whether or not potential subjects met *all* the inclusion criteria was challenging (Biernacki and Waldorf 1981; Wright et al. 1992). Moreover, the field researchers often had to rely on the male gang members or other gang-affiliated girls' verification of the eligibility of potential subjects. This process involved estimating the number of girls actively affiliated with each of the twenty-seven male gangs.[1]

For example, the field-workers would ask a gang member from the Big Cholos to give an average number of girls hanging out with their gang. The field-workers would then ask another Invaders member to provide an estimated number. If the researchers knew a young woman involved with the Invaders, they would then ask her for an estimate. For purposes of triangulation, reliability, and validity, the researchers would ask between two and five male gang members and/or their female affiliates for an average number of affiliated females within each gang. Furthermore, if one estimated twenty, another twenty, another twenty and another five, we would, for example, estimate twenty affiliates for this particular gang. In another instance, if one estimated the number at forty, another thirty, another twenty and another ten, we would average this at twenty-five. However, in most cases the number of estimates given by various informants did not differ significantly.

While the actual names for the estimated number of girls was not always known, this did not matter for our sampling purposes as long as there were identifiers (street name, boyfriend's name) associated with the girl. What was important at this point was, for example, that approximately twenty girls were associated with the Invaders. This entire process was both field extensive and time intensive.

Stratified Random Sampling

After estimating the number of affiliated girls for each gang, a list of 519 names were identified as potential study subjects. This was our roster of girls from which we would subsequently sample. The estimated "membership" for females associated with each of the gangs ranged from a low of five to a high of sixty. We aimed to actually interview one hundred and fifty of these young women. To ensure proportionate representation based on size of each of the twenty-seven gangs and to reflect the diversity within and among gangs, stratified random sampling (a probability sampling procedure that involves dividing the population into groups, or strata, defined by the presence of certain characteristics and then random sampling from each strata) was used to obtain a list of one hundred and fifty young women to interview. Table A.1 notes the roster of 519 young women along with the prevalence estimate of the number of young women affiliated with each gang and the number eventually interviewed within each gang.

To avoid selection bias on the part of the field-workers, they were unaware of the identity of the one hundred and fifty young women selected as possible participants. The community outreach specialists did not need to locate all 519 young women unless specified through randomization. For example, in gang #14 there were an estimated fifteen affiliated girls and the randomizer generated three numbers.

Table A.1 Roster of Gang-Affiliated Girls: Estimated Number for Each of the Twenty-seven Gangs and Number of Interviews Completed through Stratified Random Sampling

Gang/Gang Number	Estimated Number of Girls	Number Interviewed
1	30	9
2	20	7
3	50	16
4	10	3
5	25	7
6	10	2
7	10	2
8	20	6
9	5	1
10	60	19
11	10	3
12	39	12
13	10	3
14	15	3
15	20	6
16	10	2
17	12	3
18	40	12
19	12	3
20	5	1
21	10	3
22	11	3
23	20	6
24	15	4
25	20	6
26	12	3
27	18	5
	N = 519	n = 150

Randomizer Replacement

After the list of 519 gang-affiliated girls was generated, one hundred and fifty were selected through a stratified random sampling process.

However, we knew this hidden population would be difficult to locate and highly mobile. Initially, we devised a system that would allow for a replacement if one of the original one hundred and fifty young women could not be located. Of the one hundred and fifty young women on the original list, several could not be located, moved out of the area, were incarcerated, were not interested in the study, or were not permitted to participate in the study as a result of parental refusal. We again used stratified random sampling through the randomizer to substitute the original names with replacements.

To illustrate, youths #2, #9, and #10 from gang #4 (N = 10) were selected as the ones to interview. However, youth #10 could not be located. Using this randomizer Web site, we would then change the parameters/number range from 10 to 9 and then generate one number. Once the replacement number was produced, the field-workers would complete the process of locating her for an interview.

Data Collection Procedures

Data collection procedures were done with two distinct methods: a paper and pencil survey of a battery of self-report psychometric scales and a comprehensive life-history interview. The paper-and-pencil survey consisted of a brief two-page demographic section and ten psychometric scales measuring various psychological and behavioral constructs. The instruments were the Multigroup Ethnic Identity Measure (MEIM), the Childhood Trauma Questionnaire (CTQ), the Plutchick Feelings and Acts of Violence Scale (PFAV), the Masculinity Ideology Scale, the Mother-Daughter Relationship Scale (MDREL), the Attitudes Towards Women Scale (AWS), the Family Crisis Oriented Personal Scales (F-COPES), the Center for Epidemiological Studies Depression Scale (CESD), the Hispanic Stress Inventory (HIS), and the Conflict Tactic Scale (CTS). The psychometric instruments were administered to the gang-affiliated sample on a one-on-one basis, with guidance from a female community researcher who oversaw the interviews.

We conducted an intensive two-hour interview to determine each girl's life history. Using female interviewers enhanced both the reliability and validity of the study given the sensitive nature of the study.[2] Consent from parents or legal guardians was obtained from each subject prior to interviewing subjects. A fifty-dollar incentive was given to subjects for their participation. Each of the life-history interviews was audio taped and transcribed.

Community Survey: Life Histories/Intensive Interview

The life history interview was designed to provide qualitative and quantitative data through the use of open- and closed-ended and scenario questions. The interview included gathering basic demographic information (e.g., date of birth, place of residence) and nine other sections of questions on subjects including family history, neighborhood and community/institution relations, gang affiliation, drug-use history, violence perpetration and victimization, participation in illegal activities, social networks of friends and adults, school experience, sexual and intimate-partner violence, and sexual behavior.

The initial section of the study's questionnaire described the respondent's past and current family structure and relationships. Subjects were asked about their childhood family experiences including residential patterns, primary caregivers, involvement in illegal activities, alcohol and drug use, and domestic violence. Current family facts were also obtained such as current household makeup and description of subject's children, if applicable. The neighborhood and community/institution section determined the extent to which the respondent participates and is incorporated in local community organizations, agencies, and institutions. Likert scales were included to measure the extent of specific problems in the respondent's respective neighborhood.

The third section focused on the respondent's gang affiliation. The nature and extent of the subject's affiliation with a gang or gang members was determined by using both open- and closed-ended questions, including such items as whether the subject knew a gang member, if and how often they hung out with the gang member, what activities they did together, and so on. The drug-use history section of the questionnaire contained a standardized measurement that captured drug-use patterns for lifetime, past year, and current use. This matrix included self-reported lifetime use, age of initial use, frequency of use (including injection), and source of drugs within the previous thirty days. Drugs included in the matrix were marijuana, crack, cocaine, heroin, the combination of heroin and cocaine (speedball), acid, inhalants, benzodiazepines, opiates, and amphetamines. Overdosing, suicide attempts, and drug treatment were included in this section.

The section on violence and illegal activities began with a measurement of illegal activities committed during middle school, during the previous year, and the person with whom most of these activities were committed during that period. In addition, data was collected on each subject's experience with the police and judicial system. A scenario question asking the respondent to describe in-depth the last fight that she was personally involved with outside of her home was included as well.

The section on networks of friends and adults asked the girls about their closest friends and/or relatives and up to five adults they talked to on a regular basis. Detailed information was obtained, including demographics, drug use, illegal activities, relationship, etc. The section on school experience further explored educational attainment, as well as suspensions, expulsions, and family support.

The section on intimate-partner violence established whether the respondent was currently in an intimate-partner relationship with someone; if not, questions were asked about the respondent's most recent boyfriend. Items such as duration of the relationship and the boyfriend's drug use, age, employment, education, and so on were collected. In addition, in-depth responses were obtained by asking respondents about the last physical fight between her and her partner. The Relationship Power Scale, a widely used assessment, was included at the end of this section (Pulerwitz, Gortmaker, and DeJong 2000).

Finally, there was the section on sexual experience. This provided in-depth information on the respondents' past and current sexual activity. Included in this part of the interview were initial sexual experience, current sexual activity, condom use, and number of sexual partners. HIV/AIDS knowledge was also assessed.

Qualitative Analysis

Qualitative data for this study consisted of field notes, observations, and responses to open-ended life history and scenario questions. A scenario question is a combination of an open-ended question and a matrix of closed-ended questions that is coded at the end of the interview (Page 1990). These data were used in the chapters of the report that have a qualitative focus.

The data from the scenario questions used a more grounded theoretical approach. This allowed us to collect, code, and analyze data simultaneously. After conducting an initial twenty interviews, the research team (including interviewees, outreach staff, transcriber, and me) examined all data collected through the scenarios of violence and sexual assault. In discussing the data, several topics emerged that were not being collected consistently throughout the interviews. Consequently, I developed codes that identified topics that were characteristic of themes that emerged through this process. The scenario questions in the life-history study questionnaire were modified to include these topics or codes as probes in the subsequent interviews. These theme codes included the following:

- *Violence scenarios.* Location, time, activity, events, nature of relationship, characteristics of adversaries and bystanders, fight, drugs/alcohol, weapons, resistance, and severity
- *Sexual-assault scenarios.* Location, time, activity, events, nature of relationship, victim, perpetrator, bystanders, assault, drugs/alcohol, weapons/threats, resistance, severity, gang involvement, immediate, long-term effect, family involvement and length of incident

Transcriptions of open-ended and scenario questions allowed us to produce "thick descriptions" of violent and sexual incidents. A computer software program, NVivo, was used to analyze the qualitative data and produce all coding. This software allows support in handling qualitative textual (nonnumeric, unstructured) data through routine processes of indexing, searching, and theorizing.

Notes

1. For a more detailed description of estimating the size of hidden populations for sampling purposes, see Ove Frank and Tom Snijders (1994) and G. Edward Codina, Zenong Yin, David S. Katims, and Jesse T. Zapata (1998).
2. Research on topics such as political issues, gender equality, culture, drug use, and mental health suggests that interviewer characteristics (i.e., gender, race, or age) determine the amount and accuracy of information disclosed (Fendrich, Johnson, Shaligram, & Wislar, 1999; Huddy et al., 1997; Johnson & Parsons, 1994; Pollner, 1998; Thompson, Worthington, & Atkinson, 1994; Webster, 1996).

References

Abramson, A. J., and M. E. Fix. 1993. Growth without prosperity reveals surprising trends. *Partnership for Hope Newsletter 3*, 1–5.

Adler, P., C. Ovando, and D. Hocevar. 1984. Familiar correlates of gang membership: An exploratory study of Mexican-American youth. *Hispanic Journal of Behavioral Sciences* 6 (1): 65–76.

Agnew, R., T. Brezina, J. P. Wright, and F. T. Cullen. 2002. Strain, personality traits, and delinquency: Extending general strain theory. *Criminology* 40 (1): 43.

Alan Guttmacher Institute. 1995. *Teenage pregnancy and the welfare reform debate.* New York: Alan Guttmacher Institute.

Alva, S. A. 1995. Psychological distress and alcohol use in Hispanic adolescents. *Journal of Youth & Adolescence* 24 (4): 481–97.

Alva, S. A., and M. Jones. 1994. Psychosocial adjustment and self-reported patterns of alcohol use among Hispanic adolescents. *Journal of Early Adolescence* 14 (4): 432–48.

Alvirez, D., F. D. Bean, and D. Willams. 1981. The Mexican American family. In *Ethnic families in America*, eds. C. H. Mindel and R. W. Habenstein, 271–92. New York: Elsevier North Holland.

Amaro, H. 1995. Love, sex, and power: Considering women's realities in HIV prevention. *American Psychologist* 50 (6): 437–47.

Amaro, H., L. E. Fried, H. Cabral, and B. Zuckerman. 1990. Violence during pregnancy: The relationship to drug use among women and their partners. *American Journal of Public Health* 80:575–79.

Amaro, H., and C. Hardy-Fanta. 1995. Gender relations in addiction and recovery. *Journal of Psychoactive Drugs* 27 (4): 325–37.

Anderson, E. 1999. *Code of the street.* New York: W. W. Norton and Company.

Anderson, K. L. 2002. Perpetrator or victim? Relationships between intimate partner violence and well-being. *Journal of Marriage & Family* 64 (4): 851–63.

Archer, J., and K. Browne. 1989. Naturalistic approaches and the future of aggression research in psychology. In *Human aggression: Naturalistic approaches*, eds. J. Archer and K. D. Browne, 361–273. New York: Routledge.

Bailey, K. D. 1994. *Typologies and taxonomies: An introduction to classification techniques.* Thousand Oaks, CA: Sage.

Barrera, M., S. A. Li, and L. Chassin. 1993. Ethnic group differences in vulnerability to parental alcoholism and life stress: A study of Hispanic and non-Hispanic Caucasian adolescents. *American Journal of Community Psychology* 21 (1): 15–36.

Bauder, H. 2002. *Work on the West Side: Urban neighborhoods and the cultural exclusion of youth.* Boulder, CO: Lexington Books.

Berk, R. A., and S. C. Ray. 1982. Selection biases in sociological data. *Social Science Research* 11 (4): 352–98.

Bettie, J. 2000. Women without class: Chicas, cholas, trash and the presence/absence of class identity. *Signs* 26 (1): 1–35.

Biernacki, P., and D. Waldorf. 1981. Snowball sampling: Problems and techniques of chain referral sampling. *Sociological Methods & Research* 10 (2): 141–63.

Bowleg, L., F. Z. Belgrave, and C. A. Reisen. 2000. Gender roles, power strategies, and precautionary sexual self-efficacy: Implications for black and Latina women's HIV/AIDS protective behaviors. *Sex Roles* 42 (7–8): 613–35.

Bowser, D. 2003. *West of the creek: Murder, mayhem, & vice in Old San Antonio.* San Antonio, TX: Maverick.

Braunstein, M. S. 1993. Sampling a hidden population: Noninstitutionalized drug users. *AIDS Education & Prevention* 5 (2): 131–40.

Braverman, P. K., and V. C. Strasburger. 1993. Adolescent sexual activity. *Clinical Pediatrics* 32 (11): 658–68.

Breslin, F. C., D. S. Riggs, and K. D. O'Leary. 1990. Family precursors: Expected and actual consequences of dating aggression. *Journal of Interpersonal Violence* 5 (2): 247–58.

Briere, J. N. 1984. The effects of childhood sexual abuse on later psychological functioning: Defining a 'post-sexual abuse syndrome.' Paper read at the Third National Conference on Sexual Victimization of Children at Washington, DC.

———. 1992. *Child abuse trauma: Theory and treatment of the lasting effects.* Newbury Park, CA: Sage.

Brischetto, R. 2000. *Making connections on San Antonio's West Side: The Neighborhood Transformation/Family Development Project.* Baltimore: T.A.E.C. Foundation.

Brook, J. S., M. Whiteman, S. Finch, & P. Cohen. 2000. Longitudinally foretelling drug use in the late twenties: Adolescent personality and social-environmental antecedents. *Journal of Genetic Psychology* 161 (1): 37–51.

Brook, J. S., M. Whiteman, A. S. Gordon, C. Nomura, and D. W. Brook. 1986. Onset of adolescent drinking: A longitudinal study of intrapersonal and interpersonal antecedents. *Advances in Alcohol & Substance Abuse* 5 (3): 91–110.

Brotherton, D. C. 1996. 'Smartness,' 'toughness,' and 'autonomy': Drug use in the context of gang female delinquency. *Journal of Drug Issues* 26 (1): 261–77.

Bureau of Justice Statistics. 2000. Criminal victimization in the U.S.: 1998 statistical tables. *National crime victimization survey.* Washington, DC: U.S. Department of Justice.

Burton, L. M. 1990. Teenage childbearing as an alternative life-course strategy in multigeneration black families. *Human Nature* 1 (2): 123–43.

Buss, D. M., R. J. Larsen, D. Westen, and J. Semmelroth. 1992. Sex differences in jealousy: Evolution, physiology, and psychology. *Psychological Science* 3 (4): 251–55.

Caetano, R. 1994. Drinking and alcohol-related problems among minority women. *Alcohol Health & Research World* 3 (18): 233–41.

Campbell, A. 1995. Female participation in gangs. In *The modern gang reader*, eds. M. W. Kline, C. L. Maxson, and J. Miller, 70–77. Los Angeles: Roxbury.

Canino, G. 1992. Alcohol use and abuse among Hispanic women: A review of epidemiologic findings. Unpublished manuscript.

Carlson, B. E. 1987. Dating violence: A research review and comparison with spouse abuse. *Social Casework* 68 (1): 16–23.

Cascardi, M., S. Avery-Leaf, K. D. O'Leary, and A. M. Smith Slep. 1999. Factor structure and convergent validity of the Conflict Tactics Scale in high school students. *Psychological Assessment* 11 (4): 546–55.

Cepeda, A., and A. Valdez. 2003. Risk behaviors among young Mexican American gang-associated females: Sexual relations, partying, substance use, and crime. *Journal of Adolescent Research* 18 (1): 90–106.

Cervantes, R. C., A. M. Padilla, and N. S. de Snyder. 1991. The Hispanic Stress Inventory: A culturally relevant approach to psychosocial assessment. *Psychological Assessment* 3 (3): 438–47.

Charlesworth, W. R., and C. Dzur. 1987. Gender comparisons of preschoolers' behavior and resource utilization in group problem-solving. *Child Development* 58:191–200.

Chesney-Lind, M. 1993. Girls, gangs and violence: Anatomy of a backlash. *Humanity and Society* 17 (3): 312–44.

Chesney-Lind, M., and R. G. Shelden. 1998. *Girls, delinquency, and juvenile justice*. Belmont, CA: Wadsworth.

Codina, G. E., Z. Yin, D. S. Katims, and J. T. Zapata. 1998. Marijuana use and academic achievement among Mexican American school-age students: Underlying psychosocial and behavioral characteristics. *Journal of Child & Adolescent Substance Abuse* 7 (3): 79–96.

Covey, H. C., S. Menard, and R. J. Franzese. 1992. Juvenile gang violence. In *Juvenile gangs*, ed. H. C. Covey, 27–47. Springfield, IL: Charles C. Thompson.

Cox, W. M., ed. 1987. *Treatment and prevention of alcohol problems: A resource manuel*. Orlando: Academic Press.

Crowell, N. A., and A. W. Burgess, eds. 1966. *Understanding violence against women*. Washington, DC: National Academy Press.

Curry, G. D. 1998. Female gang involvement. *Journal of Research in Crime and Delinquency* 35 (1): 100–118.

Curry, G. D., R. A. Ball, and S. H. Decker. 1996. Estimating the national scope of gang crime from law enforcement data. In *Gangs in America*, ed. C. R. Huff, 21–36. Newbury Park, CA: Sage.

Daghestani, A. N. 1988. Psychosocial characteristics of pregnant women addicts in treatment. In *Drugs, alcohol, pregnancy and parenting*, ed. Ira J. Chasnoff, 7–16. Boston: Kluwer Academic.

Daly, M., M. Wilson, and S. J. Weghorst. 1982. Male sexual jealousy. *Ethology and Sociobiology* 3:11–27.

Davenport, D. S., and J. M. Yurich. 1991. Multicultural gender issues. *Journal of Counseling & Development* 70 (1): 64–71.

de Anda, R. M. 1996. Falling back: Mexican-origin men and women in the U.S. economy. In *Chicanas and Chicanos in contemporay society*, ed. R. M. de Anda, 41–50. Boston: Allyn and Bacon.

de Swaan, A. 1988. *In care of state: Health care, education and welfare in Europe and the USA in the modern era*. Cambridge: Polity.

Debold, E., L. M. Brown, S. Weseen, and G. Kearse Brookins. 1999. Cultivating hardiness zones for adolescent girls: A reconceptualization of resilience in relationships with caring adults. In *Beyond appearance: A new look at adolescent girls*, eds. N. G. Johnson, M. C. Roberts, and J. Worell, 181–204. Washington, DC. American Psychological Association.

DeKeseredy, W. S., and M. D. Schwartz. 1998. Male peer support and woman abuse in postsecondary school courtship: Suggestions for new directions in sociological research. In *Issues in intimate partner violence*, ed. R. K. Bergen, 83–96. Thoudand Oaks, CA: Sage.

Dobash, R. P., R. E. Dobash, M. Wilson, and M. Daly. 1992. The myth of sexual symmetry in marital violence. *Social Problems* 39:71–91.

Donovan, J. E., R. Jessor, and F. Marie Costa. 1988. Syndrome of problem behavior in adolescence: A replication. *Journal of Consulting and Clinical Psychology* 56 (5): 762–65.

Dougherty, D. M. 1999. Health care for adolescent girls. In *Beyond appearance: A new look at adolescent girls*, eds. N. G. Johnson, M. C. Roberts, and J. Worell, 301–26. Washington, DC: American Psychological Association.

Douglas, H. 1991. Assessing violent couples. *Familes in Society* 72 (9): 525–35.

Ellickson, P. L., R. L. Collins, and R. M. Bell. 1999. Adolescent use of illicit drugs other than marijuana: How important is social bonding and for which ethnic groups? *Substance Use & Misuse* 34 (3): 317–46.

Ellickson, P. L., and R. D. Hays. 1992. On becoming involved with drugs: Modeling adolescent drug use over time. *Health Psychology* 11 (6): 377–85.

Ellickson, P. L., and K. A. McGuigan. 2000. Early predictors of adolescent violence. *American Journal of Public Health* 90 (4): 566–72.

Erickson, P. I. 1998. *Latina adolescent childbearing in East Los Angeles*. 1st ed. Austin: University of Texas Press.

Esbensen, F.-A. 2000. Preventing adolescent gang involvement. Juvenile Justice Bulletin. Youth Gang Series. Washington, DC: Department of Justice, Office of Juvenile Justice and Delinquency Prevention.

Esbensen, F.-A., E. P. Deschenes, and L. T. Winfree. 1999. Differences between gang girls and gang boys: Results from a multisite survey. *Youth & Society* 31 (1): 27–53.

Farrington, D. P., and D. J. West. 1971. A comparison between early delinquents and young aggressives. *British Journal of Criminology* 11 (4): 341–58.

Felson, R. B., and S. F. Messner. 2000. The control motive in intimate partner violence. *Social Psychology Quarterly* 63 (1): 86–94.

Fishbein, D. H., and S. E. Pease. 1996. *The dynamics of drug abuse*. Boston: Allyn and Bacon.

Fitzgerald, J. L. 1996. Hidden populations and the gaze of power. *Journal of Drug Issues* 26 (1): 5–21.

Frank, O., and T. Snijders. 1994. Estimating the size of hidden populations using snowball sampling. *Journal of Office Statistics* 10 (1): 53–67.

Franklin, D. L. 1988. Race, class, and adolescent pregnancy: An ecological analysis. *American Journal of Orthopsychiatry* 58 (3): 339–54.

Friedman, S. R., R. Curtis, A. Neaigus, B. Jose, and D. C. Des Jarlais. 1999. *Social networks, drug injectors' lives, and HIV/AIDS*. New York: Kluwer Academic.

Furman, W., and D. Buhrmester. 1992. Age and sex differences in perceptions of networks of personal relationships. *Child Development* 63 (1): 103–115.

Garcia, M. T. 1989. *Mexican Americans: Leadership, ideology, and identity, 1930–1960*. New Haven, CT: Yale University Press.

Gavin, L. A., and W. Furman. 1996. Adolescent girls' relationships with mothers and best friends. *Child Development* 67 (2): 375–86.

Giordano, P. C., T. J. Millhollin, S. A. Cernkovich, M. D. Pugh, and J. L. Rudolph. 1999. Delinquency, identity, and women's involvement in relationship violence. *Criminology* 37 (1): 17–37.

Glueck, S., and E. Glueck. 1950. *Unraveling juvenile delinquency*. New York: Common Wealth Fund.

Goffman, E. 1959. *The presentation of self in everyday life*. Garden City, NY: Doubleday.

Golding, J. M. 1999. Intimate partner violence as a risk factor for mental disorders: A meta-analysis. *Journal of Family Violence* 14 (2): 99–132.

Goldstein, P. J. 1985. The drugs/violence nexus: A tripartite conceptual framework. *Journal of Drug Issues* 15 (4): 493–506.

Gorney, B. 1989. Domestic violence and chemical dependency: Dual problems, dual intervention. *Journal of Psychoactive Drugs* 21 (2): 229–38.

Gray, H. M., and V. Foshee. 1997. Adolescent dating violence: Differences between one-sided and mutually violent profiles. *Journal of Interpersonal Violence* 12:126–141.

Griffiths, P., M. Gossop, B. Powis, and J. Strang. 1993. Reaching hidden populations of drug users by privileged access interviewers: Methodological and practical issues. *Addiction* 88 (12): 1617.

Hagedorn, J. M., and M. L. Devitt. 1999. Fighting female: The social construction of female gangs. In *Female gangs in America: Essays on girls, gangs & gender*, eds. M. Chesney-Lind and J. M. Hagedorn, 256–76. Chicago: Lake View.

Hamberger, L. K., and C. E. Guse. 2002. Men's and women's use of intimate partner violence in clinical samples. *Violence Against Women* 8 (11): 1301–32.

Hanley, M. J., and P. O'Neill. 1997. Violence and commitment: A study of dating couples. *Journal of Interpersonal Violence* 12 (5): 685–703.

Harris, M. G. 1994. Cholas, Mexican-American girls, and gangs. *Sex Roles* 30 (3/4): 289–301.

Harway, M., and M. Liss. 1999. Dating violence and teen prostitution: Adolescent girls in the justice system. In *Beyond appearance: A new look at adolescent girls*, ed. N. G. Johnson, M. C. Roberts, and J. Worell, 256–76. Washington, DC: American Psychological Association.

Heckathorn, D. D. 1997. Respondent-driven sampling: A new approach to the study of hidden populations. *Social Problems* 44 (2): 174–99.

Heller, C. S. 1966. *Mexican American youth: Forgotten youth at the crossroads.* New York: Random House.

Henggeler, S. W., G. B. Melton, L. A. Smith, S. K. Schoenwald, and J. H. Hanley. 1993. Family preservation using multisystemic treatment: Long-term follow-up to a clinical trial with serious juvenile offenders. *Journal of Child & Family Studies* 2 (4): 283–93.

Herman, J. 1993. Sequelae of prolonged and repeated trauma: Evidence of a complex post-traumatic stress syndrome. In *Posttraumatic stress disorder: DSM-IV and beyond*, eds. J. R. T. Davidson and E. B. Foa, 213–28. Washington, DC: American Psychiatric Press.

Horowitz, R. 1983. *Honor and the American dream: Culture and identity in a Chicano community, crime, law, and deviance series.* New Brunswick, NJ: Rutgers University Press.

Hunt, G., and K. Joe-Laidler. 2001. Situations of violence in the lives of girl gang members. *Health Care for Women International* 22 (4): 363–84.

Hunt, G., K. MacKenzie, and K. Joe-Laidler. 2000. I'm calling my mom: The meaning of family and kinship among homegirls. *Justice Quarterly* 17 (1): 1–31.

Ickovics, J. R., S. E. Beren, E. L. Grigorenko, A. C. Morrill, J. A. Druley, and J. Rodin. 2002. Pathways of risk: Race, social class, stress and coping as factors predicting heterosexual risk behaviors for HIV among women. *AIDS and Behavior* 6 (4): 339–50.

Inazu, J. K., and G. L. Fox. 1980. Maternal influence on the sexual behavior of teen-age daughters: Direct and indirect sources. *Journal of Family Issues* 1 (1): 81–99.

Ironson, G., A. Friedman, N. Klimas, M. Antoni, M. A. Fletcher, A. LaPerriere, J. Simoneau, and N. Schneiderman. 1994. Distress, denial, and low adherence to behavioral interventions predict faster disease progression in gay men infected with Human Immunodeficiency Virus. *International Journal of Behavioral Medicine* 1 (1): 90–115.

Irwin, H. J. 1999. Violent and nonviolent revictimization of women abused in childhood. *Journal of Interpersonal Violence* 14 (10): 1095–110.

Jankowski, M. S. 1991. *Islands in the street: Gangs and American urban society.* Berkeley: University of California Press.

Jencks, C. 1990. Is the American underclass growing? In *The urban underclass*, eds. C. Jencks and P. E. Peterson, 28–100. Washington, DC: Brookings Institute.

Jessor, R., and S. L. Jessor. 1977. *Problem behavior and psychosocial development: A longitudinal study of youth.* New York: Academic Press.

Joe, K. A., and M. Chesney-Lind. 1995. Just every mother's angel: An analysis of gender and ethnic variations in young gang membership. *Gender & Society* 9 (4): 408–31.

Johnson, L. D., P. M. O'Malley, and J. G. Bachman. 2002. Monitoring the future national survey, 1975–2001. Bethesda, MD: National Institute on Drug Abuse.

Kaplan, C. D., D. Korf, and C. Sterk. 1987. Temporal and social contexts of heroin-using populations: An illustration of the snowball sampling technique. *The Journal of Nervous and Mental Disease* 175 (9): 566–74.

Kasarda, J. D. 1993. *Urban underclass database: An overview and machine-readable file documentation.* New York: Social Science Research Council.

Kaufman K., G. Jasinski, and J. L. Jasinski. 1998. Dynamics of partner violence and types of abuse and abusers. United States Air Force and National Network for Family (RNFR). Partner Violence Research Project: A Twenty-Year Literature Review and Synthesis.

Klein, M. W. 1995. *The American street gang: Its nature, prevalence, and control.* New York: Oxford University Press.

Kobus, K., and O. Reyes. 2000. A descriptive study of urban Mexican American adolescents' perceived stress and coping. *Hispanic Journal of Behavioral Sciences* 22 (2): 163–78.

Kruttschnitt, C., D. Ward, and M. A. Sheble. 1987. Abuse-resistant youth: Some factors that may inhibit violent criminal behavior. *Social Forces* 66 (2): 501–19.

LaFree, G., and K. A. Drass. 1996. The effect of changes in intraracial income inequality and educational attainment on changes in arrest rates for African Americans and whites, 1957 to 1990. *American Sociological Review* 61 (August): 614–34.

Latkin, C. A., and A. D. Curry. 2003. Stressful neighborhoods and depression: A prospective study of the impact of neighborhood disorder. *Journal of Health & Social Behavior* 44 (1): 34–44.

Lauritsen, J. L., R. J. Sampson, and J. H. Laub. 1991. Link between offending and victimization among adolescents. *Criminology* 29:265–92.

Leserman, J., J. M. Petitto, D. O. Perkins, J. D. Folds, R. N. Golden, and D. L. Evans. 1997. Severe stress, depressive symptoms, and changes in lymphocyte subsets in human immunodeficiency virus-infected men. A 2-year follow-up study. *Archives of General Psychiatry* 54 (3): 279–85.

Lewis, H. 1986. The community as child abuser. *The Hastings Center Report* 16:17–18.

Loeber, R., and M. Stouthamer-Loeber. 1986. Family factors as correlates and predictors of juvenile conduct problems and delinquency. In *Crime and justice: An annual review of research,* vol. 7, eds. M. Tonry and N. Morris, 29–149. Chicago: University of Chicago Press.

Long, J. M. 1990. Drug use patterns in two Los Angeles barrio gangs. In *Drugs in Hispanic communities,* eds. R. Glick and J. Moore. New Brunswick, NJ: Rutgers University Press.

Loper, A. B., and D. G. Cornell. 1995. Homicide by girls. Paper read at Annual Meeting of the National Girls Caucus at Orlando, FL.

Makepeace, J. M. 1986. Gender differences in courtship violence victimization. *Family Relations* 35:383–88.

Malik, S., S. B. Sorenson, and C. S. Aneshensel. 1997. Community and dating violence among adolescents: Perpetration and victimization. *Journal of Adolescent Health* 21:291–302.

Manov, A., and L. Lowther. 1983. A health care approach for hard-to-reach adolescent runaways. *Nursing clinics of North America* 18 (2): 333–42.

Martinez, R. 1996. Latinos and lethal violence: The impact of poverty and inequality. *Social Problems* 43 (2): 131–46.

Mayer, S. E., and C. Jencks. 1989. Growing up in poor neighborhoods: How much does it matter. *Science* 243:1441–45.

McCord, J. 1982. A longitudinal view of the relationship between paternal absence and crime. In *Abnormal offenders, delinquency, and the criminal justice system*, eds. J. C. Gunn and D. P. Farrington, *113–28*. Chichester, UK: Wiley.

McCubbin, H., A. Larson, and D. Olsen. 1982. Family crisis oriented personal evaluation scales. In *Family assessment inventories*, ed. H. McCubbin and A. Thompson, 193–207. Madison: University of Wisconson at Madison.

McFarlane, J., A. Malecha, J. Gist, K. Watson, E. Batten, I. Hall, and S. Smith. 2004. Protection orders and intimate partner violence: An 18-month study of 150 black, Hispanic, and white women. *American Journal of Public Health* 94 (4): 613–19.

McNeece, C. A., and D. M. DiNitto. 1998. *Chemical dependency: A systems approach*. 2nd ed. Boston: Allyn & Bacon.

Miller, J. 1998. Gender and victimization risk among young women in gangs. *Journal of Research in Crime & Delinquency* 35 (4): 429–53.

———. 2001. *One of the guys*. New York: Oxford University Press.

Miller, J. B. 1986. *Toward a new psychology of women*. 2nd ed. Boston: Beacon.

Miller, J., and N. A. White. 2003. Gender and adolescent relationship violence: A contextual examination. *Criminology* 41 (4): 1207–48.

Miller, W. B. 1958. Lower class culture as a generating milieu of gang delinquency. *Journal of Social Issues* 14 (3): 5–19.

———. 1975. Violence by youth gangs and youth groups as a crime problem in major American cities, ed. National Institute for Juvenile Justice and Delinquency Prevention. Washington, DC: U.S. Department of Justice.

Molidor, C. E. 1996. Female gang members: A profile of aggression and victimization. *Social Work* 41 (3): 251–60.

Molidor, C. E., and R. M. Tolman. 1998. Gender and contextual factors in adolescent dating violence. *Violence Against Women* 4 (2): 180–94.

Montejano, D. 1987. *Anglos and Mexicans in the making of Texas 1836–1986*. Austin: University of Texas Press.

Moore, J. W. 1988. Gangs and the underclass: A comparative perspective. In *People and folks: Gangs, crime, and the underclass in a rustbelt city*, ed. J. M. Hagadorn, 3–17. Chicago: Lake View.

———. 1990. Mexican-American women addicts: The influence of family background. In *Drugs in Hispanic communities*, eds. R. Glick and J. Moore, 129–53. New Brunswick, NJ: Rutgers University Press.

———. 1991. *Going down to the barrio: Homeboys and homegirls in change.* Philadelphia: Temple University Press.

———. 1994. The chola life course: Chicana heroin users and the barrio gang. *International Journal of the Addictions* 29 (9): 1115–26.

Moore, J. W., and J. M. Hagedorn. 1996. What happens to girls in the gang? In *Gangs in America,* ed. C. R. Huff, 205–18. London: Sage.

———. 2001. Female gangs: A focus on research. *Juvenile Justice Bulletin.* Youth Gang Series. Washington, DC: Department of Justice, Office of Juvenile Justice and Delinquency Prevention.

Moore, J. W., and R. Pinderhughes, eds. 1993. *In the barrios: Latinos and the underclass debate.* New York: Russell Sage Foundation.

Moore, J. W., and J. D. Vigil. 1989. Chicano gangs: Group norms and individual factors related to adult criminality. *Aztlán* 18 (2): 27–44.

Morales, A. 1982. The Mexican American gang member: Evaluation and treatment. In *Mental Health and Hispanic Americans,* eds. R. M. Becerra, M. Karno, and J. I. Escobar, 130–55. New York: Grune and Stratton.

Morenoff, J. D., and M. Tienda. 1997. Underclass neighborhoods in temporal and ecological perspective. *Annals, AAPSS* 551 (May): 59–72.

Morgan, P. 1996. Unknown, unexplored, and unseen populations: An introduction into the truly hidden worlds of drug and alcohol research. *Journal of Drug Issues* 26 (1): 1–4.

Morse, B. J. 1995. Beyond the Conflict Tactics Scale: Assessing gender differences in partner violence. *Violence and Victims* 10 (4): 251–72.

Murphy, S. 1978. A year with the gangs of East Los Angeles. *Ms.* (July): 55–64.

National Center for Injury Prevention. 2003. *Intimate partner violence fact sheet.* Centers for Disease Control, National Center for Injury Prevention, Feburary 28. http://www.cdc.gov/ncipc/factsheets/ipvfacts.htm (accessed June 5, 2003).

Newton, R. R., C. D. Connelly, and J. A. Landsverk. 2001. An examination of measurement characteristics and factorial validity of scores on the revised Conflict Tactics Scale. *Educational and Psychological Measurement* 61 (2): 317–35.

Office of National Drug Control Policy (ONDCP). 2006. Girls and drugs: A new analysis: Recent trends, risk factors and consequences. Washington, DC: Office of National Drug Control Policy, Executive Office of the President.

O'Keefe, M. 1997. Predictors of dating violence among high school students. *Journal of Interpersonal Violence* 12 (4): 546–68.

O'Keefe, M., and L. Treister. 1998. Victims of dating violence among high school students. *Violence Against Women* 4 (2): 195–223.

Page, J. B. 1990. Shooting scenarios and risk of HIV-1 infection. *American Behavioral Scientist* 33 (4): 478–90.

Palmer, C. T., and C. F. Tilley. 1995. Sexual access to females as a motivation for joining gangs: An evolutionary approach. *The Journal of Sex Research* 32 (3): 213–17.

Phinney, J. S. 2002. The Multigroup Ethnic Identity Measure (MEIM). http://www.calstatela.edu/academic/psych/ftp/meim.doc (accessed June 6, 2002).

Plutchik, R., and H. M. van Praag. 1990. A self-report measure of violence risk, II. *Comprehensive Psychiatry* 31 (5): 450–56.

Portillos, E. L. 1999. Women, men, and gangs: The social construction of gender in the barrio. In *Female gangs in America: Essays on girls, gangs, and gender*, eds. M. Chesney-Lind and J. M. Hagedorn. Chicago: Lake View.

Pulerwitz, J., S. L. Gortmaker, and W. DeJong. 2000. Measuring relationship power in HIV/STD research. *Sex Roles* 42, no. 7/8 (April).

Quane, J. M., and B. H. Rankin. 1998. Neighborhood poverty, family character-istics, and commitment to mainstream goals: The case of African American adolescents in the inner city. *Journal of Family Issues* 19 (6): 769–94.

Quicker, J. C. 1983. *Homegirls: Characterizing Chicano gangs*. San Pedro, CA: International University Press.

Radloff, L. S. 1991. The use of the Center for Epidemiologic Studies Depression Scale in adolescents and young adults. *Journal of Youth and Adolescence* 20 (2): 149–66.

Rankin, J. H. 1983. The family context of delinquency. *Social Problems* 30 (4): 466–79.

Redlinger, L. J., and J. B. Michel. 1970. Ecological variations in heroin abuse. *Sociological Quarterly* 11:219–29.

Rickets, E., and I. V. Sawhill. 1988. Defining and measuring the underclass. *Journal of Policy Analysis and Management* 7:316–325.

Riggs, D. S., K. D. O'Leary, and F. Curtis Breslin. 1990. Multiple correlates of physical aggression in dating couples. *Journal of Interpersonal Violence* 5 (1): 61–73.

Robbins, M. S., and J. Szapocznik. 2000. Brief strategic family therapy. Juvenile Justice Bulletin. Family Strengthening Series. Washington, DC: Department of Justice, Office of Juvenile Justice and Delinquency Prevention.

Rosales, R. 2000. *The illusion of inclusion: The untold political story of San Antonio, Center for Mexican American Studies*. History, Culture, and Society Series. Austin: University of Texas Press.

Rosenbaum, M. 1985. *Women on heroin*. New Brunswick, NJ: Rutgers University Press.

Ross, C. E., J. Mirowsky, and S. Pribesh. 2001. Powerlessness and the amplifica-tion of threat: Neighborhood disadvantage, disorder and mistrust. *American Sociological Review* 66 (August): 568–91.

Ross, C. E., J. R. Reynolds, and K. J. Geis. 2000. The contingent meaning of neighborhood stability for residents' psychological well-being. *American Sociological Review* 65 (4): 581–97.

Rotheram-Borus, M. J., C. Koopman, and A. A. Ehrhardt. 1991. Homeless youths and HIV infection. *American Psychologist* 46 (11): 1188–97.

Salovey, P. 1991. *The psychology of jealousy and envy*. New York: Guilford.

Sampson, R. J., and J. L. Lauritsen. 1994. Violent victimization and offending: Individual-, situational-, and community-level risk factors. In *Understanding and preventing violence, social influences*, ed. J. A. Roth, 1–114. Washington, DC: National Academy Press.

Sampson, R. J., J. D. Morenoff, and F. Earls. 1999. Beyond social capital: Spatial dynamics of collective efficacy for children. *American Sociological Review* 64 (5): 633–60.

Sampson, R. J., S. W. Raudenbush, and F. Earls. 1997. Neighborhoods and violent crime: A multilevel study of collective efficacy. *Science* 277:918–924.

Sampson, R. J, and W. J. Wilson. 1995. Toward a theory of race, crime, and urban inequality. In *Crime and inequality*, ed. J. Hagan and R. D. Peterson, 37–54. Stanford, CA: Stanford University Press.

San Antonio Housing Authority. 2003. ORR-Request for public housing information. San Antonio, TX, May 22.

San Antonio Independent School District. 2003. SAISD parent-student handbook 2002–03, section III: Student code of conduct. http://www.saisd.net/Parent/Handbook/hb3.shtm (accessed on July 17, 2003).

San Antonio Metropolitan Health District Director's Office. 1997. Selected facts for Bexar County: Health and demographic statistics. San Antonio, TX: City of San Antonio and Bexar County.

Sandefur, R. L., and E. O. Laumann. 1998. A paradigm for social capital. *Rationality & Society* 10 (4): 481–501.

Sanders, W. B. 1994. *Gangbangs and drive-bys: Grounded culture and juvenile gang violence.* Chicago: Aldine.

Santisteban, D. A., J. D. Coatsworth, A. Perez-Vidal, W. M. Kurtines, S. J. Schwartz, A. LaPerriere, and J. Szapocznik. 2003. Efficacy of brief strategic family therapy in modifying Hispanic adolescent behavior problems and substance use. *Journal of Family Psychology. (Division 43)* 17 (1): 121–33.

Santisteban, D. A., J. Szapocznik, A. Perez-Vidal, W. M. Kurtines, E. J. Murray, and A. LaPerriere. 1996. Efficacy of interventions for engaging youth/families into treatment and some variables that may contribute to differential effectiveness. *Journal of Family Psychology* 10:35–44.

Short, J. F. 1985. The level of explanation problem in criminology. In *Theoretical methods in criminology*, ed. R. F. Meier, 51–74. Beverly Hills, CA: Sage.

Silverman, J. G., A. Raj, L. A. Mucci, and J. E. Hathaway. 2001. Dating violence against adolescent girls and associated substance use, unhealthy weight control, sexual risk behavior, pregnancy, and suicidality. *Journal of the American Medical Association* 286 (5): 572–79.

Simmel, G. 1971. *On individuality and social forms: Selected writings*, ed. D. N. Levine. Chicago: University of Chicago Press.

Singleton, E. G., and D. A. Grady. 1996. Lack of co-occurring interpersonal violence-related emotional difficulties and alcohol or other drug problems among African American youth with conduct disorder. *Journal of Negro Education* 65 (4): 445–53.

Smith, D. 2001. When workplaces shut down. *Monitor on Psychology* (July/August): 50–51.

Snijders, T. A. B. 1992. Estimation on the basis of snowball samples: How to weight? *Bulletin de Methodologie Sociologique* 36:59–70.

Soja, E., R. Morales, and G. Wolff. 1983. Urban restructuring: An analysis of social and spatial change in Los Angeles. *Economic Geography* 59:195–230.

Spergel, I. A. 1995. *The youth gang problem: A community approach.* New York: Oxford University Press.

Stets, J. E., and D. A. Henderson. 1991. Contextual factors surrounding conflict resolution while dating: Results from a national study. *Family Relations* 40 (1): 29–37.

Straus, M. A., and R. J. Gelles, eds. 1990. *Physical violence in American families.* New Brunswick, NJ: Transaction.

Straus, M. A., S. L. Hamby, S. Boney-McCoy, and D. B. Sugarman. 1996. The revised Conflict Tactics Scales (CTS2): Development and preliminary psychometric data. *Journal of Family Issues* 17 (3): 283–316.

Strauss, A. L., and J. M. Corbin. 1990. *Basics of qualitative research: Grounded theory procedures and techniques.* Newbury Park, CA: Sage.

Substance Abuse and Mental Health Services Administration. 1996. Summary of findings from the 1985–1995 national household survey on drug abuse. Rockville, MD: U.S. Department of Health and Human Services.

Sugarman, D. B., and G. T. Hotaling. 1989. Dating violence: Prevalence, context, and risk markers. In *Violence in dating relationships,* eds. M. A. Pirog-Good and J. E.Stets, 3–32. New York: Praeger.

———. 1997. Intimate violence and social desirability. *Journal of Interpersonal Violence* 12 (2): 275–91.

Thompson, S. K., and L. M. Collins. 2002. Adaptive sampling in research on risk-related behaviors. *Drug & Alcohol Dependence* 68 (1): S57–S67.

Thompson, S. K., and G. A. F. Seber. 1996. *Adaptive sampling.* 1st ed. New York: John Wiley & Sons.

Thornberry, T. P., M. D. Krohn, A. J. Lizotte, and D. Chard-Wierschem. 1993. The role of juvenile gangs in facilitating delinquent behavior. *Journal of Research in Crime & Delinquency* 30 (1): 55–87.

Thrasher, F. M. 1963. *The gang: A study of 1,313 gangs in Chicago,* ed. J. F. Short. Chicago: University of Chicago Press.

Tsukashima, R. T. 1985. Institutional completeness and interpersonalties among Japanese-American immigrants. *Sociology Inquiry* 51 (Spring): 131–53.

U.S. Bureau of the Census. 2003a. Annual demographic survey March supplement: Table 2. Age, sex, household relationship, race and Hispanic origin by ratio of income to poverty level: 2001. September 23. http://ferret.bls.census.gov/macro/032002/pov/new02_001.htm (accessed on July 17, 2003).

———. 2003b. Poverty in the United States: 2001 current population reports. U.S. Government Printing Office 2002. http://www.census.gov/prod/2002pubs/p60-219.pdf.

———. 2003c. Quick tables: QT-PL. Race, Hispanic or Latino, and age: 2000 for San Antonio city, Texas. http://factfinder.census.gov (accessed on July 16, 2003).U.S. Department of Justice. 1995. Crime in America. Uniform Crime Reports, FBI 213.

Valdez, A. 1993. Persistent poverty, crime, and drugs: U.S.-Mexican border region. In *In the barrios: Latinos and the underclass debate,* eds. J. Moore and R. Pinderhughes. New York: Russell Sage Foundation.

Valdez, A., and J. A. Halley. 1996. Gender in the culture of Mexican American conjunto music. *Gender and Society* 10 (2): 148–67.

Valdez, A., and C. D. Kaplan. 1999. Reducing selection bias in the use of focus groups to investigate hidden populations: The case of Mexican American gang members from South Texas. *Drugs and Society* 14 (1/2): 209–24.

Valdez, A., C. D. Kaplan, and A. Cepeda. 2000. The process of paradoxical autonomy and survival in the heroin careers of Mexican American women. *Contemporary Drug Problems* 27 (Spring 2000): 189–212.

Valdez, A., A. G. Mata, E. Codina, K. Kubicek, and S. Tovar. 2001. Childhood trauma, family stress, and depression among Mexican American gang noninjecting heroin users: An exploratory study. San Antonio: Final Report to the Hogg Foundation Submitted by the Center for Drug and Social Policy Research, University of Texas at San Antonio.

Valdez, A., J. P. McCray, and D. Thomas. 1994. The impact of the North American Free Trade Agreement on Mexican American workers in South Texas. San Antonio: Hispanic Research Center, University of Texas at San Antonio.

Valdez, A., and S. J. Sifaneck. 2004. Getting high and getting by: Dimensions of drug selling behaviors among U.S. Mexican gang members in South Texas. *Journal of Research in Crime and Delinquency 41 (1): 82–105.*

Van Meter, K. M. 1990. Methodological and design issues: Techniques for assessing the representatives of snowball samples. In *The collection and interpretation of data from hidden populations*, ed. E. Y. Lambert, 31–43. Rockville, MD: U.S. Department of Health and Human Services, National Institute on Drug Abuse.

Viguel, J. D. 1988a. *Barrio gangs: Street life and identity in Southern Calfornia.* Austin: University of Texas Press.

Walker, L. E. 1984. *The battered woman syndrome.* New York: Springer.

Walker-Barnes, C. J., and C. A. Mason. 2001. Perceptions of risk factors for female gang involvement among African American and Hispanic women. *Youth & Society* 32 (3): 303–36.

Wang, J. Z. 2000. Female gang affiliation: Knowledge and perceptions of at-risk girls. *International Journal of Offender Therapy & Comparative Criminology* 44 (5): 618–32.

Watters, J. K., and P. Biernacki. 1989. Targeted sampling: Options for the study of hidden populations. *Social Problems* 36 (4): 416–30.

Watts, C., and C. Zimmerman. 2002. Violence against women: Global scope and magnitude. *Lancet* 359 (9313): 1232–38.

Weiler, J. 1999. *An overview of research on girls and violence, choice briefs.* Institute for Urban and Minority Education, Teachers College, Columbia University. http://iume.tc.columbia.edu/choices/briefs/choices01.html (accessed on July 17, 2003).

Werner, E. E. 1983. Vulnerability and resiliency among children at risk for delinquency. Unpublished manuscript.

West, A. D. 2001. HIV/AIDS education for Latina inmates: The delimiting impact of culture on prevention efforts. *Prison Journal* 81 (1): 20–41.

White, G. L., and P. E. Mullen. 1989. *Jealousy: Theory research and clinical strategies:* New York: Guilford.

Whitfield, C. L., R. F. Anda, S. R. Dube, and V. J. Felitti. 2003. Violent childhood experiences and the risk of intimate partner violence in adults: Assessment in a large health maintenance organization. *Journal of Interpersonal Violence* 18 (2): 166–85.

Whyte, W. F. 1973. *Street corner society: The social structure of an Italian slum.* Chicago: University of Chicago Press.

Widom, C. S. 1989a. Child abuse, neglect, and violent criminal behavior. *Criminology* 27:251–272.

———. 1989b. The intergenerational transmission of violence. In *Pathways to criminal violence,* eds. N. A. Weiner and M. F. Wolfgang. Newbury Park, CA: Sage.

Wiebel, W. W. 1990. Identifying and gaining access to hidden populations. In *The collection and interpretation of data from hidden populations.* Rockville, MD: U.S. Department of Health and Human Services, National Institute on Drug Abuse.

Williams, N. 1990. *The Mexican American family: Tradition and change.* Dix Hills, NY: General Hall.

Wilson, W. J. 1980. *The declining significance of race: Blacks and changing American institutions.* 2nd ed. Chicago: University of Chicago Press.

———. 1987. *The truly disadvantaged: The inner city, the underclass, and public policy.* Chicago: University of Chicago Press.

———. 1996. *When work disappears: The world of the new urban poor.* New York: Random House.

Wind, T. W., and L. Silvern. 1994. Parenting and family stress as mediators of long-term effects of child abuse. *Child Abuse & Neglect* 18 (5): 439–53.

Winick, Charles. 1962. Maturing out narcotic addiction. *Bulletin on Narcotics* (January/March): 1–7.

Winship, C., and R. D. Mare. 1992. Models for sample selection bias. *Annual Review of Sociology* 18:327–350.

Wolfe, D. A., K. Scott, C. Wekerle, and A.-L. Pittman. 2001. Child maltreatment: Risk of adjustment problems and dating violence in adolescence. *Journal of the American Academy of Child and Adolescent Psychiatry* 40 (3): 282–89.

Wright, R. T., S. H. Decker, A. K. Redfern, and D. L. Smith. 1992. A snowball's chance in hell: Doing fieldwork with active residential burglars. *Journal of Research in Crime & Delinquency* 29 (2): 148–61.

Wyatt, G. E., D. Guthrie, and C. M. Notgrass. 1992. Differential effects of women's child sexual abuse and subsequent sexual revictimization. *Journal of Consulting & Clinical Psychology* 60 (2): 167–73.

Yablonsky, L. 1962. *The violent gang.* New York: Macmillan.

Yin, Z., A. Valdez, A. G. Mata, and C. D. Kaplan. 1996. Developing a field-intensive methodology for generating a randomized sample for gang research. *Free Inquiry-Special Issue: Gang, Drugs and Violence* 24 (2): 195–204.

Index

measure of intimate-partner
violence, 136, 155–56; overview,
155–56; substance use variables
and, 161–65
control, 146–48
criminal adult-dependent gangs, 26–30
criminal non-adult-dependent gangs,
30–35
Crips, 28, 39
Curry, David, 84
cycle of violence, 62

dating violence, 112, 136–39;
precursors to, 141–51
de Anda, Roberto M., 19
delinquency, violence and, 85–86;
fights, 90–91; gang-affiliated,
86–90; sexual behavior, 93–94;
subtance use, 91–93
Devitt, Mary, 84
disrespect, 148–51
divorce, 10, 61–62, 81
Douglas, Harriet, 153
drug abuse. *See* cocaine; heroin;
marijuana; Rohypnol

education: disinterest in, 78–79;
female gang members and, 55–56;
lack of opportunities for, 9, 20, 108,
176; Mexican American families
and, 79, 81, 176, 179, 189

families: cycle of dysfunction and, xi;
development of gangs and, 60; normalization of negative habits and,
68–73; relationships to institutions,
77–81; role of, 59; single-parent, 10,
62, 105, 126, 160, 161; structure and
process, 61–68, 156–57; substance
abuse and, 73–77; violence and, 62
Family Crisis Oriented Personal Scale
(F-COPES), 74–77, 187
family process variables, 157–59;
Conflict Tactics Scale (CTS)
analysis and 157–60

Felson, Richard, 138
female gang members, study of:
acquiring access to gangs, 49–50;
establishing rapport, 53–54; maintaining visibility, 52; research team,
47–49; results, 55–56; selecting the
sample, 55
femininity: ideological expectation of,
133; oppositional, 5, 84; traditional
notions of, 110
Flores, Raquel, xiii, 13

gang leaders, 27, 29, 32, 33, 40, 41, 46
Gangs of New York (Asbury), ix
Gangsters, The, 28–30, 67, 107, 119;
adult family criminal connections,
28–29; distinct characteristics,
29–30; drugs and, 29–30; membership, 28
gang studies, 4; eligibility, 55, 184;
establishing rapport, 53–54; female,
4, 47–49; gatekeepers and, 49–51;
maintaining visibility and, 52; male,
45–47; overview of samples' characteristics, 55–56; research process, 55
gang typologies, construction of, 24;
adult influence, 25; drug-use patterns, 25; illegal activities, 24–25;
organizational structure, 25; violence, 26
gendered power dynamics, precursors
to, 139–40
gender roles, 180–81; as etiology of
violence, 178–79; beyond-risk and,
2; female gang members and, 6–7,
122, 152, 180; intimate-partner violence and, 55; power dynamics, 139;
socialization and, 153; shifts in, 5,
59, 61; traditional, 61, 113, 180–81;
victimization and, 132, 133
girlfriends: control and, 147; defined,
94–95; disrespect and, 148–53; drug
use, 96–97; illegal activities and,
98–99; intimate-partner violence
and, 123–28, 138; jealousy and, 103,

18–19; Frio City Road community, 21–22; historical background of barrios, 16–18; increase in gang activity, 12; Mexican American community, 15–22; poverty in, 18–20; social etiology of barrios, 16–18; West Side, 15–23, 45–47, 70, 175–76; youth gangs, 22–24
San Antonio, TX, gangs: adult influence, 25; drug use patterns, 25; illegal activities, 24–25; organizational structure, 25; violence, 26
Sanchez, Mark, 31, 33
Santisteban, Daniel, 113
school boys, 80
serial residency, 65, 81
sexual and physical violence, 111–14; boyfriends, 112; family, 112–14; gangs, 114
sexually transmitted diseases, 94, 107–8, 123, 178
sexual relationships, 105–8
sexual victimization: by boyfriends, 115–18; fear of jeopardizing relationships and, 4; female gang association and, 6, 114–15; gang rape, 114; history of sexual abuse and, 166–67; intimate-partner violence and, 112; rationalization of behaviors, 121–22; substance use, 122–23; within gang context, 118–21. See also rape
Shaw, Clifford R., 8
Short, James, 11, 135
Simmel, George, 61
single-parent households, 10, 62, 105, 126, 160–61
situational level processes, 11, 135
substance use, study of, 160–65; variables, 161; variables and Conflict Tactics Scale (CTS) analysis, 161–65

tattoos, 5, 112
Tecatos, 29, 101
Thompson, Steven, 183
Thornberry, Terence, 108

Thrasher, Frederic, ix, 60
Tilley, Christopher, 139
transitional gangs, 38–41
Treister, Laura, 138

underclass, 9, 14, 22, 42
unemployment: impact on families, 55, 56, 63; impact on communities, 1, 21–22, 176; intimate-partner violence and, 55, 189; Mexican American community and, 7; normative view of, 3; San Antonio and, 17, 18–19, 21–22. See also poverty; working poor
Up And Above (UAA), 39–40; drugs and, 39; evolution into gang, 39–40; tagging, 39
U.S.-Mexico border region, 15, 17

Valdez, Avelardo, x–xi, 184
Varrio La Paloma (VLP), 33–35, 119–20; drugs and, 35; gang war, 34–35; leadership, 35; location, 34; membership, 34; organization, 34
Vigil, James, 60
violent confrontations: associations with a male gang, 102–4; jealousy, 104–5; physical, 126, 128, 141–51; sexual relationships, 105–8; talking shit/maddoging, 100–102
violent social interaction: instigation, 140; progression to confrontation, 140–41
violent victimization, 109–13
virginity, 6, 80, 120

Watters, John, 184
Weiler, J., 113
welfare dependency, 1, 9, 22, 42, 176
White, Norman, 138, 152, 153
Whitfield, Charles, 166
Whyte, Williams Foote, 43
Wilson, William, 9
working poor, 18–19. See also poverty; unemployment

LaVergne, TN USA
24 July 2010
190689LV00001B/35/P